PAPAL
JUSTICE

PAPAL JUSTICE

*Subjects and Courts in
the Papal State, 1500–1750*

Irene Fosi

Translated by Thomas V. Cohen

The Catholic University of America Press
Washington, D.C.

The paper used in this publication meets the minimum requirements of
American National Standards for Information Science—Permanence
of Paper for Printed Library Materials, ANSI Z39.48-1984.

∞

Library of Congress Cataloging-in-Publication Data
Polverini Fosi, Irene.
Papal justice : subjects and courts in the Papal State, 1500–1750 /
Irene Fosi ; translated by Thomas V. Cohen.
p. cm.
Includes bibliographical references and index.
ISBN 978-0-8132-1858-8 (pbk. : alk. paper)   1. Justice, Administration
of—Papal States—History—Modern period, 1500–
2. Courts—Papal States—History—Modern period, 1500–
3. Civil procedure—Papal States—History—Modern period, 1500–
I. Cohen, Thomas V. (Thomas Vance), 1942–   II. Title.
KKH6743.4.P65 2011
347.456—dc22   2010041496

CONTENTS

v

ILLUSTRATIONS

PREFACE TO THE
ENGLISH-LANGUAGE EDITION

When, in 2002, I published my essay "Il governo della giustizia" (The Governance of Justice) in the anthology *Roma moderna* (Early Modern Rome), one volume in a series of several on the history of the city, the publisher of that collection suggested to me that I write a book that addressed the theme of justice not only in Rome itself but in the whole Papal State. The project attracted me. It seemed a way finally to round out and solidify research that, over many years, I had been conducting on judicial sources in Rome and elsewhere. But then all the problems started to emerge. I would have to write a synthesis rather than a detailed study; I would thus have to leave out all sorts of themes and unsolved problems. I would be forced to give a very partial picture of a phenomenon tightly bound up with the problems of sovereignty, the governance of the state, and the control of its territory. Meanwhile, I would also have to deal with questions posed by the sources: how did the state's subjects perceive justice, and how did they themselves make use of it? This book's analysis of procedures, of the "cruel" justice of the ancien régime, practiced by the sovereign pontiff, as it was by other monarchs, carries with it no moral condemnation—to blame or criticize would be presentist and ahistorical. To understand, to put in context—those are the historian's tasks Marc Bloch has set us. The Counter Reformation papacy did not only have to contrive to defend orthodoxy. By its double nature, it had also to manage to govern its temporal domains. In that latter domain, papal monarchy was little different from other territorial states of the same period. This book attempts to respond to some of the multiple questions around this story and to show the complexity of an effort that tried, not always successfully, to make theory and practice bear fruit, and to operate comprehensively to assure good order, both moral and social.

When, in 2007, my Italian book came out, North American and English scholars received it well. And it was clear to me that in English-language scholarship there was no synthesis of the sort that I had written. So I proposed a translation adjusted to the needs of a different readership. Accordingly, I added some material, the better to lay out and clarify issues already well known in the Italian literature. I also updated

my notes and bibliography, adding useful references, in English wherever possible. The present edition is therefore fuller and richer than the
Italian original. But this work of translation and revision, and, in some
cases, of adaptation, in both style and substance, would not have been
possible without the intervention of Thomas V. Cohen. His translation
has not been of the straightforward, anonymous, detached variety. A
historian with a deep knowledge of the sources and problems discussed
here, he has known how to read and interpret my pages and give them
an English-speaking voice. This has been a work of very close collaboration, carried on by ongoing e-mail dialogue and then by long conversations, as Roman spring pushed into early summer. It is the fruit of a
friendship born, many years ago, at the work tables of the Archivio di
Stato di Roma, when we were enchanted by the same documents. I am
also grateful to Simon Ditchfield, who first suggested the idea of turning to the prestigious Catholic University of America Press; to Thomas
Kuehn, for thinking well of what I have written; to John Tedeschi for
precious suggestions and advice; and to Laurie Nussdorfer, a very dear
friend and splendid scholar on Roman subjects, who very generous-
ly read and reviewed the translation. And of course I extend my sincer-
est thanks to David McGonagle, director of the Catholic University of
America Press, who welcomed and championed this book's translation.

ROME, OCTOBER 2009

ABBREVIATIONS

AC	Archivio Caetani, Rome
ACDF	Archivio della Congregazione per la Dottrina della Fede
ACSS	Archivio Colonna, Monastero di S. Scolastica, Subiaco (Rome)
ASF	Archivio di Stato di Firenze
ASR	Archivio Stato, Rome
ASV	Archivio Segreto Vaticano
ASVR	Archivio Storico del Vicariato di Roma
BAV	Biblioteca Apostolica Vaticana
BC	Biblioteca Casanatense, Rome
BL	British Library, London
HHST-A	Haus-, Hof- und Staatsarchiv, Vienna
S.O.	Sant'Offizio

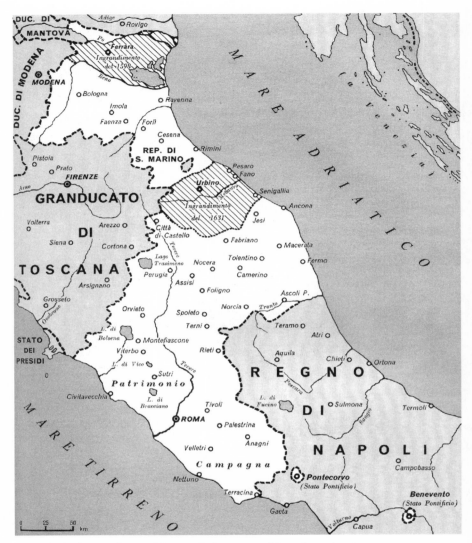

Map of Italy showing the Papal State at the beginning of the eighteenth century.

PAPAL JUSTICE

Introduction

> In the Church State they have made arrests everywhere, without respecting any baronial lands, and they say that in the past few days the *bargello di Campagna* [chief constable of the countryside] has carried out his duties in Marino, a Colonna town, for the pope wishes to be recognized as the lord of all.[1]

That is how, in October 1667, an attentive Roman diarist stressed his belief that papal justice could now control territory that for centuries had been under the jealous, obtrusive jurisdiction of barons. But he was overly optimistic, as we can see by what turns up later in his own chronicle, recording disorder and mayhem in the city and the countryside. All told, at the seventeenth century's end, Roman control of papal territory was still troubled, and this was not always just the fault of feudal lords.

By the middle of the Seicento, after having grown haphazardly and jelled late, the pope's temporal domains were a composite form. The state's heterogeneity and unusual structure made the center's conquest and affirmation of power evolve differently in one place and another. The struggle for control played out mainly outside the cities, in the mountains and in other impenetrable zones short on roads and tracks and low on security. Rome's progress went slowly in the rural communities, where, more than elsewhere, the state faced habits of vendetta, of private peace pacts, and of all those practices of parallel justice that drew their raison d'etre and support from local power relations, social ties, and family bonds. Among the state's subjects, justice called into play a defense of those venerable privileges, prerogatives, and customs that ever more often collided with Rome's own power.

This book has a double theme and deals with two phenomena that were very tightly linked: the control of the state's territory and the governance of its machinery of justice. Governance had more to it than the mere "administration of justice." That expression is too modern, evoking as it does a coherent rationality and clear sense of

---

1. Archivio di Stato di Rome (henceforth ASR), Cartari Febei, no. 86, f. 115r.

purpose still lacking in the early modern period. In the old regime, rather, the power to judge was not at all autonomous and separate. It was deeply embedded in all powers of any sort lodged anywhere in the swarm of persons, bodies, institutions, and lesser "states" that made up a territorial entity. The early modern Papal State was, in this regard, no different from any other. To speak of justice thus means to observe from one angle the institutions called on to bring it into being. We must survey the mechanisms of recruitment of the state's servants, the shape of their careers, and the information channels that conditioned their adaptation to their jobs. The same sources that show the law's workings also reveal crime's protagonists, both individuals, whether anonymous subjects or gentlemen of famous name, and whole families or communities. One must untangle their fraught, contradiction-laden relations with official justice. The justice under discussion here is hegemonic— "apparatus-justice," as one scholar has defined it.[2] It was the justice of the courtrooms (often neither especially grand nor particularly well lit), the justice of tribunals. But our subject also embraces the other means and practices used against all those who, to rejigger their own position with the authorities, or with their family, community, or social group, broke the law.

The two centuries between 1500 and 1700 saw major shifts in the perception of society, of hierarchic structures, of political authority, and of the state's assorted duties. But governance's main task remained the vouchsafing of God's good order. The state, therefore, had to assure justice, the backbone of *buon governo* (good governance). This image, spun by theory and spread by propaganda, conflicted with reality. Whoever was called upon to rule and govern had to live with reality's demands, often sharply at odds with the culture and official policies formulated in cities, above all in Rome, and exported and imposed elsewhere. This imposition owed not only to force, but also to negotiation, through the compromise and mediation necessitated by widespread local opposition.[3] In the early modern period, social order and public order were two closely linked and interdependent ideas and realities. So-

2. Mario Sbriccoli, "Giustizia criminale," in *Lo stato moderno in Europa. Istituzioni e diritto,* ed. M. Fioravanti, 163–205 (Rome: Laterza, 2002).

3. Paolo Prodi, "Presentazione," in *Disciplina dell'anima, disciplina del corpo e disciplina della società tra medioevo ed età moderna,* ed. Paolo Prodi, 12 (Bologna: Il Mulino, 1994).

cial order was often tested and put at risk by social forces, but it also was modified by public order. Between the two, the authority of the sovereign—in our case, of the sovereign pope—stepped in, or, perhaps, did its best to insert itself as an umpire or guardian.

But to guarantee good order and *buon governo* also meant to be resourceful and watchful to thwart the spread of heresy, to punish scandalous behavior, and to unearth and quell suspect ideas, cults, beliefs, and practices. In the early modern period, many alleged crimes had no touchstone distinguishing moral and spiritual delinquency from political felony or everyday misdemeanor. The Papal State was firmly committed to an order based on the Catholic principles it championed.[4] The double nature of the sovereign made this vigilance necessary, as did the structure of a state largely in the hands of churchmen. The role of the Inquisition here was of fundamental importance. It had complex relations with other judicial bodies, both in Rome and around the state, with the ecclesiastical authorities, and with bishops' and legates' courts.

Treatises, pamphlets, and iconography all proclaimed that the pontiff's territories and cities embodied justice and good order. Reality was different; the pope's principality was far from a working model for other Italian states. So the gulf between theory and practice, between political culture and propaganda on the one hand and the realities of governance and discipline on the other, was clear indeed. The same was true in other states of the time, but it was more evident in the papacy, a non-hereditary monarchy, eternally unstable. Thus, Foucault's famous term "discipline" should not be applied to Rome's transformation of social order without qualification and distinctions. We have to keep in mind the intrinsic, inseparable connections of society with religious power, with political institutions, and with the diverse, lively political nuclei scattered across the motley territory under the pope's sway.

Seen from below, from society, papal justice had conflicting meanings. Between the sixteenth and eighteenth centuries, the pope's sphere of control kept growing, in an attempt to master banditry, vagabondage, and poverty, three conditions deleterious to order and justice in city and country alike. Meanwhile, in the minds of the state's subjects the idea of *buon governo* differed from the sovereign's,

---

4. Adriano Prosperi, *Tribunali della coscienza. Inquisitori, confessori, missionari* (Turin: Einaudi, 1996).

as is clear from their letters and petitions and from the words of witnesses before any official of the courts. "To live in peace": this formula summed up the image of *buon governo* as it looked from below, where one appraised power by asking just how much it let a person "mind my own business" (*fare i fatti miei*). These words expressed a popular ideal of authority—distant, unobtrusive, and adroitly balanced between imposing more modern norms and tolerating behaviors and customs increasingly at odds with the new concept of order. More and more, these traditional behaviors were destined to be stigmatized and prosecuted as crime, deviance, or sin. But the selfsame subjects of the state, for all that they shied away from the state, also sought this delicate balance, invoking the sovereign's clemency and grace with petitions to the pope and to his tribunals, imploring order and justice. Clemency and grace were a foundation of sovereign power, and a safe haven for subjects plagued by punishment's frequent misalignment with guilt. During the whole early modern period, lay and ecclesiastical courts operated by wielding both punishment and forgiveness. So did the well-trained or slovenly police, the inquisitors, and the overzealous or overcautious bishops. The results were thoroughly irregular, thanks to the heterogeneity of the political landscape, and the great variety of city, town, and local identities. The populace therefore did its best to cope.

This book's point of view is mainly Roman. But it works not only with the city's internal papers. Much of what appears here is based on letters between the center and the periphery. This vast correspondence was like a perpetual, circular ocean current, flowing out from Rome and coursing back, passing through a hinterland that tossed in its requests, protests, and suggestions. In the flux of everyday events, and in the practices of courts and jurists, the letters and petitions show us very plainly how managing disorder and making justice work required continual compromise and expedient repair work.

Whatever theories said, when confronting the workings of justice, both authorities and subjects needed to make accommodations. Everyone had to integrate ill-fitted parts, to mix old ways with new, and to negotiate with competing interests. It was a process of slow adaptation; there was no systematic, radical destruction of a social order and its interpersonal relations. Governance did not unmake the older forms of justice. Regulated and supervised by higher authorities, these sometimes survived and continued to guarantee peaceful coexistence and the common good.

This book begins with a look at the composite geography of the lands of the Papal State (chapter 1). It then turns to Rome itself to show how its varied courts, in the sixteenth and seventeenth centuries, defined and reinforced their jurisdictions, and it examines the impression that the justice of the pope's own city made on his subjects (chapters 2 and 4). We give particular attention to the tribunal of the Inquisition and to its relations with other judicial institutions in Rome itself (chapter 3). We also examine the Inquisition's relations on the periphery, studying its engagement, and its sometimes prickly collaboration, with other courts, both lay and ecclesiastic (chapter 6). We devote considerable space to the control of the nobility, which was often rebellious and sometimes heterodox (chapter 5). Chapters 7 through 9 examine a variety of crimes, in society in general, inside the family, and among clergy. Through case studies, these chapters try to offer a panorama of the gamut of behavior, and of the values, habits, and social arrangements confronting justice. It turns out that the web of institutions and doctrines that sustained justice in its work had far more holes and weak spots in its mesh than state theory, and especially propaganda, would lead us to believe. The culture of *buon governo* kept butting up against reality, with all its logistical problems, its conditions on the ground, its strenuous defense of privileges—by nobles, cities, and towns, against Rome and its ministers, both lay and ecclesiastical (chapters 10–11). The frictions of this daily confrontation stimulated the continual conversation between the center and the periphery, between power and its subjects. This dialogue was translated into a busy correspondence, and a tide of petitions, a great river of ink that flooded all institutions, not just the courts alone (chapter 12). By this flood of letters between the center and the periphery power was consulted, legitimated, and received, via compromises and agreements. And these letters could impose the state's will dramatically, reminding subjects where they really stood.

All told, the pope's justice tried to find its sure perch and field of action, while smoothing things down, mediating, and making its peace with local conditions. It did not always succeed. In this crucial project of mediation, the best prepared were always the churchmen, governors, legates, judges, and inquisitors. But prudence and mediation did not always prevail. There were brutal impositions, repressions, corruption, and ignorance. These marks of maladministration and bad governance, far more than the state's better traits, have lived on in memory as icons of the clericalization of governance in the early modern Papal State. This bad reputation gave rise to a perduring tradition of hostile history writing marked by the scornful term "a government of priests" (*governo di preti*). But earlier, in the sixteenth century, justice and *buon governo* also had been the subjects of an intense and pervasive official propaganda campaign via painting cycles, coins, and medals. Alongside these images directed toward the illiterate and literate alike there appeared in cheap printed editions lively broadside stories inextricably entangled with propaganda for the Roman church and pope. Tales of famous executions broadcast an image of papal justice aiming to educate the state's subjects and to fete good's triumph over evil (chapter 13). Nevertheless, with its gory scenes, this literature also contributed in the eighteenth and nineteenth centuries to the sorry picture—almost a black legend—of the pope's justice as bloodthirsty, vindictive, and grasping. The stories would help paint the turbid image of Italian decadence, where the Papal State figured as a main protagonist.

At the end of this work I am obliged to thank all those who, directly or not, have helped my research in archives and libraries to bear fruit: the Archivio di Stato di Roma, the Archivio Segreto Vaticano, the Archivio della Congregazione per la Dottrina della Fede, the Biblioteca Apostolica Vaticana, not to mention many Roman libraries, especially the Biblioteca Casanatense and the Biblioteca Corsiniana. The friends and colleagues with whom I have discussed themes and problems appearing here are many and I am grateful for their precious advice and their stimulating suggestions and answers to my many doubts.

I

A Complex Geography

At the end of the fourteenth century, the geography of the pope's domain was in constant evolution. Despite the great antiquity of its name, we can label the Renaissance Papal State, in Machiavelli's words, a "new" principality. From decade to decade, its borders, and indeed the whole territory, kept swiftly changing shape. International affairs, the onset of the Italian Wars for instance, contributed to the frontiers' continual shifting, as did dizzying changes in papal politics. So, for example, the Borgia project to build a "family state" was undone by Julius II (1503–1513), and then Leo X (1513–1521) waded in to set right his predecessor's work. But then came the Sack of Rome (1527). That catastrophe forced a break with earlier politics and put an end to the sudden oscillations, the gain or loss of substantial territories. So, when it comes to the Papal State—its institutions and its whole administrative and political apparatus—one can speak of a "Long Fifteenth Century" ending only in 1530, when change slowed down. The papal domain, however, continued to grow. In 1539 came the creation of the Farnese state of Camerino. Then, in 1598, came Ferrara's "devolution" into papal hands, and in 1631 came Urbino's. Furthermore, Avignon and the nearby county of Venassin remained under papal administration, as did the little enclaves of Benevento and Pontecorvo, both in Neapolitan territory. In the seventeenth century, the duchies of Castro and Ronciglione returned to direct papal rule. With so many assembled parts, this was a truly composite state, and would remain so down to its eventual disappearance.

How did contemporaries regard this shifting geography? We can find our answer in descriptions of the landscape, both maps and geographic writings, some of them in the humanistic tradition and others that, risking anachronism, we might call geopolitical. At the beginning of the sixteenth century, unlike their geographer predecessors, and very much unlike the humanists, geographers began to investigate the real conditions in the papal dominions.

They scrutinized the cities and their histories, but also looked beyond them, at their hinterlands, betraying a nascent awareness of the cities' belonging to a region and a landscape. But these early works showed little interest in the political borders in play at the hands of the popes of the first half of the sixteenth century.[1] It was only later, as the century went on, after the central papal offices had assumed sharper shape and clearer function in governing the state's assorted territories, that the geographers began to mind the borders. In this process, the activities of the Congregazione del Buon Governo (1592) were crucial.[2] Founded for fiscal and economic ends, this office soon came to have geographic and cartographic knowledge of the territory, of the traits and powers of towns and villages, and even of the privileges of the feudal lords. This awareness of boundaries was interwoven with alertness to local roots and to the concrete identity that sprang from local usages and privileges, forming a shared social and religious heritage that very often collided with the justice brought, and imposed, by Rome. The success or failure of papal rule, of its administration of justice, and of social discipline all depended on the play of these local differences and on the state's dialogue with its subjects' inherited modes of attachment and belonging. The state's growth was a long, slow business, a piecemeal advance, with steps forward and concessions, and with acts of mediation. There was also repression, some of it quite harsh.

At the end of the fifteenth century, the Papal State was divided into five provinces: the Patrimony of Saint Peter, the Duchy of Spoleto, the March of Ancona, the Romagna, and Campagna e Marittima. These divisions were already evident in 1357, anticipated by the *Constitutiones Aegidianae*, administrative decrees promulgated at Fano in a *parlamento generale* by Cardinal Gil de Albornoz. The cardinal's decrees aimed to extend to all papal territories the political and administrative model already in vigor in the Marches. These regulations controlled the activities of the *rettore*, who represented the pope and whose task it was "to direct the resources of the

1. For this topic, see Roberto Volpi, *Le regioni introvabili. Centralizzazione e regionalizzazione nello stato Pontificio* (Bologna: il Mulino, 1983).

2. Gabriella Santoncini, *Il Buon Governo. Organizzazione e legittimazione del rapporto fra sovrano e comunità (secc. XVI–XVIII)* (Milan: Giuffrè, 2002); Stefano Tabacchi, *Il Buon Governo. Le finanze locali nello Stato della Chiesa (secoli XVI–XVIII)* (Rome: Viella, 2007).

province towards the consolidation of papal authority while maintaining the consent of the governed."[3] So the *rettore*'s job was fundamentally political from the start, and would become ever more so, for the *rettore* worked alongside the *legato*, the legate, a cardinal endowed with ample political and judicial powers and sent on one or another mission, often a delicate one. As time went on, in some provinces, the legate replaced the *rettore* altogether. The rules laid out the jurisdictions, both civil and penal, for keeping public order and defending the territory, and stressed the roles of both justice and the legate's administration, both fundamental for the pope's authority. On the other hand, there were no ground rules for the activities of the *tesoriere* (the treasurer), the other key figure in the running of the provinces. It fell to the *tesoriere* to raise the taxes and all the income of the *Camera Apostolica* (Apostolic Chamber, i.e., the central treasury), not to mention to pay the papal officials active in his province. He was a dependent of the *Camera Apostolica*, and a papal appointee. The treasurer had growing ties with the major merchant-banker houses active in the papal curia—Sienese, Florentine, and Genoese.

Meanwhile, in the Middle Ages, the provincial *parlamenti* were still active. Assemblies representing social groups and towns, they had not yet lost their function—discussion and political negotiation with the representative of papal rule. Relations between the legate, or the *rettore*, and the local *parlamento* were not always smooth. Good relations depended on the personality of the pope's man and on his skill at mediating, and at imposing his will on local quarrels and conflicts fed by faction, by feudal power, and by the rivalries of cities. From the fifteenth century on, as papal officials were more often afoot in the provinces and as Rome gained the power to force consensus and began to draw local oligarchs to the capital, these representative bodies faltered and faded. The division of competencies never had the clarity of an organization chart. Rather, wars, international politics, and the internal workings of papal politics at the end of the fifteenth century left provincial administration ever more uncertain and unstable. Only toward the middle of the sixteenth century would things finally jell.

---

3. Andrea Gardi, "L'amministrazione pontificia e le province settentrionali dello Stato (XIII–XVIII secolo)," *Archivi per la storia* 13, nos. 1–2 (2000): 43.

RESTLESS BORDERLANDS

The northern border best exemplified the process of fragmentation and reconfiguration of the landscape. Behind the territorial shifts lay, on the one hand, the state-building campaign launched by Alexander VI (1492–1503) on behalf of his son Cesare Borgia, and on the other, the warlike policies of popes like Julius II. In 1503, Julius retook Cesena and other Romagna towns, among them the castle at Forlì, which Cesare had held, along with the title "Lord of the Romagna." The pope's campaign demonstrated that it did not suffice to heap up cities in the Borgia mode to make oneself master of a territory; one needed, rather, to build a coherent political unit. By the time Julius died, in 1513, he had succeeded in winning back territories that had been in Venetian hands, like Faenza and Rimini. And then, after Venice's catastrophic defeat at Agnadello (1509), the papacy took back the other Romagna cities: Ravenna, Rimini, Cervia, Faenza, Russi, Brisighella, Meldola, and Mercato Saraceno.[4] But, already three years earlier, Julius II had subjected Bologna, chasing out the ruling Bentivoglio, even though, thereafter, the reconquered city would still enjoy a privileged position in the state. Julius had appeared at Bologna's walls with an imposing army and then gone on to Perugia to drive off its ruler, Giampaolo Baglioni. The whole campaign looked like little less than a triumphal cavalcade, or, perhaps, like a pomp-filled *Possesso* march (the coronation parade at Rome), contrived to affirm papal authority on the lands and towns it traversed.[5]

At the turn of the sixteenth century, with the breakdown of the Italian balance of power, international affairs had required the popes to expand their domains northward to exploit a political map reduced to rubble and confusion, taking advantage of factional fights and of the general instability that invested the Lombard Plain, from the Apennines up to the Alps. Even after the papal authorities retook the Romagna lands and broke up the remnants of

4. For a comprehensive survey of early modern Romagna, see Angelo Turchini, *La Romagna nel Cinquecento*, vol. 1, *Istituzioni, comunità, mentalità* (Cesena: Il Ponte Vecchio, 2003).

5. For the symbolic and political meaning of this ceremony: Irene Fosi, "Court and City in the Ceremony of the *Possesso* in the Sixteenth Century," in *Court and Politics in Papal Rome, 1472–1700*, ed. Gianvittorio Signorotto and Maria Antonietta Visceglia, 31–52 (Cambridge: Cambridge University Press, 2002).

the Borgia state, they worked long and hard to master local conditions. The factional fights in cities had their echoes in the countryside, feeding disorders and violent habits that, toward the century's end, unleashed a great wave of banditry, most often led by feudal lords who, keen to grab back powers lost to the Borgias and still largely free of papal rule, battled one another in private feuding between locally powerful families sometimes labeled "private warfare and affirmation of force."[6] Gradually, in the course of the sixteenth century, intensely local forms of power and dominion would give way to others defined by factions or broader familial alliances. Local power was fostered too by the nature of the landscape, by the distance from Rome and its officials, by the decrepit or absent roads that hindered or barred the intervention of papal officials and judges. In the second half of the sixteenth century, the state tried to cope with this situation, hardly unique to the Romagna, but especially common in papal zones near borders. The recourse was to break the territory into manageable pieces and to coordinate policy from the center, using the new Roman congregations like the Buon Governo and Sacra Consulta, administrative councils staffed by cardinals. In this period, papal authorities undermined the bonds of faction and fealty, the old glue between the peasants and their lords, by supplanting these feudal links with relationships of service and with exchanges between local elites and representatives of the Holy See.[7] In 1524, the northern territory, all the way from Rimini west to Piacenza, finally recovered by papal authority, at least in theory, was reorganized under two "legations," each with its legate. One was called Bologna, and contained the Romagna; the other, Gallia Cispadana, included Parma and Piacenza. In each city sat a governor. Moreover, there came changes in fiscal administration; the job of provincial treasurer, for the first time ever, was auctioned off.

The situation was still in flux; the popes lost some territories. In 1530, Modena and Reggio went back under Este rule, and in 1545, the Farnese family, Paul III's kinsfolk, hived off Parma and Piacenza to build themselves a duchy. The Romagna remained a ter-

6. "Guerra privata e affermazione di forza": as labeled by Cesarina Casanova, *Gentiluomini ecclesiastici. Ceti e mobilità sociale nelle Legazioni pontificie (sec. XVI–XVIII)*, 39 (Bologna: Clueb, 1999).

7. Ibid., 18.

ritory in pieces, bereft of a center to pull all parts together. One can calibrate the efficacy of papal governance by its capacity to impose itself, via officialdom, as the superior body and reference point for both elites and underlings. Down to the end of the seventeenth century, legates, governors, or presidents ran the Romagna. The first of these, usually cardinals, had more forceful authority and more autonomy; the others, as inferiors in rank, were more beholden to rulings from Rome, especially after the end of the sixteenth century, when the regime reorganized and elaborated its structure. But we shall see below how, even later, legates could fall into struggles with local bodies, above all when the thing at stake was justice.

SOLDIERS' LANDS: THE MARCHES AND UMBRIA

In the Marches too, sitting on the Adriatic and thus bound up, in economics and politics, in often uneasy relations between Rome and Venice, early modern politics could be far from smooth. In the sixteenth century, the old, wide unity set out by the Egidian Constitutions succumbed. Between 1501 and 1610, Ascoli, Ancona, Fano, Fermo, Jesi, Montalto, Fabriano, San Severino, and Matelica all acquired papal governments. This fragmentation reflected the need to break down districts, the better to rule directly through men run by Rome. It also bore witness to particular agendas in papal politics, as when Sixtus V (1585–1590), himself from Grottammare (Montalto, in the Marches), wished to reorganize the city regimes in his land of birth. Such endeavors aimed to create consensus among local ruling circles, and also to impose, via the papal governor, a more than merely symbolic Roman authority, and to brandish its strength and centralizing ambitions.

The Marches were a richly urban region, but lacked one center that outranked the rest. Macerata, the seat of papal administration, never acquired political or economic hegemony over the other towns. With so many competing towns, a parliament remained active. It was an intercity institution, representative in nature from the start, and it eventually took the name Congregazione della Marca. The papal government found it a useful interlocutor, especially for settling quarrels about taxation. As the early modern period went on, this function faded, while the Roman congregations gained strength. They included the Buon Governo of Clement VIII (1592–1605), and the Sacra Consulta, founded in 1559 and charged with smoothing out the rule of papal provinces and making governance uniform across the board.

The strong sense of civic identity that surfaced in factional conflict, tied as it was to feudal nobles with urban ties, often caused violent clashes between towns and the men of Rome. In the first half of the sixteenth century, when papal administration was still just settling down and politics and warfare were still turbulent, urban revolts against Rome were common. Paul III (1534–1549) trampled Perugia after it rebelled in the so-called Salt War, but, in fact, years earlier the Papal State had already aspired to curtail the political autonomy of Umbria's biggest town. Leo X had waded in forcefully, interfering in the internal fights of Perugia's factions, but between 1527 and 1530, before Malatesta Baglioni returned to town, the republican magistrates obtained for themselves their own Tribunal of the Rota, to make clear to all the autonomy of civic justice in the face of the pope's own courts. But the faction fights made it easier for Paul III to gain lasting submission, and, in 1540, the place lost its autonomy entirely. Perugia's relations with the papacy were regulated by two documents: the Capitoli of 1424 and a 1553 bull of Julius III that redefined the city's subjugation. The city had had its legate, but now it received a mere governor, who ran the whole of Umbria, with Perugia as his seat. Under this new regime, the elite families, product of a vital local economy, continued to play prestigious roles.[8] As has been said, Perugia's government was "a sort of co-dominion of papal officials and local patricians," as is easily seen from the correspondence of Perugian agents at the papal court, who reported back not only to the governors, but also to the city's own priors, who were an emblem of lost liberty and fine representatives of collective identity.[9] The legates and governors, face to face with city politics, found ways to mediate and compromise with local elites as they sought consensus around the new power of Rome. But it was far harder to impose justice and order in Perugia's more remote towns

8. Erminia Irace, *La nobiltà bifronte. Identità e coscienza aristocratica a Perugia tra XV e XVII secolo* (Milan: Unicopoli, 1995); and "'L'Atlantico peso del Pubblico,' Patriziato, politica e amministrazione a Perugia tra Cinque e Settecento," *Archivi per la storia* 13, nos. 1–2 (2000): 177–90.

9. Erminia Irace, "Una voce poco fa. Note sulle difficili pratiche della comunicazione tra il centro e le periferie dello Stato Ecclesiastico (Perugia, metà XVI–metà XVII secolo)," in *Offices, écrits et papauté (XIIIᵉ–XVIIᵉ siècle)*, ed. Armand Jamme and Olivier Poncet, 273–99 (Rome: Ecole Française de Rome, 2007).

and villages, in the inaccessible mountains far from lines of communication. And in Perugia itself, even if in the seventeenth century
things no longer blew up violently, there was no lack of friction and
unease with Rome. This was especially true in the 1640s, as the Barberini papacy trailed off and the ill-advised Castro war ruined precarious finances and undercut the wobbly old consensus between
popes and high and mighty local families.

THE GOVERNO OF THE LEGATES:
FERRARA, BOLOGNA, ROMAGNA

In major cities, the papacy used its very highest administrative
official, the legate. For instance, from 1598 on, with the local Este
dynasty now extinct, Ferrara and its territory were in papal hands.
To take firm possession of the old ducal city, Clement VIII had first
resided there himself, living alongside his officials, the new authorities. But the pope could not stay forever; in Ferrara, as in Bologna
and in the Romagna, he installed a legate, a cardinal ruling for three
years in his name. Though medieval in origin, over the centuries the
legate had evolved considerably in his role. By the end of the sixteenth century, one could define him as "a bureaucrat of the highest
rank who, in his career, found prestige in holding responsible positions, but looked as well for honor and for the advantages they offered."[10] Legates were churchmen drawn from the world of papal
finance, or linked to it tightly. In Bologna, for instance, the seventeenth-century legates were mostly Genoese, members of banking
families active at the papal court.[11] They found ready opportunity to
insert their fellow Genoese to serve under contract as administrators of the province's finances, or to assign them government jobs,
especially in towns under their own jurisdiction.

The legate represented papal authority *in provincia*, charged
above all with fostering justice and good governance. The nomination briefs were explicit, listing all the circumstances in which "the
superior"—as they called him—could wield his power. He also had
considerable authority in matters spiritual, so long as he respected

10. Andrea Gardi, "Il mutamento di un ruolo. I legati nell'amministrazione interna dello Stato Pontificio dal XIV a XVII secolo," in *Officiers et Papauté (XIVᵉ–XVIIᵉ).
Charges, hommes, destins*, ed. Armand Jamme and Olivier Poncet, 418 (Rome: Ecole
Française de Rome, 2005).
11. Nicole Reinhardt, "Bolonais à Rome, Romains à Bologna? Carrières et stratégies
entre centre et périphérie. Une esquisse," in *Officiers et Papauté*, 237–49.

the decrees of the Council of Trent. As for justice itself, the legate could pass judgment on the clergy, both regular and secular, conduct investigations, pass sentence in criminal matters, and use the secular arm to arrest, to jail, and to put to death. As the pope's representative in the province, by proxy he had the pope's own double sovereign power, secular and spiritual. In theory. In fact, however, the legate did not meddle in spiritual affairs and did not clash with bishops. In the seventeenth century, when episcopal power, redefined at Trent, became firmer, the legate abandoned interest in matters of faith and stopped colliding with diocesan powers. In the sixteenth century, however, bishops often had to struggle to impose their will in spiritual and temporal affairs. Gabriele Paleotti's conflicts with Bologna's governor, on the issue of installing Trent's reforms, are a well-known case in point. At times like that, legates did intervene on the bishops' behalf, even in spiritual affairs.[12] Inevitably, then, friction and conflict sprang up, kindling factional rivalries that undermined the pope's power in his trickier cities. The legate's sway in Bologna was represented, symbolically and practically, by the Tribunale of the Torrone, where the he dealt out justice in criminal matters. Established in the 1530s under Clement VII (1523–1534), when the historian Francesco Guicciardini was legate there, the Torrone stood for papal authority, and for Rome's coercive power, facing down the city's inveterate quest for autonomy. The pope's Bolognese subjects never liked this tribunal, and saw the legate's power, especially over justice, as oppressive despotism.[13]

The Ferrara legation, founded at a more stable time in the growth of the papal monarchy's territorial and institutional sway, benefited from a firmer equilibrium, in the province itself, between the bishop's old powers and the legate's new ones. And the legate was inserted into a social situation where the old noble resistances to Roman power had not flickered out, or even simmered

12. Paolo Prodi, *The Papal Prince. One Body and Two Souls: The Papal Monarchy in Early Modern Europe* (Cambridge: Cambridge University Press, 1987), 123–56.

13. For a complete analysis of this tribunal, see Cesarina Casanova, "L'amministrazione della giustizia a Bologna. Alcune anticipazioni sul Tribunale del Torrone," *Dimensioni e problemi della ricerca storica* 2 (2004): 267–92; Giancarlo Angelozzi, "Il tribunale criminale di Bologna," in *La Legazione di Romagna e i suoi Archivi. Secoli XVI–XVIII*, ed. Angelo Turchini, 737–74 (Cesena: Il Ponte Vecchio, 2006); Giancarlo Angelozzi and Cesarina Casanova, *La Giustizia criminale in una città di antico regime. Il tribunale del Torrone di Bologna (secc. XVI–XVII)* (Bologna: Clueb, 2008).

down, for their old masters, the Este, still held power at Modena, not very far away. From the moment of his entry into town, therefore, he was wrapped in a symbolism—of sovereign justice, good order, and social peace—that stressed his superior role as pacifier of faction, discord, and disorder and that fed the consensus his governance required.[14] So the legate's function in Ferrara was, as elsewhere, eminently political, but it could flip into a delicate diplomatic mission, especially when international politics menaced the papal borders. Relations with the Republic of Venice, with the Duchy of Milan—and thus with Spain—and even with the House of Savoy put the reins of policy in legates' hands. One example was the war over Monferrato and the Mantuan succession (1627–1631). As France, Spain, and the German Empire collided, the papacy struggled to hold to a neutral line and to keep their subjects from signing up to fight on one or another side. Meanwhile, thanks to war's confusion and destruction, plague and famine raged. Extraordinary times aside, it fell to the legate to impose papal power on the city, its hinterland, and its dependent towns and villages, without colliding with local privileges and, above all, without alienating the nobles of the zone. To rekindle their factions and all the disorders they entailed would have sapped Rome's authority. So the exercise of justice served both as an instrument of social control and a device for political uniformity. Assorted "instructions" and treatises for "those who went off to govern" and the briefs of investiture all underlined the task: to protect the weak, and women, and those legally dependent on others. Justice, evenhanded and superior, thus should inspire the legates' course of action. The dichotomy between theory and practice, between the instructions they received and the realities they faced, demanded of the cardinal legates caution, prudence, and tact.

Faced with the looming dangers posed by widespread banditry, and by the nobles' smoldering rebelliousness, at Bologna toward 1600 the legates' justice tried to suppress insubordination by banishing anyone tainted with lèse-majesté (high treason). They repressed harshly the families that led factions—for example, the

---

14. Irene Fosi, "'Parcere subiectis, debellare superbos': la giustizia nelle cerimonie di possesso a Roma e nelle legazioni dello Stato Pontificio nel Cinquecento," in *Cérémonial et rituel à Rome (XVIe–XIXe siècle)*, ed. Maria Antonietta Visceglia and Catherine Brice, 90–115 (Rome: Ecole Française de Rome, 1997).

Pepoli and Malvezzi. They also intervened to put down petty criminality, via "composition," a money settlement to compensate a misdeed's victim and close the case. To bring proceedings to a quicker end, before a judgment, they had complaints withdrawn and made a private "peace" (una pace) between the parties.[15] But sometimes conflicts arose, and there were formal protests against a cardinal's judicial actions, when they were harsh, repressive, or downright brutal. From Bologna came complaints against the harshness and brutality of the birri (police) and of the agents of justice sent across the countryside chasing after troublemakers. There were complaints as well against notaries' greed and corruption. At the end of the seventeenth century, all such laments stemmed from the city's, and its magistrates', diffuse but deep discontent with the actions of legate Buonaccorso Buonaccorsi, who, among other things, was persecuting certain nobles.[16] Bologna's complaints often arrived at Rome via its ambassador, but generally failed to win a hearing. Rome's position sometimes seems biased against Bologna's requests, as if to demonstrate, by a hard line, Rome's superiority over all "privileges" and "liberties" conceded to the subject city since 1500.[17]

In theory, the pope's representative, in his daily work, was supposed to trim norms to fit his practices and to modulate his actions with an eye to the authority he represented and to local traditions. True, this difficult equipoise between two often warring realities was the mark of buon governo. But, in cities like Bologna, Ferrara, and even Perugia, with strong traditions of communal rule and local lordship, this delicate balance demanded "suitability" and prudence, virtues sometimes scanty in men sent out to govern provinces.

The starting point for public order was to nail down the provisioning of foodstuffs, to ban forbidden arms, and to control the

15. Andrea Gardi, Lo stato in provincia. L'amministrazione della Legazione di Bologna durante il regno di Sisto V (1585–1590) (Bologna: Istituto per la Storia di Bologna, 1994), 212–18.

16. Angelozzi, "Il tribunale criminale di Bologna," 762–74.

17. Angela De Benedictis, Repubblica per contratto. Bologna, una città europea nello Stato della Chiesa (Bologna: il Mulino, 1995). On the difference between the relations of Bologna and Ferrara with Rome, see Birgit Emich, "Bologneser libertà, ferrareser decadenza: Politische Kultur und päpstliche Herrschaft im Kirchenstaat der Frühen Neuzeit," in Staatsbildung als kultureller Prozess. Strukturwandel und Legitimation von Herrschaft in der Frühen Neuzeit, ed. Ronald G. Asch and Dagmar Freist, 117–34 (Vienna: Böhlau, 2005).

poor, the vagabonds, and other social elements that risked disturb-
ing the quiet of city and hinterland. The pope's representative, sitting in the seat of governance, made his presence felt to his subjects
by confirming and repeating the decrees *(bandi)* of his predecessors, as well as reaffirming the general decrees *(bandi generali)* that
laid out in no uncertain terms all crimes and punishments. Published at the outset of each legate's term of office, these general decrees were designed to forge continuity, in ideal and practice, with
his predecessor's actions and to reinforce papal power, expressed
concretely in his representative. But the proof in the pudding—of
the quality of the regime and of the severity of its justice—was expressed, from the outset, in the threats of severe punishments and
executions issued against transgressors and criminals. Severity was
a sign of good provincial administration, but of control too, and of
vigilance against misgovernance by official underlings that could
spark revolts and fuel popular discontent. It fell to the legate to assure that there be no abuses or illicit acts by officials in the lesser
towns: local protests came his way and he had to forward them to
Rome. Throughout the modern period, the legates' letters to the
"cardinal nephew," a kinsman of the pope elevated to the college to
act as his de facto first minister, bear witness to continual mediation between center and periphery, amidst the many complex and
often conflicting local power arrangements.[18] For the rich diversity
of the legate's activities in law-and-order matters, one should read
his correspondence with the governors of the many cities in his territory, where he often stresses the difficulty of bringing "his" justice
to his domain's far corners.

The cardinal legates of Bologna, Ferrara, and the Romagna usually received, alongside their letters of investiture, an extra brief, itself
almost a ritual of taking office, that specified ample *facultates contra
bannitos* (powers against banished men), granting them extraordinary authority, to strengthen Rome's local hand. The legate kept a
keen eye on the nobles' deviant behavior, watching over their vendettas and their alliances for faction's sake, which might undercut *buon
governo.* As the seventeenth century went on, steps against the banished more and more took on the appearance of police work directed

18. See, for Ferrara, *La Legazione di Ferrara del Cardinale Giulio Sacchetti (1627–
1631),* ed. Irene Fosi with the collaboration of Andrea Gardi, 2 vols. (Rome: Archivio
Segreto Vaticano, 2006).

at outlaws who, exiled to the countryside, smuggled, preyed on peasants, stole livestock, and kidnapped or killed travelers. It was endemic border banditry that flared up in times of crisis.

Rome itself, in the seventeenth century, still looked on this campaign in the distant *legazioni* for *buon governo* and peace with rebellious nobles with skepticism or veiled irony. The author of *Istruzione curiosa et utile data al legato di Romagna al tempo di Urbano VIII* (Curious and Useful Instruction Given to the Legate of Romagna at the Time of Urban VIII) wrote:

As for the jurisdiction that the legate has over places directly under his control, it is easier to make people believe that he can exercise it than it is to put it into effect, but it is always good not to dangle incentives, for if there be among the barons some who make themselves heard, they will be less likely to allow their subjects to have recourse [to the law] or let them have their cases seen to by the courts, and they [the barons] will trouble both themselves and the legate with petitions and appeals to Rome under pretext of the violation of their privileges.

The author went on to remark that all sorts of "governing cliques" (*brighe di governo*) and activities—from the grain office to the office over the waters, from the maintenance of roads to the control of public order—served the interests of "private passions" (*passioni private*).[19]

AROUND ROME: PATRIMONIO,
CAMPAGNA E MARITTIMA

The polymorphous regions right near Peter's Seat, sutured to papal rule at various times in diverse ways—the Patrimony, and Campagna and Marittima (and add to the list Sabina, hived off from Campagna and autonomous from 1605)—in the early modern period still featured that rich diversity of political, juridical, geographic, and social make-up that limited and shaped papal power elsewhere. Besides these lands, or, to put it precisely, sitting atop them, was the District (*Districtus Urbis*), a zone stretching forty Italian miles from Rome, where the governor of Rome had full jurisdiction. As we shall see, to do justice his court very often over-

19. Archivio Segreto Vaticano (henceforth ASV), Misc. Arm. III, t. 15, f. 181r. See also Cesarina Casanova, "La giustizia penale in Romagna e a Bologna nella seconda metà del Seicento. Alcune ipotesi e molte incertezze," in *La Legazione di Romagna*, ed. Angelo Turchini, 699–735 (Cesena: Il Ponte Vecchio, 2006).

stepped this somewhat theoretical outer boundary, especially in the sixteenth century.

The Patrimony of Saint Peter, north of Rome, was, among these territories, the most marked by cities' presence, but it also had ancient feudal holdings and autonomous "states" like the Farnese Duchy of Castro and the Orsini Duchy of Bracciano. The situation of cities, towns, and villages varied: some were direct dependents of the Holy See (*immediate subiectae*), subject to taxation by the Apostolic Chamber. But communities let out as fiefs, or subject in any way to a signiorial regime, owed instead a payment (*censo*) straight to the See itself, an updated form of their old feudal dues. As for Campagna e Marittima, at the beginning of the early modern period the district contained the lands of many barons, extensive and often contiguous. These took the form of real feudal "states" where papal authority long struggled to make even the faintest presence felt. Sermoneta, fief of the Caetani, like the nearby towns Sezze, Ninfa, and Norma, perched on the Monti Lepini, strategic high ground that overlooked and controlled the coastal route to the Kingdom of Naples. The principality of Paliano, a town further east, with its many lands nearby, some coastal, others inland, was a veritable state of the Colonna, one that its masters, proud and alert to their prerogatives, defended jealously. The Colonna lands bordered on those of the Conti, and, nearer Rome in the Alban Hills, touched the lands of the kindred Zagarolo Colonna branch, and of the Savelli, a family of once-potent Roman barons who still held scattered holdings to the city's south and in the Sabina mountains east and north of Rome.[20] As the sixteenth century went on, these families gambled their own futures and territorial power, and their positions in the papal court, by playing international politics, taking one or the other side with factions backing France or Spain. Their eventual fates were subject to the blows and counterblows of Italy's politics, and depended too on mastery of the art of war, and on the unencumbered exercise of feudal power, which was turbulent and violent.

So, south of Rome, governors of cities directly subject to the

20. For a fuller picture, see Giovanni Pizzorusso, "Una regione virtuale: il Lazio da Martino V a Pio IV," in *Atlante storico-politico del Lazio*, 63–87 (Rome: Laterza, 1996). For the Orsini of Bracciano, see Caroline Murphy, *The Pope's Daughter: The Extraordinary Life of Felice della Rovere* (New York: Oxford University Press, 2006).

Holy See always had to cope with the power that mighty and meddlesome clans of Roman barons wielded, directly or indirectly, over towns, magistrates, and subjects. Control was also hard because of the mountainous landscape on the Naples border, a fertile ground for outlaws, who found ready baronial hosts. This zone was impervious to repeated futile bulls and decrees by which, from the late fifteenth century on, the popes strove to break up this noble-bandit alliance by threatening punishments, severe but seldom used, and thundering out excommunications that rarely worked. Toward the baronage—those great feudal families that since the Middle Ages had shaped the power and the policies of the bishop of Rome—papal strategies, even in the early modern age, remained wavering and contradictory. In the second half of the sixteenth century, the pontiff strove to prevent the fragmentation of feudal holdings and reserved to himself the right of conceding fiefs and of defending his own authority in the face of lordly powers. That is the significance of Pius V's 1567 bull "De non infeudando" (his reign: 1566–1572), which recognized, explicitly, feudal jurisdiction and protected the economic aspect of feudal justice. In fact, "it was in the pope's interest that the wealth of barons recover, or, at least, that the crisis in which they found themselves be eased."[21] The capital's provisioning with grain depended, mostly, on the nobles' lands; so did the smooth working of the Annona, the Grain Office, whose efficiency was crucial to urban order. Clement VIII returned to the matter of the economic problems of the baronage, setting up the Congregazione dei Baroni (1596) to keep an eye out for crises and to force debt-laden barons to auction off their lands. By the end of the sixteenth century, the Roman baronage was indubitably in a crisis—an economic and political upheaval that affected caste identity. Against their inveterate anarchy and violence the state had unleashed a wide-reaching, if sometimes wobbly campaign. We will see later how this would evolve into a real political process.[22] From the last decades of the sixteenth century, there was a slow but unceasing transformation, and in some cases erosion, of feudal pow-

21. Pizzorusso, "Una regione virtuale," 73.

22. See chapter 5. For the Barberini, one of the new families, see Caroline Castiglione, *Patrons and Adversaries: Nobles and Villagers in Italian Politics* (New York: Oxford University Press, 2005); for the Borghese see Bertrand Forclaz, *La famille Borghese et ses fiefs. L'authorité négociée dans l'Etat Pontifical d'ancien régime* (Rome: Ecole Française de Rome, 2006).

er. Meanwhile, new papal families kept inserting themselves into Rome's political and social scene. The Boncompagni, Peretti, Aldobrandini, Borghese, Chigi, Barberini, and Pamphili wove lines of intermarriage with the old baronage, taking many territories off their hands, in both the Patrimony and Campagna e Marittima, and, as they did so, forging a transformed feudal geography destined to endure long after the early modern period ended.

2

Roman Tribunals in
the Early Modern Period

Life, honor, and our capacity to act are all in the hands of judges: for, given that honorable conduct and charity are in short supply, violence is on the increase, as is the cupidity of men of ill will; and if judges do not defend us against them, our affairs will go badly . . . and what is more important, justice these days is never done without the help of hard cash.

That is how, at the end of the sixteenth century, the political theorist Giovanni Botero described the expectations, operations, and interests that converged on the administration of justice.[1]

In the papal territories, justice issued from the center, Rome, from institutions both old and new. As time went on, thanks to assorted factors, as justice gained force it reached the periphery. Given the composite nature of the Papal State, Rome was not the only center. There were cities with strong communal traditions, feudatories with well-rooted power, and frontier zones still troubled and wobbly. From the late 1400s, thanks to the growth of papal power, when Roman justice wrestled with this complex, diverse state of affairs it was centralized in structure and hegemonic in spirit.[2]

The reorganization of the administration of justice was crucial for papal policy. After the popes' return from Avignon, now that Rome was the stable home of the papacy itself, of its court, and of its nascent machinery of state, the city saw a progressive and often radical restructuring of its judicial apparatus. This was no simple operation; it lasted long; the slowness of the process was one clear sign of the tricky business of balancing papal power with that of

1. Giovanni Botero, "Delle cause della grandezza delle città," in *Della Ragion di Stato libri X*, 341–43 (Venice: Gioliti, 1598). We translate here from the Italian. For a version of this passage in Botero in a seventeenth-century English edition, see *The Cause of the Greatnesse of Cities*, bk. 2, ch. 6, 79–80 (London: E. P. for Henry Seile, 1635), available online from Early English Books Online.

2. Mario Sbriccoli, "Giustizia criminale," in *Lo stato moderno in Europa. Istituzioni e diritto*, ed. Maurizio Fioravanti, 163–205 (Rome: Laterza, 2002).

the city's own magistrates of the Capitol—the senator and the con-servatori—heirs, or pale shadows, of the fading power of the urban commune. The late fifteenth century and the century that followed witnessed seesaw progress, strung between the desire to control the commune and the impulse not to obliterate the city's own institu-tions. Their functions did indeed live on, if now diluted, and kept their symbolic meaning as the bulwark for liberty and civic iden-tity against papal power. Rome was a paragon, or mirror, of a po-litical process that, with local differences, went on in other parts of the *Stato della Chiesa* (State of the Church) as well, wherever tradi-tions and civic identities were ill reconciled with intrusive Roman power.[3]

In the Italian ancien régime, governance, administration, and jus-tice could not be sundered. Our modern sensibility, with an eye to nineteenth- and twentieth-century models, would see the old mul-tiplicity of judicial bodies as chaos, but, for the time, it was entire-ly normal. The world expected jurisdictions to multiply and func-tions to tangle, thanks to a gradual accumulation of roles, so that, in institutions' daily work, conflict was routine. To this confusion early modern popes responded, like other sovereigns in Italy and elsewhere, with an unbroken, if shifting, campaign to make things simpler and more uniform, and to guarantee justice's more persua-sive, effective, and coherent delivery. They did not always succeed. Still, it seemed to the provinces, towns, and villages scattered across the state that Rome with its many courts could deliver reliable, fair justice, free of the pressures, bullying, incompetence, and corrup-tion of local courts. But, in fact, day-to-day practice proved beyond a doubt that in Rome too justice worked mostly via composition-settlements in cash, quiet agreements on the side, and, above all, private resolutions of interpersonal conflicts. So justice managed to reconcile interests, to mediate tension and rivalry, and to enable di-vergent social and judicial languages to cohabit. The law might use one or another idiom, depending on the circumstances and inter-locutors, and on the chances of guaranteeing one or another legal mode of operation the upper hand. Moreover, much always hung on the moods and drift of the pope in power—and, likewise, on

3. On the political space of the Capitoline municipality in the modern period see Laurie Nussdorfer, *Civic Politics in the Rome of Urban VIII* (Princeton, N.J.: Princeton University Press, 1992).

the play of interstate relations, interfaith politics, family conflicts, and factional struggles, and much hung too on each judge's decisions. In sum, before the courts, nothing was a sure thing.

Let us then talk of Rome, of its numberless tribunals, its tangled jurisdictions, and its inevitable quarrels.

BUONA GIUSTIZIA

At the beginning of the sixteenth century, as a powerful sign of its institutional renewal, the papacy took in hand the governance of justice; Julius II actually dreamed of uniting all Rome's tribunals on Via Giulia, the city's Renaissance main street, built by him and named in his own honor. Thanks largely to the hostility of the

FIGURE 1. The Via Giulia, where Julius II wanted to gather together all of Rome's courts. In the mid-seventeenth century new prisons (*carceri nuove*) were opened on this street.

city's large Florentine community, the project fell through.[4] Nevertheless, in the first half of the sixteenth century, Rome's two most important tribunals saw their prerogatives rearranged. In 1514, Leo X with one bold stroke reinforced the powers of the governor, shunting to his jurisdiction Rome's citizens' cases, both civil and criminal, both spiritual and temporal, and granting him the right to override the statutes whenever he saw fit. Soon thereafter, the Sack of Rome of 1527 threw the city and its institutions into chaos. Amidst epidemic, rapine, and appalling atrocity, the cessation of justice represented, amidst darkness, the very collapse of governance itself.

Rome, when times were normal, enjoyed a reputation for "*buona giustizia.*" As the next two centuries went on, increasingly citizens in fact said so and came running to the Roman tribunals, petitions and letters in hand, to escape the "partiality" of local courts, to denounce other judges and notaries for corruption, and to shortcut procedural delays. In Rome there were many courts; this very multiplicity—no rare thing in cities elsewhere in Italy and Europe either—thanks to the contradictions and confusions it engendered, actually seems more often than not to have advantaged the courts' public. Justice's good repute also had its symbolic roots. Perhaps Romans believed that justice would be better near the seat of the sovereign pontiff. He, like any other prince, was a fount of justice and grace, but all the more so thanks to the dual nature, both spiritual and temporal, of his power. Thanks to the capital's spectacular rites of punishment, its congregations of cardinals, and its pope, Rome, in the collective popular imagination, was a paragon of true justice and equity.

The popes took steps to make their justice more effective. The reorganization of the competences of the Roman congregations of cardinals, a gradual, fitful process, was central to the policies of Sixtus V, a pontiff especially preoccupied with justice. The bull *Immensa aeterni Dei* of 22 January 1588 renewed, amplified, and defined the functions of these congregations, by then the principal organs of governance, both spiritual and temporal. Sixtus's bull signified the desire to centralize papal power. But the congrega-

---

4. Irene Fosi, "Pietà, devozione, politica: due confraternite fiorentine nella Roma del Rinascimento," *Archivio Storico Italiano* 149 (1991): 119–62.

tions never canceled earlier structures and activities; they just sat atop them, and the same was true of the work they undertook with regard to justice both at Rome and in the provinces; the old powers lived on and fought back.

The pope, with his bulls and constitutions, was not the only source of rules. Administration, governance, and judging were all deeply personalized. Accordingly, at the beginning of a stint in office, each officeholder issued decrees, constitutions, and orders to recall the standing rules, and to correct them and bring them up to date. But this ceaseless, disorderly proliferation of rules and precepts posed a problem: which rule took precedence over others, and how did it all connect to who held what office? This confusion was a fundamental problem, especially because it conditioned the center's imposition of power on the outlying territories, the cities, and the zones under feudal jurisdiction. What was the force of papal constitutions, and of the decrees of legates and governors, in the face of the statutes and custom collections and of the unwritten practices that governed life in the countryside, and in cities and lesser centers? And, above all, who saw to it that these rules would be respected? The problem affected the whole Papal State, with its stepwise spread of central power. But Rome itself, supposed model for other places, suffered too from overlapping jurisdictions, and the disorder grew as time when on, so that rules, magistrates, and police forces competed, wrangled, and even fought.

TRIBUNALS NEW AND OLD

At Rome, in the sixteenth and seventeenth centuries, the tribunals of the papal curia itself, called courts of the Camera—collegial bodies with competence to judge cases involving commerce, agriculture, and stock raising, and the business of leasing out the tax collection—coexisted with the courts of the city itself, and then there were the many congregations that, often, in opposition to ordinary courts, interwove or superimposed their own jurisdictions.[5]

5. For the whole picture, see Gabriella Santoncini, "Il groviglio giurisdizionale dello Stato ecclesiastico prima dell'occupazione francese," *Annali dell'Istituto Storico Italo-Germanico in Trento* 20 (1994): 82–102, and the rich bibliography cited there; Alberto Martini, "Dal tribunale al patibolo: il teatro della giustizia a Roma in antico regime," in *I Cenci: nobiltà di sangue*, ed. Michele Di Sivo, 255–308 (Rome: Colombo, 2002).

In the course of the sixteenth century, the Tribunal of the Governor—who was always both a bishop and also the pope's vice chancellor—became, de facto, the city's most important judicial organ. The governor had jurisdiction *in criminalibus* over the whole populace of Rome and its District (within the radius of some forty miles), and over both clerics and laymen, over both the privileged and the lowly. He could wield summary justice and had the power to apply ecclesiastical censure, and he was free to violate city statutes.[6] Cases initiated before his tribunal could be hauled into no other courts. Rather, thanks to a right granted him, he could pass judgment on cases already in process elsewhere, or under the jurisdiction of another court. The sentences he handed down could not be challenged or revoked, and could be canceled only on the express wishes of the pontiff.[7] In spite of the governor's superiority, recognized and sanctioned since 1514 by papal policy, the city's other courts kept up their own intense activity, even if they sometimes collided with Rome's senior criminal court. The governor, as judge, was not a total autocrat; it was his duty to discuss cases and to pass judgment after hearing the views of the Congregation for Crime (*Congregazione Criminale*). Its members were, besides the governor himself, the two lieutenant judges for criminal cases (*luogotenenti criminali*), the fiscale (the public prosecutor, or *procuratore fiscale*), the advocate for the poor, and two procurators of the poor (one nominated by the pope, the other chosen by the Archconfraternity of San Girolamo della Carità). This council met weekly at the governor's own house, bringing together the public and private sides of justice's *buon governo*. Even at the end of the seventeenth century, this mixture would strike the institutional commentator, Cardinal Giovanni Battista De Luca, as a tangible expression of the pope's good justice. He wrote: "Those rules of *buon governo* come under a lot of pressure . . . in that there is a push to have punishment come as fast as possible, while the memory of the crime is still fresh. But this [deliberate pace], rather, is the true way of administering justice in criminal matters."[8]

On the sixteenth-century Roman scene, other courts were nim-

6. Giovanni Battista Fenzonio, *Adnotationes in Statuta, sive ius municipale Romanae Urbis* (Rome: Camera Apostolica, 1636).

7. For a general institutional picture of this magistracy, see Niccolò Del Re, *Monsignor Governatore di Roma* (Rome: Istituto Nazionale di Studi Romani, 1972).

8. Giovanni Battista De Luca, *Il Dottor volgare*, vol. 6, bk. 15, ch. 33, p. 360, cited in Martini, "Dal tribunale al patibolo," 363–64.

ble, keen to defend their own jurisdictions in the face of "new" tribunals born of the pope's desire to centralize his powers. Already in 1473 Sixtus IV had tried to find a fair balance between the senator's tribunal, an older court that embodied municipal traditions, and the governor's, the newer body. Sixtus ended by favoring the senator's, which from its inception had shouldered the tasks of guaranteeing justice in the city, distributing cases among assorted Roman courts, and keeping an eye on judges and especially on the lower magistrates and notaries—a major bridge between high justice and the pope's subjects.

The Court of the Senator, also called the Tribunal of the Campidoglio, had civil and criminal jurisdiction over residents (*incolae*, non-citizens) and over Roman citizens (*cives*), with the exception of churchmen, men of the papal curia, and all others who, for one or another reason, were attached to the curia's officialdom, to the court around the pope, or to the Apostolic Chamber. What was on this tribunal's docket? Theft, for one thing, especially of basic commodities—food, clothing, shoes, sheets, or tools; this was the typical thievery of a poor society where, if famished, one stole just anything. Also fraud. And there were crimes against the person, from homicide to wounding and deliberate facial scarring to plain assault. These were the most common accusations; they bear witness to an everyday violence fed not only by hunger and precarious conditions, but even more by the defense of honor and by vendetta's bloodshed.[9] The senator's tribunal, heir and relic of the old commune, in the sixteenth century felt pressure from the popes to bring into its own hands all justice within Rome's walls. Therefore the two main criminal courts, governor's and senator's, clashed over jurisdiction, especially in the first decades of the sixteenth century, often in strident tones. The struggle of these two served as a sounding board for political tensions as the papacy waded into the Italian Wars, all the while fretting that the nobility might once more rebel and plunge Rome into anarchy.

In 1550 came the Court of the Borgo, the narrow urban district across the Tiber where streets approached Saint Peter's Square and the portals of the Vatican. The new tribunal's foundation under-

9. For the functions of the senator's tribunal, see Michele Di Sivo, "Il tribunale criminale capitolino nei secoli XVI–XVII: note da un lavoro in corso," *Roma moderna e contemporanea* 3 (1995): 201–16.

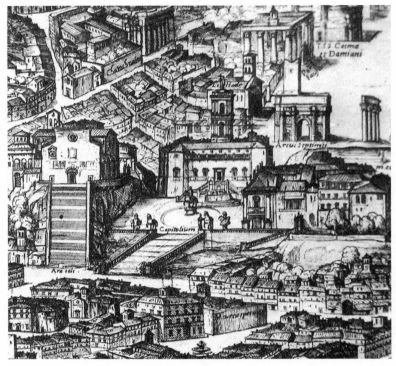

FIGURE 2. The Capitoline Hill, with the Senatorial palace, home of the Tribunal of
the Campidoglio.

lined the political fact that curia and court had become the privileged power axis inside the city. The Borgo court had powers like
the governor's, but a snugger zone of operation—right around the
Apostolic Palace, thick with curial officials and with merchants
scouting career-enhancing moves and profits. This tribunal, with
its narrow spatial scope and explicit jurisdiction, was charged with
whisking a privileged population tied to the curia out from under
the surveillance of Rome's other judges. Indeed, it was the cardinal
nephew, the pope's prime minister, who kept an eye on the judge
of the Borgo. The fact is clear from the letters of Giovanni Salvi,
who between 1635 and 1645 held the post.[10] That judge routine-

10. Biblioteca Apostolica Vaticana (henceforth BAV), Barb. lat. 8994. Salvi would
be dismissed in 1645, and, writing to Cardinal Francesco Barberini to remind him of

ly kept Cardinal Francesco Barberini, Urban VIII's nephew, well posted about all his official business, informing him of quarrels and violent acts, and asking his guidance on how to proceed, especially when cases involved persons close to the court or papal household. Barberini then spun these matters off to his major domo and trusted henchman Fausto Poli. The Borgo tribunal was suppressed in 1667, when both curia and papal court were entering a period of difficult adjustment.

In the sixteenth century, and indeed in the seventeenth as well, there survived in Rome other courts that represented a feudal sphere not yet supplanted. Curia Savelli, the tribunal of the marshall of the church, fit the picture well; it was an ancient heirloom, a privilege long enjoyed by the Savelli, one of Rome's primordial clans of barons. Its jurisdiction was circumscribed to lay curials, men attached to the Roman curia (*romanam curiam sequentes*); this group was larger than one might expect. The city hosted both the papal court and a financial market of global scope, thanks to the pope's role as sovereign and head of the church; men of many kinds "followed the curia." As this tribunal's few remaining papers show, before its judges appeared mainly the protagonists of local crimes: acts of aggression or verbal attacks, usually wounds inflicted to repay some blow to the honor of a person, family, or class. The scene for these dramas was the street, with windows and doors always ajar or about to open to let Romans speak, or spy, or watch, often on the sly, their enemies and friends, their neighbors, and strangers. In November 1629, Jacobo Castiglioni, a *procuratore*, denounced a woman who had come rushing into his house in search of certain documents, "and I have no idea what things, and because in my house there was nothing. I told her to be off and to attend to her own affairs, and she went out and when she was in the street she tossed me a bundle of insults like 'ass-hole procuratore' and other things of that sort, and because I hold a doctorate, am a person of honor, and an official, and I saw how a lowly woman was putting me beneath her, I am putting in a formal legal complaint and I ask that justice do its duty."[11] Such legal complaints were lodged for the

---

his services, would recommend his "understudy," Giovanni Battista Janni, in hopes of "a job for him in Monteflavio."

11. ASV, Curia Savelli, Investigazioni, vol. 1, f. 66v (2 November 1629). On this, see Elisabeth S. Cohen, "Honor and Gender in the Streets of Early Modern Rome," *Journal*

most part in order to report offenses and, thanks to the court's intervention, to recapture lost honor.

The tribunal of the auditor of the Camera, independent of the Apostolic Chamber since 1484, already boasted broad jurisdiction over clerics and men of the curia. Pius IV (1559–1565) then increased it. Its powers, at once vast and vague, made it the most important civil court in Rome, and brought it readily into collision with the Court of the Senator. And then there were other courts, like those of the Ripa and the Ripetta, the downstream and upstream river ports of Rome. These were collegial bodies with jurisdiction over controversies arising from commerce, agriculture, stock raising, and the farming-out of provincial taxation. Meanwhile, each religious order had its own tribunal, and atop that there were supreme tribunals that expressed the universality of the pope's own jurisdiction over the church. In the early modern period, the scope of the Tribunal of the Rota just kept growing; as a court of appeal, it oversaw marriage cases, and litigation over benefices, beatification and canonization trials, and other important cases from lower courts. The Segnatura, once it split in 1492 into Segnatura di Grazia and Segnatura di Giustizia, became a supreme appeals tribunal for cases coming from the entire universal church, be they civil litigation or criminal matters, either church or lay; it had the power not only to review sentences but also to proceed in the first instance.

Every tribunal had its jail, often just a few dark, unwholesome chambers. The early modern prison had judicial uses; it was not for punishment. It served to house the malefactor, real or just suspected, at his or her expense, while the trial went on. There was isolation, *la segreta*, and there was "at large" *(alla larga)*, where one stayed with other prisoners. The windows of "at large" quarters faced streets that resounded with the shouts of friends and allies passing messages to prisoners. The noise itself was one sign of the continuity between street life and jail, a place where much of the population, at least once, had spent some time. Another place, more terri-

of Interdisciplinary History 22 (1992): 597–625. For "Corte Savelli," see Niccolò Del Re, *La Curia capitolina e tre altri antichi organi giudiziari romani* (Rome: Fondazione Marco Besso, 1993), 103–29. For a general picture, see Peter Blastenbrei, *Kriminalität in Rom 1560–1585* (Tübingen: Niemeyer, 1995), and "Violence, Arms, and Criminal Justice in Papal Rome, 1560–1600," *Renaissance Studies* 20 (2006): 68–87.

ble because sure and fateful, was the jail called "the galley slave" (*la galeotta*), where the prisoners condemned to rowing were held prior to being transferred to the naval base, Civitavecchia, and from there to the galleys themselves. In 1656, the new prisons in Via Giulia opened. Other prisons, Tor di Nona and Corte Savelli, closed soon after. Spaces in the new jail were more ample and salubrious and men and women were kept apart, solving the old problem of promiscuity. One always paid to stay. Families had to supply the cash, though in case of poverty the confraternity of San Girolamo della Carità stepped in. Overall, in the ancien régime, punishments were harsher than crimes might seem to merit. There was little use of prisons. Rather, the usual punishments, execution aside, were whippings, hoistings on the rope (*strappado*), and other humiliating physical afflictions, plus fines or full confiscation, exile, and the galleys.[12]

The governor's court, especially after the middle of the sixteenth century, tended to ignore the forty-mile radius of the District and to extend its jurisdiction over the entire state. Such a broadening of its competence was justified by the fluid political situation, and by the need to use the Roman tribunal and its judges to signal a strong papal presence in subject territories, then still riled by faction, revolt, banditry, and noble rebellion. But, even in the seventeenth century, with the emergency over and good administration well ensconced, the governor again and again was asked to intervene in cases outside his ambit in the District. In 1600, for example, an inhabitant of Todi turned straight to the governor of Rome to lodge a legal complaint against a fellow townsman, guilty, he claimed, of having seduced his daughter.

FIGURE 3. Public flogging and banishment.

12. On Rome's prison system, see Michele Di Sivo, "Sulle carceri dei tribunali penali a Roma: Campidoglio e Tor di Nona," in *Atti del Convegno (Somma Lombardo, 14–15 dicembre 2001) Carceri, carcerieri, carcerati. Dall'antico regime all'Ottocento*, ed. Livio Antonielli and Claudio Donati, 9–22 (Soveria Manelli: Rubbettino, 2006).

He hoped for sure justice, untainted by local pressures and interests. The accused countered that the court lacked standing *extra districtum* and petitioned to transfer the case to the bishop of Todi. It was hardly the first time that the governor found himself in conflict with a bishop's jurisdiction, whether casually, or, more often, by design. In 1616 Pirro Jacovacci da Vallecorsa wrote the governor for a pardon for his son, once a cleric in the diocese of Fondi, south of Rome, who had been banished for homicide from the whole province of Campagna e Marittima and who, after twelve years in exile, had finally obtained a pardon from the victim's family. In principle, to reinstall him required the bishop's consent, but the governor revoked the exile, in writing, without the least trace of episcopal assent in the surviving paperwork. Has a piece of paper gone astray? Or, more likely, did quiet conversations bring this and other cases to resolution? Not all lines ran straight: the panorama of justice, at Rome and in the Papal State, revealed its share of jumble, despite all the pope's attempts at good clear order.

The plurality of jurisdictions made for confusion in the minds of the pope's subjects. Faced with tribunals that offered complicated, arbitrary chances at obtaining justice, from all around the state—not just from Rome—they often appealed straight to the pope, whom they saw as the reliable fount of equity. In 1624, Diamante Calvi, "tormented" since 1594 by a notary of the Tribunale del Campidoglio, "with a thousand sweet-talks, sharp dealings, lies, and tongue-lashings, so that I, a poor little woman living alone, have never been able to have my due," asked the pope "as a just prince" to have her case transferred to the governor. That same year, another woman, Agnese Rainaldi, "defrauded by her husband of her dowry of 1000 scudi," asked the governor, rather than the Tribunale di Ripa, to look into her case. The priest Vincenzo Gavotto, accused of debts and jailed in Naples by order of the auditor of the Apostolic Chamber, asked the pope that his case be transferred to the *vicario*'s court, an ecclesiastical jurisdiction, "because I am a cleric, or to the governor, to both of whom, by the rules, such matters should belong." These are just a few examples; one could cite many more to demonstrate how, although the public might be baffled by the complexity of justice and the swarm of courts, the governor's supremacy had become widely known.

THE BISHOP OF ROME AND HIS TRIBUNAL

From the middle of the sixteenth century, as the Catholic Reformation took hold, the line between sins and crimes blurred; this development inevitably tangled the jurisdictions of courts already at work in the city, like the governor's and the *vicario's*, with those of some bishops in other dioceses in the state. But then, everywhere, including Rome itself, what truly shook justice's precarious equilibrium was the advent of the Inquisition (1542). Controversies flared, not only over jurisdiction, but also over precedence. These disputes further complicated the tricky insertion of the new Tribunal of the Faith in the pope's own city.

The Tribunale del Vicario was Rome's episcopal court, for the *vicario* himself officiated in the pope's stead as the city's working bishop. His court's powers were ample, but ill defined, especially over crimes. His competence extended to the vague realm of "moral" crimes, in domains of sex, family, and comportment. The *vicario's* power was thus not solely spiritual, but, in the city, material as well; he had his constabulary and his judges, who in their careers often served the city's own tribunals too. Among the magistrates was a lieutenant criminal judge, picked by the pope upon the *vicario's* nomination. To the lieutenant fell the deciding vote in the Congregazione Criminale; he reported on trials in course and drafted *monitori* (staying orders) and sentences. In his team were two "criminal substitutes," also judges, and two "substitute *fiscali*" (prosecutors), four notaries, and a band of cops under a *bargello's* command. His was a court of first instance for clerics and laymen in mixed cases where civil and canon law both applied. Matrimonial cases, sodomy, and blasphemy (if short of heresy, which fell to the Inquisition) should all have fallen to the court of the city's acting bishop. But the governor's own documents prove that in fact they often went to him instead, for he could use his power to preempt a case, and he could also cite powers granted him by the civic statutes. From 1550 on, the *vicario* also had jurisdiction over Jews and Jewish converts to Christianity. This was a claim of considerable symbolic and political power, and it came to him in the very years when, in Rome, Jews were being segregated and confined to the new ghetto. The Casa dei Catecumeni, a closed residence to produce new converts, was set up, and so began the policy of control, conversion, and marginalization of Rome's Jews that set the tone for the centuries that followed.[13]

The *vicario*'s court, as the tribunal of the acting bishop of Rome, worked hand in glove with the Inquisition, which often handed the *vicario*, for "salutary penance," persons who had proven only lightly tainted by crimes in the Holy Office's purview, even when they turned themselves in, spontaneously, out of zeal or fear, accusing themselves of some deed or action smacking of unorthodoxy. And then there were the falsely accused, thanks to ignorance, or to the malice of "enemies, rivals, and busybodies," often their own kinfolk. Moreover, because it had jurisdiction in cases of *mixto foro* (where lay and church law mingled), and because it was the bishop's court of the pope's own town, the *vicario*'s tribunal was summoned, more than courts elsewhere, to champion social discipline and morality, overseeing private behavior: sexuality, family relations, and marriage. The loss of almost all the court's records makes historical investigation hard. One lonely volume of interrogations before the *vicario*'s criminal lieutenant, from 1567, in the pontificate of stern Pius V, when control and repression of the city's life was most rigid, opens a narrow window onto what must once have been a sweeping panorama.[14] It gives a glimpse of domestic violence and neighborhood conflict, and of prostitution, this last the hallmark of a fluid society mainly male and often unmarried, where clergy and others strayed far from the moral model that the Council of Trent had hoped to impose. Every day, before the tribunal, trooped men and women, and laymen and clerics, over whose morality Pius V designed to keep close watch. The court investigated social habits, tracking emotional alliances, company kept, and deviant sex. Above all, disorderly sexuality and, in that connection, prostitution and clerical morals were the court's favorite targets for control and repression. Before the *vicario* appeared the habitual prostitutes, plus women who now and again "let themselves in for intercourse" (*si fanno negotiare*) sometimes under the indulgent eyes of husbands or others of their circle. Denunciations streamed in from neighbors, spurred by envy, ancient enmity, or an itch to stir up trouble.

13. On this theme, see Marina Caffiero, *Battesimi forzati. Storie di ebrei, cristiani e convertiti nella Roma dei papi* (Rome: Viella, 2004).

14. Archivio Storico del Vicariato di Roma (henceforth ASVR), Tribunale criminale del Vicario, Costituti, busta 102.

FIGURE 4. The public flogging and exile of Sicilian prostitute Isabella Ferri.

I live in Trastevere on the street that runs right up to San Crisogono, and in the house attached to mine there is a woman called Betta, and she keeps two women in her house, whose names I do not know, but they are whores . . . and lots of people go there, and they make too much racket and ruckus, and in my house I have a wife.[15]

The denouncer went on to ask that his neighbors be driven off, "on account of their unseemly way of life, and the many dirty words they always say, and that one can hear from down in the street." Prostitution was deeply embedded in Roman economic and social life; it was not marginal in the modern way. It served the social and emotional needs of unmarried men and the economic needs of disadvantaged women with very slender options. Nevertheless, in the

15. ASVR, Tribunale criminale del Vicario, Costituti, busta 102, f. 201r.

eyes of moralists, prostitution, whether public or hidden, was an element of disorder and of contagion. Festive parties, music, fire-arms and sharpened steel, forbidden games, and foreign clientele were the trade's habitual garnish. Such things, witnesses might claim, disturbed neighborhoods' fragile equilibrium, besmirched the senses—sight, and hearing—and undermined the good order that, with ceaseless effort, authority strove to plant in town. Even if penned by occasional decrees into marginal neighborhoods, prosti-tution, unstoppable, overlapped civic dikes and upset all the papa-cy's futile legislation.[16]

The *vicario* was also called upon to keep an eye on the Jews, whose condition stranded them on the cusp of marginality; on that account, he was mired in repeated wrangles with other Roman judg-es. The Jews were accused of failure to wear the marks newly imposed by laws, the hats and cloth badges designed to distinguish them from everyone else in Rome. They were blamed as well for receiving sto-len goods, and for taking bets—"will the river flood or subside?"—for frequenting Christian women, and for brawls and other distur-bances of good public order. The authorities pushed hard to control the Jews, with only mixed success.[17]

There is good evidence that the campaign of the *vicario*'s court to discipline the city met with failure. In the early eighteenth centu-

16. Among the various studies on the Roman courtesans and prostitutes and their world see: Monica Kurzel-Runtscheiner, *Töchter der Venus. Die Kurtisanen Roms im 16. Jahrhundert* (Munich: Beck, 1995); Elizabeth S. Cohen: "'Courtesans' and 'Whores': Words and Behaviour in Early Modern Rome," *Women's Studies* 19, no. 2 (1991): 201–8; Cohen, "Seen and Known: Prostitutes in the Cityscape of Late Sixteenth-Century Rome," *Renaissance Studies* 12, no. 3 (1998): 392–409; Cohen, "Back Talk: Two Pros-titutes' Voices from Rome c. 1600," *Early Modern Women: An Interdisciplinary Jour-nal* 2 (2007): 95–126; and Tessa Storey, *Carnal Commerce in Counter-Reformation Rome* (Cambridge: Cambridge University Press, 2008).

17. See, among others, the essays in *Quaderni storici* 99 (1998), edited by Michele Luzzati. Kenneth Stow, *The Jews in Rome (1536–1551)*, 2 vols. (Leiden: Brill, 1995); Stow, *Theatre of Acculturation: The Roman Ghetto in the Sixteenth-Century* (Seattle: Univer-sity of Washington Press, 2001); Stow, *Jewish Life in Early Modern Rome: Challenge, Conversion, and Private Life*, Variorum Collected Studies Series (Aldershot: Ashgate, 2007), where almost all the reprinted articles bear on Christian-Jewish relations in Rome; Simona Feci, "The Death of a Miller: A Trial *contra hebreos* in Baroque Rome," *Jewish History* 7, no. 2 (1992): 9–27; Jörg Deventer, "Zwischen Ausweisung, Repression und Duldung: die Judenpolitik der 'Reformpäpste' im Kirchenstaat (ca. 1550–1605)," *Aschkenas: Zeitschrift für Geschichte und Kultur der Juden* 14, no. 2 (2004): 365–85; Kim Siebenhüner, "Conversion, Mobility and the Roman Inquisition in Italy around 1600," *Past & Present* 200 (2008): 5–35.

ry, in a memorial for official eyes designed to describe and strength-
en the office, Nicolò Antonio Cuggiò, the cardinal *vicario*'s secretary
(1700–1739), wrote that, among other things:

one hears of the dissoluteness of the regular clergy [monks and friars],
who with great liberty go out alone in Rome and everywhere else as well
. . . and their clothing is hardly modest and in their churches one finds,
mostly, dissolute young men, and women of easy virtue. . . . In the nunneries good monastic discipline is not to be found . . . in the churches
they celebrate the holidays with great pomp, fancy staging, and music,
with great waste of money. . . . In the monasteries, at the celebrations for
taking the veil or the habit, they have introduced the abuse of bringing to
the ladies [who come to see the service] refreshing drinks and chocolate,
and young men carry their trains. . . . And the custom of putting on plays
in monasteries is pernicious because they do not perform spiritual works.

Cuggiò then goes on to cite all the abuses committed by the Jews,
and then observes, "The prostitutes have increased in number and
receive both priests and friars, with great scandal . . . in Rome there
are many men who keep concubines . . . the notaries of the court
are not very diligent about keeping the public records in good order, and seldom bind their papers into volumes."

The disorder depicted in this polemic suggests the weak impact of the *vicario*'s authority as guarantor of public morality, and
shows how immunities, and privileges—especially those enjoyed by
the major basilicas—and competition with other courts all applied
the brakes to his judicial incursions. Moreover, as Cuggiò wrote at
the end of his detailed catalogue of the abuses that undercut the authority of the *vicario*:

Churchmen, whether secular or regular clergy, when involved in civil or
criminal cases, make use of the secular courts . . . something that does
much to diminish the jurisdiction of your Eminence's court and does
great damage to [the income of] your notaries.[18]

MAKING PEACE

These then were the most important institutions charged with
providing justice in Rome. It was a complicated panorama. And,
especially in the sixteenth century, it felt the personal interven-

18. Domenico Rocciolo, ed., *Della giurisdittione e prerogative del Vicario di Roma.
Opera del canonico Nicolò Antonio Cuggiò segretario di Sua Eminenza* (Rome: Carocci,
2004), 60–66.

tions of the pope himself; he could decide which tribunal would hear a case, when to cancel a sentence and to have a trial's records destroyed, and whether to absolve a man plainly guilty of crimes, however atrocious. True, the governor too could excommunicate, but this power, restricted more and more, was used above all in crimes of lèse-majesté, that is, of rebellion, in all its many forms, and of banditry. The pope usually intervened in cases that involved barons and other nobles. His Holiness was unpredictable; sometimes harsh public punishment befell such men, sometimes extraordinary clemency. For other folk—for most of the pope's subjects—papal justice followed very different paths.

But how many cases were settled out of court? And how many saw only a partial intervention of "official" justice? These questions evoke a problem that has fascinated recent scholarship: can we sketch out a comprehensive picture of criminality and subject it to quantitative analysis?[19] And, in this attempt at measurement, how can we define those rough deeds that had long accompanied private disputes and quarrels, and often failed to turn up in court? Can we locate them precisely, in the shifting borderlands between public and private social regulation?[20] The sources themselves—depo-

19. On this issue, see the questions raised by Mario Sbriccoli, "Storia del diritto e storia della società. Questioni di metodo di ricerca," in *Storia sociale e dimensione giuridica. Strumenti di indagine e ipotesi di lavoro*, ed. Paolo Grossi, 127–48 (Milan: Giuffrè, 1986); Sbriccoli, "Fonti giudiziarie e fonti giuridiche. Riflessioni sulla fase attuale degli studi di storia del crimine e della giustizia criminale," *Studi storici* 29 (1988): 491–501; Edoardo Grendi, foreword to "Fonti criminali e storia sociale," *Quaderni storici* 66 (1987): 695–700; Grendi, "Sulla 'storia criminale': risposta a Mario Sbriccoli," *Quaderni storici* 73 (1990): 269–75. For English translation of Italian works that use criminal records to social historical ends, see Edward Muir and Guido Ruggiero, eds., *Microhistory and the Lost People of Europe* (Baltimore: Johns Hopkins University Press, 1991); Muir and Ruggiero, eds., *History from Crime: Selections from Quaderni Storici* (Baltimore: Johns Hopkins University Press, 1994). For works in English using court records, see for instance Thomas Kuehn, "Reading Microhistory: The Example of *Giovanni and Lusanna*," *Journal of Modern History* 61 (1989): 514–31; Trevor Dean, *Crime in Medieval Europe. 1200–1550* (Harlow: Longman, 2000); Julius R. Ruff, *Violence in Early Modern Europe* (Cambridge: Cambridge University Press, 2001); Pieter Spierenburg and Sophie Body-Gendrot, eds., *Violence in Europe: Historical and Contemporary Perspectives* (New York: Springer, 2008).

20. On the subject of Italian peacemaking and settlements that did not go to court, see Benôit Garnot, ed., *L'infrajudiciaire du Moyen Âge à l'époque moderne* (Dijon: Presses universitaires de Dijon, 1996); Ottavia Niccoli, "Rinuncia, pace, perdono. Rituali di pacificazione della prima età moderna," *Studi storici* 40 (1990): 219–61; Niccoli, *Perdonare. Idee, pratiche, rituali in Italia tra Cinque e Seicento* (Rome: Laterza 2007); Marco Bellabarba, "Pace pubblica e pace privata: linguaggi e istituzioni processuali nell'Italia

sitions offered up in trials, registers of official papers, letters, and petitions for clemency—demonstrate how the great mass of actual trials, or, to put it better, the mountain of papers that depict the procedures of cases, reflects in fact only a scintilla of the assaults and strong-arm dealings, infractions, illicit actions, and crimes committed by the early modern populace.

Though a private peace and reconciliation might arise by interpersonal negotiation, unassisted by officials, courts themselves often sponsored and guaranteed out-of-court settlements. For the pope's subjects, as for inhabitants of other states, to go to court meant a long, uncertain journey. The records in the archives suggest that, even in Rome, most complaints concluded with a solution between the parties involved, that is, with a peace agreement, or with a posted bond, a "surety about not doing harm" (*segurtà de non offendendo*). Rome's 1580 statutes foresaw the benefits of making formal peace within ten days of the offense, and this "consensus," they said, by putting an end to the quarrel, would halve the usual fine attached to the crime in question.[21] The statutes also foresaw the election, every two years, of *pacieri*, official peacemakers, but, in reality, the actual mediators between aggrieved parties were often persons external to the courts, belonging to the litigants' social group, community of workers, or neighborhood. In the second half of the sixteenth century, the courts themselves would figure more and more as legitimate protagonists in making peace. But this arrogation did not go smoothly, flying as it did in the face of customs and values that followed other logics not easily reconciled to the growing claims and competence of judges. A peace had to follow certain agreements. First came the decision of the aggrieved to withdraw his or her complaint before the courts. "By his own free will he agreed to let the complaint be quashed and gave them peace

moderna," in *Criminalità e giustizia in Germania e in Italia. Pratiche giudiziarie e linguaggi giuricidici tra tardo medioevo ed età moderna*, ed. Marco Bellabarba, Gerd Schwerhoff, and Andrea Zorzi, 189–213 (Bologna: il Mulino, Berlin: Duncker & Humblodt, 2001); Bellabarba, *La giustizia nell'Italia moderna* (Rome: Laterza, 2008), 76–81; Barbara Krug-Richter and Ruth E. Mohrmann, eds., *Praktiken des Konfliktaustrags in der Frühen Neuzeit* (Münster: Rhema, 2004); John Bossy, *Peace in the Post-Reformation: The Birkbeck Lectures 1995* (Cambridge: Cambridge University Press, 1998); Stuart Carroll, "The Peace in the Feud in Sixteenth- and Seventeenth-Century France," *Past & Present* 178 (2003): 74–115; Paolo Broggio and Maria Pia Paoli, eds., *Stringere la pace. Teorie e pratiche della conciliazione nell'Europa moderna (secoli xv–xviii)* (Rome: Viella, 2011).

21. Fenzonio, *Adnotationes in Statuta*, 584–86, 597–98.

according to the form [of the law] under penalty": so goes the Latin formula used by the notaries of the governor's tribunal.[22] Then followed the promise of the other party "not to molest [harm]" his rival. At the beginning of the seventeenth century, the jurists elaborated precise rules to legitimate and regulate recourse to these practices, adjusting their criteria with an eye to the social station of those seeking to make the peace.[23]

The act of peacemaking had symbolic and sacred weight, manifest in the rituals and gestures that accompanied it: the kiss, the handshake, the embrace in front of witnesses or even, sometimes, before the entire community gathered around. Besides cutting short vendettas, which easily could trouble the quiet and good order of the community, peace was also an essential condition for anyone who aspired to the sovereign pope's beneficence. In fact, those condemned to exile, when petitioning for pardon, had good reason to cherish hope for a gracious hearing if they had first made peace with the offended party. Hence the frequent call to judges in the further provinces, to keep in decent order the record of peace pacts. There was an almost obsessive insistence, via instructions and letters to men in charge of courts, on good order and on registration. Proper documentation guaranteed certainty, and pinned down the conditions agreed on, often after tense conflicts. The act of drafting the peace agreement was a moment of ritualized gestures and formulae, often solemnized by the presence of public authorities. It was an action that purified, and that allowed the malefactor's reintegration into society.

The many, many "consensuses and peace agreements" registered every day by the Roman courts—by the governor's tribunal, for example—especially at the end of the sixteenth century and the beginning of the seventeenth, most often concerned verbal offenses, wounds, blows, and other lesser acts of violence of the sort that daily disturbed the city's streets. Few involved homicides and other "more atrocious crimes." These merited the force of justice and exemplary punishment. The tribunal itself, and its notaries, urged the quarreling parties toward a peaceful settlement, before undertaking the long march of a formal trial. The notaries stood to gain, what with the fees and registration payments a peace pact involved,

22. ASR, Tribunale Criminale del Governatore, Registrazione d'atti, buste 152 ff.
23. Niccoli, *Perdonare*, 98–113.

and also often pocketed more under the table. Extrajudicial peace also was a fine way to cut the labor that burdened inefficient courts, short of qualified staff and prey to uncertainty and risk. Moreover, the *pax* signaled the court's authority over an essential function of justice: not punishment, but reconciliation; not exclusion, but inclusion. A relic of the medieval past and of private justice, in the late sixteenth century the peace agreement became a convenient instrument in the hands of judicial officials. They used it to flag the function of sovereign justice, the guarantee of "quiet life"—order and concord among subjects. As the early modern period went on, interpersonal reconciliation would take on an ever more sacred tinge, thanks largely to the holy value imputed to it by the actions of religious orders like the Jesuits and Capuchins, who preached peace, especially when on their rural missions.[24] Meanwhile, in society, aggrieved parties in a quarrel, at one side's prodding or by mutual consensus, might aim for an official court-sponsored peace, seeing formalization via the law as more effective than an out-of-court settlement that called solely on their social and moral capital in the city, town, or district. In that way, the law, which had public goals like peace, tranquility, and order, also served private ends of narrower scope. The termination of a quarrel, if it took the form of a "peace" and a "pardon," was a hybrid device in both ideas and institutions, at once social and legal, and, thanks to divine guarantees, also verging on the supernatural. In the private peace, three codes converged: social honor, public law, and faith.[25]

The "consensuses and peaces" took place not only before the notaries of the tribunals to which a complaint had come, or who on their own authority had undertaken an investigation. Indeed, most "peacemakers" were third parties, sometimes private—friends, workmates, clerics—and sometimes officials with public authority, like the notaries. In Rome, the ambassadors of France and Spain were often guarantors of peace, not only for their co-nationals but also for Romans and other townsfolk. In the provinces, the task often fell to the legates and governors, who represented papal authority and were keen to calm the discords and factions that disturbed their communities. "Not by trickery, but of their free will and out

24. Adriano Prosperi, *Tribunali della coscienza. Inquisitori, confessori, missionari* (Turin: Einaudi, 1996), 642–49.
25. Niccoli, *Perdonare*, 188.

of love for Jesus Christ . . . they made and delivered peace and concord" are the words, in Latin, in the documents drawn up before the many witnesses and describing, in standardized notarial terms, the solemn atmosphere of a ceremony that assembled, in piazza or in palace, both the principals and the whole community. The solemn collective ceremony built consensus with the representatives of papal authority, especially in the country and in places recently conquered. So, at Spoleto, on 27 August 1583, Cardinal Alessandro Sforza, legate *a latere* (with highest rank and powers) for the whole state (Bologna excepted), formalized a peace between city factions. Times were hard in this Umbrian town, shaken by the participation of local nobles like Pietro Leoncillo in banditry.[26] A few years earlier, in 1581, Francesco Nardo de Marano, notary and *vicario* of Monte Ottone, a small town in the county of Fermo, on the Adriatic, had registered several peace agreements made before witnesses, with all the solemn formulas and ritual gestures.[27]

In the city, it was often work companions or neighbors who took custody of good order and guaranteed quiet by offering themselves as peacemakers:

I, Baldo, give faith as I did last year, when a state of mutual dissatisfaction arose between Venantio Mancino of Civitanova and Maestro Francesco Angelino from Recanati. Urged by both parties, last August I stepped in to serve as a man of worth, to assure that nothing bad take place between them, and I first took the promise from the said Venantio to not offend Maestro Francesco, but rather to treat him as a brother and to serve him on all occasions. And I informed Maestro Francesco of the promise that the said Venantio had given me, with the said offer. And the same Francesco gave me his word he would not offend, and also offered to serve the said Venantio, and I did this work of charity at the request of the said Maestro Francesco, who showed a desire to live quietly in peace.[28]

26. ASR, Tribunale Criminale del Governatore, Processi (16 secolo), busta 201, case 14, f. 936v. Cardinal Sforza, at this point, arrogated to himself all the town's civil suits, to avoid party discord.

27. ASR, Tribunale Criminale del Governatore, Processi (16 secolo), busta 223, a small insert between folios 662v and 663r. "N.N. invicem fecerunt pacem et generalem quietationem de omnibus verbis et iniuriis tam factis quam verbis successis usque ad presentem inter eos [et] successores quam pacem promiserunt datam, ratam et firmam habere et in nullo contra facere vel venire sub pena sacris constitutionibus contentis in rubrica de poena frangentis pacem per me notarium declaratum in signo vere pacis osculum sibi dederunt ac promiserunt et renuntiaverunt et [se] obligaverunt et iuraverunt."

28. ASR, Tribunale Criminale del Governatore, Processi (16 secolo), busta 309, f. 410r–v.

That is how Baldo Ruspa, on 28 May 1598, picked his words, or, to put it better, put his name to words laid out for him. "Not knowing how to write, he has had it written by one Francesco Genovini, a doublet maker." Ruspa, a Roman, was acting as peacemaker between two men from the Marches who had quarreled in an artisan workshop, probably over harsh words or money. But Ruspa alone could not guarantee this peace: had either Francesco or Venantio broken its terms, unless, as often happened in quarrels, they repaired the breach quickly, they stood to lose their forfeit to the state.

⚜

In the 1580s, writers of treatises turned their attentions to the private peace. In 1583, Fabio Albergati penned his *Trattato del modo di ridurre a pace l'inimicitie private* (Treatise on the Manner of Bringing Private Enmities to a Peace Settlement), a work that would be reprinted in the following century.[29] This Bolognese writer was not the only one to ponder the problem; other authors in the same years dedicated treatises to peace, above all with hopes of calming the "enmities" between noble factions.[30]

In Albergati's pages, peace was defined as "the tranquil freedom of being able to live together in safety," as a foundation, therefore, of order and good governance.[31] It was a definition ripened by observation of his own times, of the nobles' turbulent quarrels, and of the need to forge a stronger sovereign authority that could guarantee justice and order above the strife of factions. Albergati stressed especially the quarrels that turned on honor, so frequent among nobles. It came at a moment when papal power had to cope with factional upheavals in the state's major cities, which fed banditry, and to repress noble behavior that sat ill with Trent's ideas of morality. Albergati was aware that "from ignoring or tolerating honor quarrels among subjects there arise enormous evils, for they try the patience of moral men, provoking them, and forcing them to be-

---

29. *Trattato del Signor Fabio Albergati del modo di ridurre a pace l'inimicitie private* (Rome: Dragondelli, 1664; first edition: 1583).

30. It suffices to cite, among the others of the time or later, the following works, many of which concerned the issue of the social status of the mediator who should ratify a peace: Orazio Volpelli, *Tractatus de pace* (Venice: Giovan Battista Guerra, 1573); Nicolò Morone, *Tractatus aureus. De fide, tregua, et pace. In quo omnia fere continentur, quae in civilibus et criminalibus iudiciis* (Venice: Z. Damiano, 1574); Sebastiano Guazzini, *Tractatus de pace, tregua, verbo dato alicui principi* (Macerata: A. Grisei eredi, 1669; originally, Rome, 1610).

31. Albergati, *Trattato*, 7.

come unjust and bad."[32] So he called on the prince to placate the
hatreds and to nudge peacewards a turbulent nobility that needed whipping into shape, to render it a model for all society. To the
pope, he argued, fell the hard but necessary task of demonstrating
to all rulers of other places how his own dominions embodied concord and good order.

And just as, in any state it is proper, for its own internal health, to extirpate so evil a custom, so, certainly, in the cities of the Church it seems all
the more certain that one should bring that [policy] about. For the cities'
lord is an example to all other princes, both of holiness and of good religious conduct. It is reasonable that his subjects reflect the same goodness
that he himself possesses, so that their goodness should be just as much
greater than other peoples', as the grandeur of the pope's majesty is greater than that of any other potentate.[33]

These words served as a faithful, but not disinterested, eulogy for
the justice policies of Gregory XIII (1572–1585). Gregory's long reign
had to wrestle with a great crime wave all around the state, thanks
to economic crisis, and, unlike his ferocious successor, Sixtus V, he
made little headway. His policies in fact were contradictory, an ineffectual mix of decisive firmness and oversupple clemency. The popes
that came after Gregory would achieve far better results.

32. Ibid., 595–96.
33. Ibid., 598–600.

3

The "New" Inquisition
and the Pope's City

How to describe the relationship between the Inquisition, "faith's tribunal," and Rome's other courts, central and peripheral? In Rome, as we have seen, the governor's claims to primacy fostered endless tensions with other agencies. The Inquisition, with its own ambitions and sweeping prerogatives, stirred up the very same kind of troubles. In the state's assorted districts, justice's administrative realignment had to resolve simmering conflicts between the pope's officials, on the one hand, and local courts on the other. These latter were linked, often, to bishops, who by 1600 or so had been bolstered in their powers by the Council of Trent's reforms. This investigation is risky if one peruses judicial theory alone and searches for the church's justice and the Inquisition's evolving role only in the ever-stiffening rules codified around the turn of the seventeenth century and deployed in "the inquisitor's arsenal," or if one looks for lay justice solely in the heaped luggage of rules for legal conduct. These rules did matter, but they were continually tested, revised, and modulated by the working habits of men at the center, who posted rulings and suggestions to the hinterland in response to shifting circumstances, with a steady eye to who now tangled with the law. Justice was in no way frozen.

This tension between mobile praxis and stubborn theory, between fluid adaptation and reformulation on the one hand and rigidly, dogmatically static written norms on the other, is a constant theme in the correspondence between congregations at the center and officials in the field.[1] This pattern was not confined to inquisi-

1. For this, see the introduction to Pierroberto Scaramella, ed., *Le lettere della Congregazione dell'Sant'Ufficio ai tribunali di fede di Napoli 1563–1625* (Trieste: Edizioni Università di Trieste—Istituto Italiano per gli Studi Filosofici, 2002), xv–xliv. On the Inquisition in general see John Tedeschi, Gustav Henningsen, and Charles Amiel, eds., *Studies in Sources and Methods: The Inquisition in Early Modern Europe* (Dekalb: Northern Illinois University Press, 1996); John Tedeschi, *The Prosecution of Heresy: Collected Studies on the Inquisition in Early Modern Italy* (Binghamton, N.Y.: Medieval and Renaissance Texts and Studies, 1991); Francisco Bethencourt, *L'Inquisition à l'epoque mod-*

torial administration or to the control of faith and morality; rather, it pervaded the whole of justice. In officialdom, cultural roots ran deep: tentativeness, flexibility, and authoritative judgment well tempered by prudence were elements of "good governance" derived from training in canon law, and from reading the classics through a Christian and Neo-Stoic double lens. The Apostolic Constitutions, decrees *(bandi)*, and many tracts on "good governance"—these last a harbinger in Italy and the Papal State of the spreading science of administration—came ever thicker as the seventeenth century progressed, but they voiced theory and intentions only. A similar yen for discipline and theory appears in the constitutions, published at the hand of bishops, of diocesan synods that in much of Italy also shouldered inquisitorial roles. To dominate consciences, to foster tattling, to keep an eye on thought were policies widely accepted and desired, but they often stumbled on inconvenient obstacles. Hence the need to mediate. For historians, it is the letters and petitions, rather than the verdicts of trials, that demonstrate how hard it was to square real practices with norms.

CONTROLLING ROME

In 1542, a commission of cardinals, established by Paul III and chaired by Gian Piero Carafa (the future Paul IV), reshaped the original Tribunal of the Inquisition, established in the Middle Ages, renaming it the Roman Inquisition to distinguish it from Spain's own supreme tribunal of the faith. Rome's judicial scene was already complex, with many tangled and overlapping courts. The injection of a new high court for the faith was certain to stir up tension and conflict. What image did this tribunal and its powers have across the Papal State? And what of the pope's own city, where justice already wore the robes of fearsome efficiency, and of solemn, sovereign equity, thanks to boastful iconography and to the solemn pomp of public executions? In the face of such claims to majesty, could the Inquisition boast of absolute and unquestionable superiority over rival courts? The Inquisition's path to primacy was, from the outset, far less smooth and straight than popes might have wished or claimed. Indeed, in the two hundred years from its foundation, the

---

erne. Espagne, Portugal, Italie, XV–XIX siècle (Paris: Fayard, 1996); Francesco Beretta, *Galilée devant le Tribunal de l'Inquisition. Une relecture des sources* (Fribourg: Université de Fribourg-Suisse, 1998).

tribunal followed a parabola, rising and
falling with the flood and ebb of discipline's overall power over the consciences of the pope's subjects.

Despite its yen for superiority, the
Roman Inquisition was thoroughly entangled with other judicial bodies in the
city. In the seventeenth century, it met
all over town, in the pope's summer palace on the Quirinal Hill, or in his Vatican palace by Saint Peter's, or at the Dominican head church, Santa Maria della
Minerva, or even in the house of its own
cardinal secretary. In Rome itself, there
are many signs of collaboration with
other courts—with the Tribunal of the
Vicario and with the great courts of the
curia, especially the Apostolic Penitentiary, which oversaw cases reserved to
the pope's own judgment.[2] This collaboration between *vicario* and Penitenziere,

FIGURE 5. The beheading of
Silvio di Giulio of Armeria,
a conventual Franciscan, for
counterfeiting.

dating from the 1470s, the time of Sixtus IV, was already smooth and
substantial seven decades before the establishment of the Roman Inquisition.[3] Legal experts helped consolidate this synergy with other
Roman courts; judges (*luogotenenti criminali*) like Pietro Belo, notaries like Claudio della Valle, or prosecutors (*procuratori fiscali*) like
Francesco Persico often lent a hand at once to both the Holy Office
and the governor's and senator's courts. This circulation of legal experts, both clerical and lay, attests to a scarcity of personnel equipped
with the training and skill to navigate the law's complex procedures.
The major cities—Rome especially, but also Bologna, Ferrara, and
Perugia—could guarantee a supply of men "experienced in the af-

2. For the shape and tasks of this tribunal, "reference point for moral theology, for
the new normative system of ecclesiastical life," see Paolo Prodi, *Una storia della giustizia. Dal pluralismo dei fori al moderno dualismo fra coscienza e diritto* (Bologna: il Mulino,
2000), 306–13.

3. For this, see Elena Brambilla, *Alle origini del Sant'Uffizio. Penitenza, confessione e
giustizia spirituale dal medioevo al XVI secolo* (Bologna: il Mulino, 2000). For a synthesis, see Andrea Del Col, *L'Inquisizione in Italia dal XII al XXI secolo* (Milan: Mondadori, 2006).

fairs and styles of courts."[4] Meanwhile, for justice in the outer districts, things were often harder. At the same time, this busy traffic of judges, prosecutors, lawyers, and notaries slipping from tribunal to tribunal served to forge a single judicial web of serried links. In its fine mesh, ecclesiastical merged with lay and sin with crime.

Paul IV (1555–1559), aware of the new tribunal's novel and delicate tasks, had ruled that its "office has precedence over all the other tribunals, and its ministers must be revered by all the others, and in all things all must defer to it and obey it."[5] The Inquisition's superiority was also to be evident in the zone of ceremony—in gestures of precedence and in the "reverences" that other Roman judges were expected to show. Meanwhile, in October of 1555, in a climate of persecution against the Jews in Rome and the Papal State, the Carafa pope handed the Inquisition all current trials against the Judaizing New Christians at Ancona, suspending the fines that, via judicial blackmail, customarily allowed Jews an out. Meanwhile, if anyone appeared before the governor for blasphemy against Christ or the Virgin, a notary of the Holy Office had to examine him. Three years later, another new rule instructed Roman judges to send all cases of simony, the purchase of grace or sacred office, to the Inquisition.[6]

Authorities took particular care to preserve the Inquisition's authority in times of a Vacant See, when, after a pope's death, a power vacuum fed disorder, rampage, and sack, and when the blurring of jurisdictional powers posed a special menace to this new tribunal.[7] Even though most papal moves to consolidate the role of the Holy Office occurred early, in the first decades of the second half of the sixteenth century, the desire to assure its respect and precedence, and its power during Vacant See, would be reasserted over and over in later years. The events of 1559, when Paul IV

---

4. "Reso pratico dagli affari e stili forensi": quoting Pietro Giannone (1676–1748), Neapolitan jurist and intellectual, enemy of the church's temporal power and so persecuted and exiled. Sergio Bertelli, ed., *Vita scritta da lui medesimo* (Milan: Feltrinelli, 1960), 72.

5. This quotation is from a later document that compiled all the prerogatives of the Inquisition. Archivo della Congregazione per la Dottrina della Fede (henceforth ACDF), S.O. [Sant'Offizio], St. St., LL 5-h, ff. IV–25.

6. Ibid.

7. Carlo Ginzburg, "Saccheggi rituali. Premesse ad una ricerca in corso," *Quaderni Storici* 22 (1987): 615–36; Laurie Nussdorfer, "The Vacant See: Ritual and Protest in Early Modern Rome," *Sixteenth Century Journal* 18 (1987): 173–89.

died—the assault that burned the Inquisition's palace, the riots that swept the city—were a vivid specter haunting the institution's memory. So Pius V, mindful of his own past as a severe inquisitor, on 6 June 1566 boldly underlined the superiority of faith's tribunal over all the others, in Rome and in his state, and, under threat of excommunication, ordered all his ministers to obey it in every matter in its scope.[8] Such excommunication, Pius asserted, could be issued only by the Inquisition. Moreover, neither the governor's *bargello* nor other police officials could pocket the usual stipend when fetching prisoners from their Roman jail to the Holy Office prison.

Excommunication, the Inquisition's great prop, was a drastic instrument. The pope's subjects perceived it as extraordinary pressure by sovereign force, a means to bend consciences toward submission and compliance. Other tribunals too, the governor's for instance, had the power to invoke it. But from the early seventeenth century they used it ever less, until it became the Inquisition's alone. Nevertheless, improper uses of excommunication, even sacrilegious ones, abounded; authorities kept a sharp eye out and punished severely its abuse. In 1608, for instance, Ippolito Fabiani, bishop of Civita Castellana and an Augustinian monk, reported uneasily that a policeman of Bassiano's *podestà* (civic magistrate) named Giovan Pietro had knelt before that community's notary asking him to confess him, "and, on his knees, he [the notary] made the sign of the cross on his head and told him, 'Arise, and depart with God, for you have been absolved.' And Giovan Pietro, in his official work, threatened others with excommunication in matters both civil and criminal."[9] These improper uses always preoccupied bishops and inquisitors, for the offense and scorn they inflicted on the powers and practices of the holy tribunal.

Meanwhile, throughout the sixteenth century, the effort to define and array repression's instruments never ceased. For easier proof of guilt, torture had become an established method to extract confessions from suspects who failed to answer judges' questions clearly. It is true that, from the late sixteenth century on, the corre-

---

8. On 1 April 1569 Pius V once more reaffirmed the superiority of the holy tribunal, threatening with the severest punishment anyone who impeded its activities, and who offended, not assisted, its ministers: *Bullarum diplomatum et privilegiorum Sanctorum Romanorum Pontificum Taurinensis Editio*, vol. 7 (Turin: Dalmazzo, 1862), 744–46.

9. ACDF, S.O., St. St., Q 3-a.

spondence of the Inquisition's congregation does contain appeals to judges to use moderation and discretion, but these are no real clue to torture's actual application, especially in distant zones. Meanwhile, the repeated assertions of the superiority of the Inquisition are a sure indicator of its struggles to arrogate to itself the power to judge, and not in matters touching faith alone. In the zone where lay met sacred (cases of *mixtum forum*), the tribunal of the cardinal *vicario* staked out its own solid claims, as it was the court of the bishop of Rome; many cases actually ended up there. The governor's own court, with its increasingly well-articulated, extensive power, also put in claims.

In the minds of subjects, both Romans and foreigners, whether from the local countryside or from distant parts, the jurisdictional competence of the Inquisition was far from clear. Many persons came before the Holy Office of their own accord "to unburden their consciences" and to accuse themselves of crimes in fact not punishable there; that shows how confused, even in the seventeenth century among Rome's own denizens, were notions about its scope and powers. These autodenunciations also show how widespread was the fear it aroused. Fear of the Inquisition sometimes pushed presumptive suspects to adopt a preemptive strategy: better to be let off with an early finding—not culpable, no grounds—than to be fished out of some city jail and hauled to court later. This was the very opposite of dealings with the other branches of criminal justice; whenever possible one dodged and shirked them.

The crime of sodomy illustrates this pattern well. In the seventeenth century, the statutes defined it, and the tribunals of the *vicario* and governor had jurisdiction. The Inquisition became involved only when heresy was suspected or proven. Clearly, only a fine-knit effort at surveillance and diligent collaboration between confessors, parish priests, and tribunals—*vicario*, governor, and Inquisition—could guarantee the repression of this private crime. Even some Spaniards, who, remembering their own national Inquisition, denounced themselves to the Holy Office, accusing themselves of sodomy and bestiality. They were sent over to the *vicario* "to impose on them great penances for their own good."[10] For, as we shall see, unlike the Spanish Inquisition, the Roman institution did not proceed against such crimes. In Rome, instead, against

10. ADCF, S.O., St. St., I 2-d, ff. 457r–458r.

"the unspeakable vice" it was the governor's tribunal that turned its repressive force, as many trials and denunciations prove. This is one more demonstration of how the governor's sphere of action kept expanding, invading zones of *forum mixtum* once reserved to the *vicario's* docket.[11]

The governor's competence stretched yet further into what might seem Inquisition turf. His right of intervention let him judge, or at least set a trial in motion, for "the keeping of prohibited books," "claims to alchemy," and concubinage, fortune telling, and apostasy, as his rich records show.[12] This tribunal, Rome's most important, represented, in the city, the District, and often in the rest of the state, the pope's own authority. As its power grew, from 1600 on, like an octopus it reached out ever further, and ever more forcefully, repressing not only morally deviant behavior, crimes of blood, and verbal offenses, but also transgressions that smacked of heresy. But it did pass these last across to the Inquisition itself.

SCANDALS, NOT HERESIES

As we have seen, the papers that once traced the sixteenth- and seventeenth-century business of the Criminal Tribunal of the Vicario no longer survive. The unruly French Jacobins may have destroyed them in the two years when they controlled Rome. It is therefore hard to puzzle out how things worked when cases moved the other way: how many cases, first examined by the vicario, then shuffled across to the Inquisition?

A rare surviving vicario trial, the story of Diamante and of her husband, Paolo, poses many questions, both about procedures and about the fates of persons forced to recount crimes of various kinds

---

11. For assorted cases of sodomy, and of "leading girls astray" (*sviamento*), see ASR, Tribunale Criminale del Governatore, Processi (17 secolo), busta 86, case 29; busta 88, case 9; busta 147, case 15; busta 158, cases 14, 18, and 19.

12. ASR, Tribunale Criminale del Governatore, Processi (17 secolo), busta 55, case 3; busta 67, case 1; busta 84, case 5; busta 99, case 23; busta 114, case 6; busta 115, case 19; busta 135, case 27, are some examples of such trials from the early seventeenth century. On the subject of sodomy, see Marina Baldassari, *Bande giovanili e "vizio nefando." Violenza e sessualità nella Roma barocca* (Rome: Viella, 2005). His investigation uses only the records of the governor's court. For this problem in European culture: Kent Gerard and Gert Hekma, eds., *The Pursuit of Sodomy: Male Homosexuality in Renaissance and Enlightenment Europe* (New York: Haworth Press, 1989); Michael Rocke, *Forbidden Friendship: Homosexuality and Male Culture in Renaissance Florence* (New York: Oxford University Press, 1996); Guido Ruggiero, *Machiavelli in Love: Sex, Self and Society in the Italian Renaissance* (Baltimore: Johns Hopkins University Press, 2007).

in domestic space. On 29 January 1567, Diamante, by then eleven years married, deposed against her husband, Paolo of Spoleto, accusing him of forcing her to eat meat on Fridays. "And he says that it is not a crime, and that he does not wish to throw it out, and when I scold him . . . he swore upon the bread that he would kill me." The husband's violence, which the neighbors also noticed, was not limited to his grave defiance of religion's rules or to his repeated blasphemy. "When he is angry, he always curses with all sorts of blasphemy," says the wife, who also records the sacrilegious gestures of her violent husband. "And when he is angry he takes the Madonna and he rips her [clothing?] and he puts the crucifix under his feet." The court also investigates his sexuality, asking his wife if he has tried "to know her against nature." The answer is affirmative. Within the domestic walls there is also suspicion of incest; the victim is the little daughter, Pantasilea. The girl affirms in court, "When my mother goes to mass he comes close to me and wants to do disgusting things, and this has happened twice, and he says, 'I want to marry you and to kill your mother and we will go to the village and we will empty out our house.'" Jailed in Corte Savelli prison, the man claimed not to know the reason for his detention—the normal dodge when one first faced a judge. In the neighbors' eyes, the man was difficult. "I have heard it said that he is a Lutheran and that he eats meat every day," says a witness.[13] Still, although branded by a bad reputation that could leave no Roman court indifferent, Paolo was not sent over to the Inquisition. His crimes, though grave if true, showed no sign of heresy. There was no false doctrine in his blasphemies, nor was he polygamous, despite some scandalous impulses in that direction. Immoral, but no heretic! His case remained before the tribunal of the cardinal vicario.

Synergy and collaboration between the governor's court and the Inquisition was indeed possible, and it certainly had official favor. It blossomed fast in matters of lèse-majesté—where the state's authority was assaulted. A case from 1588 is a good example. On 7 April 1588, Sixtus V sent the governor copies of the Inquisition's interrogations of a Spaniard from Salamanca, Martino de Cardines, now *auditore* (feudal judge) of Cardinal Colonna. He instructed the governor "to proceed secretly, as is done in cases of the Holy Of-

13. ASVR, Tribunale Criminale del Vicario, Costituti, vol. 102, ff. 46v–47v.

fice."[14] Cardines had been denounced by Florentine and Genoese merchants in the wood trade, who also brought timber to Rome from the Conca estate, a possession of the Holy Office. They had asked permission to bring some timber to Astura, a Colonna fief, but Cardines had made them pay a tax, something the merchants argued was against the rules. The Spaniard, as a faithful Colonna servant, had retorted that "Cardinal Colonna is master of his estate, not the Holy Office, nor the pope, and as for his property, neither the pope, nor any man alive, nor even God can take it from him, and I [here the Florentine merchant, Domenico Vivaldi] was not ever going to be bringing it to him if I did not pay up."[15] The Genoese merchant, Giorgio Sauli, confirmed these words; he also appealed to the rulings of the bull *In Coena Domini*, which threatened with excommunication all who impeded the transport of commodities to Rome. In the pontificate of Sixtus V, a time of trenchant defense of the authority and powers of the pope against the claims of Roman barons like the Colonna family, the affirmations of the noble cardinal's *auditore* sounded like a provocation, a challenge to papal authority.

BLIND OBEDIENCE

By the beginning of the seventeenth century, Roman tribunals' collaboration seemed better regulated and more harmonious. Many persons captured by the police of the governor or the senator were transferred to the Inquisition because they had been found with papers for working superstitious magic, with unknown names, or "some inscriptions with incantations" in their pockets, as happened with Matteo, a Roman held in the jail of the Curia Capitolina and then transferred to the Inquisition.[16] In 1612, Paul V (1605–1612) with his constitution *Universi agri dominici* redefined the tasks and jurisdictions of the Roman courts, reaffirming the central role of the Holy Office.[17] Still, the conflicts among the courts did go on, ready to flare up even over petty details, punctilios that touched

---

14. ASR, Tribunale Criminale del Governatore, Processi (16 secolo), busta 223, ff. 668r–680v.

15. ASR, Tribunale Criminale del Governatore, Processi (16 secolo), busta 223, f. 670r.

16. ADCF, S.O., St. St., H 6-f, ff. not numbered (7 January 1603).

17. For the constitution of Paul V and the reform of the Roman courts, see "Tribunali, giustizia e società nella Roma del Cinque e Seicento," special issue edited by Irene Fosi, *Roma moderna e contemporanea* 5, no. 1 (1997): 7–184.

one or another tribunal's prestige and the reputation of its servants. In the late seventeenth century, a memorandum to both Clement X (1670–1676) and Cardinal Alderando Cibo, secretary of state, reviewed the rules that had assured the superiority of the Inquisition over all other Roman courts. It observed acerbically that, in the past, whenever prisoners had been suspected of crimes pertaining to the Holy Office, one sent them across at once. Now, instead, not only were rival courts obstructing such procedures, but they were also asking that an official of the holy tribunal come over in person to request the suspect's consignment.[18] The memorandum went on to lament:

how much this new pretension is prejudicial to the supreme authority and dignity of the Sacred Congregation . . . it gives the worst possible example to secular princes . . . who among other things are extremely attentive to the rules observed in Rome, so as to be able to deduce, by example, what to do in cases that arise in their states. If, with Monsignor Governor, it proves necessary to give up the usual practice and dicker with him in a matter where he ought to show blind obedience as a subordinate, the princes will not obey as they have until now but deny us in the matter, and there would be lost that majesty and reverence that has been till now conserved by the supreme pontiffs with much studious effort and application.[19]

Thus, even at the end of the seventeenth century, there was still a lively desire to bolster Rome's own model obedience and tacit submission to the Inquisition. By then, though, under the weight of threatening, irrepressible new ideas about the free circulation of persons and of "very pernicious books," its real authority had begun to creak.

18. "On these principles, which are so stable, when any suspect jailed in the secular tribunals is discovered to be suspected of a crime concerning the Holy Office, the order is given for the transportation of that same suspect into the prisons of the Holy Office with a warrant. . . . Similar warrants, both in Rome and in the states of secular princes, have always been obeyed and held in due regard and no governor or judge or other minister has ever disobeyed them. But now I have met with Monsignor the Governor of Rome, given that Pietro Bosco, jailed at Tor di Nona, has been denounced at the Holy Office, for having certain writings with supernatural formulae [on them]. Even though the usual warrants were sent to the wardens of the said prison, monsignore Governor makes the claim that, besides the warrant which he can receive from that same warden, an official of the Holy Office should go there, in which case he shows himself ready to consign him [the prisoner]": ADCF, S.O., St.St., H 6-f, ff. not numbered (7 January 1603).

19. ACDF, S.O., St.St., H 6-f, ff. not numbered (7 January 1603).

By the end of the seventeenth century, on the wider political scene, not only the Inquisition but the papacy itself was losing
ground both in international affairs and in the delicate equilibrium
of the Italian states. Nevertheless, at Rome itself, the supremacy
of the Inquisition could still be imposed, even if it stirred up resistance. It proved harder to keep up the pressure in the provinces
of the Papal State. The laconic records of the Inquisition's sessions
confirm, even for Rome itself, that the tribunal pursued a cautious
line of conduct. This has been found as well by recent studies on
other parts of Italy. Prudence was the rule, for instance, when it
came to holding public readings of the court's sentences, especially
if the occasion promised a big crowd, or even worse, if the gathering might stimulate hearers to copy the crimes in question. The Inquisition was aware of the dread power of the word. In 1597, and
again in 1602, some of the decrees of the cardinals of the congregation suggested not spelling out in judicial sentences the whole
catalogue of crimes condemned. Better not to descend to the particulars, putting on paper the convict's actual words, lest they be
obscene or blasphemous! Even at the beginning of the seventeenth
century, it seems, the formal ceremony of public abjuration was
not yet well defined. Abjuration was a spectacle designed to sum
up and lay out the entire power of the sacred tribunal, and to warn
and instruct all those who came. But the congregation resolved, on
27 May 1603, that for public abjurations at Saint Peter's, before the
pope, one should consult the papal master of ceremonies, Paolo
Alaleone.[20] This move was less a sign of an unsteady hand than an
expression of the Inquisition's desire to reconcile abjuration's rites
with the ever more rigid rules of papal ceremony, inserting them
adroitly.

But, meanwhile, note the court's ambivalence; it oscillated between desire for the imposing stagecraft of exemplary punishment,
a terrifying admonition, on the one hand, and on the other its fear
of contagion via bad examples set by the words and gestures of
stubbornly defiant prisoners. Accordingly, comforters for the condemned and the execution companies that seconded their consola-
tory labors, throughout early modern times, disciplined the ritual of capital punishment, both for the Inquisition's victims and for
others on the scaffold. They were important mediators between

20. ACDF, S.O., St. St., H 6-f (27 May 1603).

the institutions of punishment and the condemned, and between both of those and the mass of fearful, curious spectators.[21] Roman executions took place in many places: at the downtown end of the Sant'Angelo Tiber bridge, on the Capitoline Hill, at Campo de' Fiori market, in Piazza Giudea by the ghetto's chief gate, at the city wall by Porta Latina, and also in the jail at Tor di Nona and inside the massive fortress on the Tiber bank, Castel Sant'Angelo.

In Rome it was the Archconfraternity of San Giovanni Decollato (Saint John the Baptist Beheaded), also called della Misericordia (of Mercy), that shouldered the task of comforting the condemned, of converting them and making them accept "the good death," of accompanying them to the scaffold, and finally of collecting their bodies for burial in the confraternal cemetery. The confraternity was founded at the end of the fifteenth century by members of Rome's Florentine community. It had been strongly influenced by the penitential spirituality of the late medieval *Bianchi* movement and had counted among its members Michelangelo, when he was working on the Medici tombs. Its members from the start obeyed their basic statutes, and then, with the passage of time, they drew up ever fatter manuals with instructions about assorted cases, offering persuasive strategies if, for instance, one had heretics to deal with, or common criminals. The central task was to prepare the convict spiritually: the later choreography of death would fall to the execution's master of ceremonies. But, obviously, for a successful execution "spectacle," the condemned had to face

21. There are many good recent studies on the theme of executions. See for example Vincenzo Paglia, *La morte confortata. Riti della paura e mentalità religiosa a Roma nell'età moderna* (Rome: Edizioni di Storia e Letteratura, 1982); Pieter Spierenburg, *The Spectacle of Suffering: Executions and the Evolution of Repression: From a Preindustrial Metropolis to the European Experience* (Cambridge: Cambridge University Press, 1984); Richard van Dülmen, *Crime and Punishment in Early Modern Germany* (Cambridge: Cambridge University Press, 1990); Giovanni Romeo, *Aspettando il boia. Condannati a morte, confortatori e inquisitori nella Napoli della Controriforma* (Florence: Sansoni, 1993); Vic A. C. Gatrell, *The Hanging Tree: Execution and the English People 1770–1868* (Oxford: Oxford University Press, 1994); Adriano Prosperi, *Dare l'anima. Storia di un infanticidio* (Turin: Einaudi, 2005), especially 301–58; Prosperi, "Morire volentieri: condannati a morte e sacramenti," in *Misericordie. Conversioni sotto il patibolo tra Medioevo ed età moderna*, 3–70 (Pisa: Edizioni della Normale, 2007); Claude Gauvard and Robert Jacob, eds., *Les rites de la justice. Gestes et rituels judiciaires au Moyen Age occidental* (Paris: Léopard d'or, 2000); Florike Egmond, "Execution, Dissection, Pain and Infamy—A Morphological Investigation," in *Bodily Extremities: Preoccupations with the Human Body in Early Modern European Culture*, ed. Florike Egmond and Robert Zwijnenberg, 92–128 (Aldershot: Ashgate, 2003).

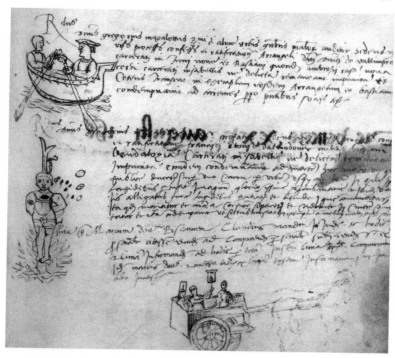

FIGURE 6. Various punishments: galley slaves; a convict burning at the stake; the condemned being transported to the scaffold or execution accompanied by members of the Archconfraternity of San Giovanni Decollato.

the crowd as repentant, redeemed, and ready for the "good death." The solemn ritual was needed to frame justice's civic pedagogy— the body's destruction would redeem the soul. The confraternity did not restrict itself to solemn executions and public abjurations; it also lent other good offices to a dense network of parishes, convents, and nunneries.[22]

The Congregation of the Inquisition, in the mid-seventeenth century, had to revert to the issue of ceremony. In a quest for precedence and a desire to reaffirm the superiority of its judges to those of secular princes, a backer opined: "Inquisitors more perfectly represent the person of the supreme Pontiff than the representatives of the

22. Peter Schmidt, "De Sancto Officio Urbis: Aspekte der Verflechtung des Heiligen Offiziums mit der Stadt Rom im 16. und 17. Jahrhundert," *Quellen und Forschungen aus italienischen Archiven und Bibliotheken* 82 (2001): 404–89.

prince represent his person, because Inquisitors deliver their sentences with authority and they speak law *(ius dicunt)*. Above all," writes the anonymous author of this seventeenth-century memorandum, "it seems to me that it would serve the reputation and the seemly conduct [*decoro*] of the aforesaid lords [the princes] in their domains if as secular persons they honored the ecclesiastical Inquisitors, who are apostolic delegates, and gave them precedence."[23] If Rome desired to resolve conflicts decisively, to draw sharp boundaries around jurisdictions, and to offer itself as a firm example to the rest of the Papal State and the rest of Italy, it had to control the varied conditions in the provinces, in inquisitorial matters as in others. This was no easy task. One example: a memorandum of 1678 by the cardinal legate in Ferrara, Galeazzo Marescotti, suggested prudent ways of remodeling ceremonies. He did not disguise his unease in the face of awkward matters:

In Ferrara there is a tribunal of the Holy Office in the monastery of San Domenico, with a father inquisitor, and with his officials and accredited officers, as in any other tribunal. With these men, when there is a dispute over jurisdiction, it is necessary to tread with great delicacy, so as not to become badly entangled with the General Congregation of the Holy Office in Rome, which is accustomed to support its privileges and its warrant-holders with great energy so as not to give a bad example to the secular princes in the neighborhood. For this reason it will always be laudable to settle with the Father Inquisitors on friendly terms any disputes that arise. The Cardinal Legate customarily invites the Father Inquisitor to take a seat, and escorts him the whole way through the antechamber, but if he came often, he would not always ask him to take his seat, especially in the mornings, as his walking through is both permissible and useful. Rather, it would be best if the Cardinal Legate gave instructions to his Chamber-master that whenever the Father Inquisitor comes he should expedite things for him, ahead of all the others, without making him wait long in the antechamber.

In other words, the legate, who, in the early seventeenth century, more and more stood in for the pope in temporal matters in the governance of his province, strove to reduce to a minimum or to eliminate outright any chance for conflict, lest it besmirch the local image of the pope's power and of his justice.

23. ACDF, S.O., St. St., UV 11, ff. 90r–91v.

4

The Theater of Justice

THE BASICS OF COURT PROCEDURE

Inquisitorial procedure took firm hold, we know well, as the late Middle Ages shaded into early modern times.[1] It represented the triumph of an asymmetric model of procedure, hard on the defendant, where the judge himself, also an inquisitor, played an active role. He could start proceedings on mere shreds of evidence: a "notice of a crime" sufficed to launch a case *ex officio*, that is, on the court's initiative, in the absence of a public complaint. To start rolling, the machinery of justice relied on the reports of the police and the "reports of barber surgeons" (*relationes barbitonsorum*), and of the assorted other barbers and surgeons on staff at the many Roman hospitals or at the little clinics housed in confraternities. Under orders from the tribunal's chief, these medical men kept a vigilant eye on both the hospitals and on the constabulary's operations, reporting in sharp detail all wounds or victim corpses. The reports of barber surgeons help us scholars trace the precise starting point of inquisitorial procedure. They are also useful to us because they let us gauge the level of interpersonal violence—at a given historical moment, or with the season, or during holidays like carnival, or as part of those unscheduled conflicts that marked the city's life. One good example is the violence against Jews, near the ghetto, especially during carnival. These same sources also serve medical history; they illustrate surgeons' ability to distinguish among wounds, and also assay the courts' medical awareness and link it to the official medicine taught at university.

1. For a general panorama, see Ettore Dezza, *Accusa e inquisizione dal diritto comune ai codici moderni*, vol. 1 (Milan: Giuffre, 1989); Giorgia Alessi, *Il processo penale: un profilo storico* (Rome: Laterza, 2004); Mario Sbriccoli, "Giustizia criminale," in *Lo stato moderno in Europa. Istituzioni e diritto*, ed. Maurizio Fioravanti (Rome: Laterza, 2002). For Rome and the Papal State in particular, see "'Pro tribunali sedentes'. Le magistrature giudiziarie dello Stato Pontificio e i loro archivi," in *Archivi per la Storia* 4, nos. 1–2 (1991); *Giustizia e criminalità nello Stato Pontificio*, ed. Monica Calzolari, Michele Di Sivo, and Elvira Grantaliano, in *Rivista storica del Lazio*, 9, no. 4 (2001), a special issue published as a monograph.

An *inquisitio* started when the court first caught wind of crime. But, for all their zeal, magistrates could never know all that happened in the city. Rome was too varied, too obscure, too crammed with places sheltered by immunity from jurisdiction—churches, convents, embassies, and noble palaces; Rome also was too full of foreigners, pilgrims, and vagabonds aswarm in wine shops and taverns. In the streets, the cops *(birri)* made their presence felt, often raucously, brawling and assaulting the populace. More hidden, but no less intrusive, was the secret action of the "friends of the court," the ubiquitous spies eternally on their toes to sniff out and report the least hint of disorder and deviation.

The second stage in *inquisitio generalis* was formal investigation. This task fell to a notary, sometimes an official attached to the pertinent tribunal, sometimes just the fellow who happened to receive the crime's legal denunciation. The notary might call on the prisoner on his own initiative *(motu proprio,* to use the formal term), or he might arrive with a warrant *(mandato)* to accredit him, from the governor or from whatever other court he served. Notaries had other missions: they ran the grisly errand called "recognition of the cadaver," and they also sallied forth to collect testimony about the who and what of crimes that came to the court's notice. Most of their "investigations" dealt with brawls and woundings; in these affairs, the notaries and assistant prosecutors who sometimes joined them enjoyed scant success, thanks to the code of silence and the fear and defensiveness of those they interrogated. These notaries were the judicial system's bottom rung. Of all, they were corruption's easiest prey, given their own uncertain pay, easily supplemented by pressure on those who, with a prudent bribe, might shorten a trial's tortuous run or even buy their way to freedom.

Justice's next formal stage was the interrogation of the suspect and of witnesses. The transcript of that stage, in the language of the time, was called "the trial" *(il processo* in Italian, *processus* or *inquisitio specialis* in Latin). If the suspect was too poor to afford a lawyer, at this stage the tribunal might assign, free of charge, an "advocate of the poor" *(avvocato dei poveri).*[2] The defense lawyer, however,

2. For the genesis of this figure, see Marina D'Amelia, "Il buon diritto, ovvero dell'accesso alla giustizia per i poveri. Prime riflessioni su un problema rimosso," in *Povertà e innovazioni istituzionali in Italia. Dal medioevo ad oggi,* ed. Vera Zamagni, 335–54 (Bologna: Clueb, 2000).

never cross-examined witnesses face to face, nor did he appear at his client's side in court. His job was largely confined to paper—devising questions to be put to witnesses and suspects and drafting arguments to lay before the judge. At the trial's end came the submission of lawyers' written briefs and then, at last, the sentence.

It is often hard to follow a case from beginning to end, from the curtain's rise with the first denunciation down to the final act, the sentence. Often, a paper version never came out, not with capital cases, for instance, nor even with condemnations to the galleys. The suspect always had to ask, and pay, and the tribunal's price, if one were poor, could be too steep. And yet, if one had been absolved, a paper declaration was reprieve's and closure's only sure proof.

The neat itinerary sketched here is a mere model; reality was complex and various. In Bologna, for instance, only one denunciation in ten ever led to a proper trial.[3] What we historians now call a "trial" is in fact a fragmented paper trail, a culled assortment of official documents marking some stages of justice's march across a case. At any point judges might purge the record of papers that no longer served them. Furthermore, official proceedings were only the tip of the iceberg; a trial was part of a larger story. People turned to the courts only after trying self-help, hoping to settle matters on their own, with the aid of family, workmates, or social circle. Certainly, when one did turn to the judge for help, one did so with small expectation of staying the course through the procedure's every step. Rather, the turn to justice was a feint; it signaled the will to go one-on-one with an offender. One still hoped to settle out of court. And, indeed, when the crime was less than grave, the tribunal was wont to summon the quarreling parties to resolve their contention on their own, withdraw the formal complaint (the *querela*), and make a formal peace agreement (*una pace*).

This tangling of formal justice with extrajudicial negotiations and settlements is one reason for the fragmentary nature of the

---

3. Giancarlo Angelozzi, "Il tribunale criminale di Bologna," in *La Legazione di Romagna e i suoi Archivi. Secoli XVI–17*, ed. Angelo Turchini, 737–74 (Cesena: Il Ponte Vecchio, 2006); Cesarina Casanova, "L'amministrazione della giustizia a Bologna. Alcune anticipazioni sul Tribunale del Torrone," *Dimensioni e problemi della ricerca storica* 2 (2004): 267–92, shows how theory and practices shaped the workings of the Bologna criminal court. For similar matters in Marseilles two centuries earlier, Daniel Lord Smail, *The Consumption of Justice: Emotions, Publicity, and Legal Culture in Marseille, 1264–1423* (Ithaca, N.Y.: Cornell University Press, 2003).

surviving paper record. Intermediate solutions could halt a case, often with no recorded reason why. The sworn settlement, with penalties attached in case of breach (the *fideiussione*), and the peace
with a surety forfeited if flouted (the *sicurtà de non offendendo*), and
even the pope's grant of official grace and pardon, snuffing out a
trial wherever mercy alighted, were common resolutions of judicial
proceedings. Especially in the sixteenth century, there was even
direct intervention by the pope himself, and above all by his chief
minister the cardinal nephew, to correct the trial, shift its legal
principles, or revise the sentence. Such intrusions, thwarting justice's desire and will, flaunted the papacy's authority and power.

A second reason for unclear documentation and spasmodic proceedings lay in Rome's scrambled and competing institutions. To
the minds of subjects, as we will show repeatedly, the spheres of
competence of the diverse Roman courts were far from clear. Why
then turn to one and not another? Sometimes one court was clos-
est; sometimes it, or its staff, had a reputation for clemency, or perhaps it was the cheapest in sight, or one might have a friend there—
a judge or, more often, a notary. We seldom really know, but now
and then the vaguely hinted suggestion of a motive jumps off a page
of depositions.

❧

"I have heard it said, but I don't remember!" These words, uttered in 1567 by one Antonio Sanchez before the notary of the *vicario's* tribunal, give in a nutshell the general stance of those called
as accused or witness to depose in court. The words express a stab
at self-defense before an alien justice, to preserve one's own social
relationships, and to ward off accusations hurled at any witness
who collaborated, denounced, and betrayed. Whoever cozied up
to the courts broke fragile ties—with family, neighbors, and workmates—admitting outsiders who carried in their baggage unfamil-
iar rules and might defend and impose them by brute force. Far
wiser was it to declare, from the outset, that the case was none of
one's business. Indeed, a trial's verbal opening gambit, almost always,
ran: "I don't know for what reason I find myself under inquiry."

Court records are fascinating, especially the trials (*processi*).
Their pages seem to peel away the veil from daily life—unmasking
the very feelings and telling marks of a colorful, violent world. But
keep a watchful eye to mediation! When we remember all those

things that mediated between thought or speech and paper and all that shaped the drafting, as spontaneous documents these writings lose all credibility. It is obvious now, for instance, that such papers cannot be used, by themselves, to tally crime's level and trace its movement across time. The officers of justice sifted and selected papers. How many official documents were destroyed by magistrates themselves because, in mid-case, a pope intruded? And how many criminals were never denounced or prosecuted? Then add the courts' selection, in mid-trial, of materials they found useful to a case. Have they preserved all the interrogations? The defense? The sentence? The answer, usually, is no! And what of voice? The notary, a linguistic mediator, sometimes selected, or transformed, interrogation's actual words. So did men and women say precisely what is written down? The notaries, we know, took notes during interrogations, for a later draft "in good copy" (*in bella copia*), with an eye to rhetoric's conventions, putting into the witness's mouth more correct locutions, more seemly not only for a dictionary; imprecations, screams, and wailings, under torture, are always noted, and punished, but a victim might blurt things so raw one dared not write them. The depositions of suspects are the most dubious. How true are their confessions? But this is a matter for a later chapter, as it regards more than just the nature of court papers.[4]

There are other reasons to beware all-too-easy enthusiasm for judicial sources, for they hide as much as they reveal. For one thing, all historians, not just historians of crime, struggle to catch the true drift of oral exchanges: subtle rhythms of instant rapport, things said but never written, informal conversations—both in the theater of a trial and elsewhere too—all these things were milestones on some judicial pathway. Other subtle things, fleeting but sometimes caught on paper, could shape the fate of a proceeding, and be decisive, for instance, for the success of a policy of surveillance and

---

4. For the use of sources, see, among others, Dominick LaCapra, "*The Cheese and the Worms*: The Cosmos of a Twentieth-Century Historian," in *History and Criticism*, 45–70 (Ithaca, N.Y.: Cornell University Press, 1985); Thomas Kuehn, "Reading Microhistory: The Example of *Giovanni and Lusanna*," *Journal of Modern History* 61 (1989): 514–31; Thomas V. Cohen and Elisabeth S. Cohen, *Words and Deeds in Renaissance Rome: Trials before the Papal Magistrates* (Toronto: University of Toronto Press, 1993), 3–31; Paul Ricoeur, *Memory, History, Forgetting*, trans. Kathleen Blamey and David Pellauer (Chicago: University of Chicago Press, 2004); Carlo Ginzburg, *Il filo e le tracce. Vero, falso, finto* (Milan: Feltrinelli, 2006).

of efforts to control and discipline social spheres that resisted the intrusion of courts and judges. A second problem: the legal action was seldom the whole story. Social relationships both vertical and horizontal, such as friendship, acquaintanceship, and fealty and clientage, marked ancien régime society and institutions. Assuring governance, and bolstering justice, they were crucial to any policy to control territory. Moreover, to go to court cost money, precious cash that the protagonists of everyday violence could seldom spare. Not only that. To go to court was a time-consuming way to solve questions that involved individuals, families, neighborhoods, social relationships, and finances, and, above all, that touched on honor. Was it not better to find a private solution, with a peace pact? The border between private settlements, voluntary and recognized, on the one hand, and official justice on the other remained vague and slippery. Private settlements met sometimes with official favor, sometimes with suspicion, especially if they reflected the dangerous turbulence of the nobles, who resented all attempts to oversee and discipline their riotous violence.[5]

So it does not suffice to know the rules and structures. One must go beyond the geographic and institutional framework—so useful for understanding governance—and the varieties of officials and architecture of institutions. One must survey as well the parallel, informal channels, supplementary, not hostile, to the formal ones, and crucial for making rules bite, judges reign, and good governance flourish. Everything was up for negotiation: compromises, side agreements, and potent meddling marked not only justice but also the whole of social life and politics. At Rome and in the hinterland, such dealings helped shape the construction of consensus.

"BECAUSE IT VIOLATES THE PROVISIONS OF THE BANDI"

"Yesterday night, six hours after sundown, I found Michellangelo [sic] Salluccelli, a Roman, who was going down Via del Babuino. He was disguised as a puppet, even though he had a mask on his face, and because he was in violation of the *bandi*, I brought him to jail at Tor di Nona." So did Corporal Ascanio Tigri, constable

5. Giancarlo Angelozzi and Cesarina Casanova, *La nobiltà disciplinata: violenza nobiliare, procedure di giustizia e scienza cavalleresca a Bologna nel 17 secolo* (Bologna: Clueb, 2003), 219–25.

of the governor, relate in bare-bones language how he had "done his duty," arresting people who were amusing themselves in the city streets late in the evening of 11 February 1611, in mid-carnival. The control of the cityscape was not without its uncertainties and problems, as is clear from the drumbeat of reports by the chief constable (*bargello*) and by the constabulary, and from the legal complaints, court investigations, and notaries' visits to hospitals. The constables, especially in their nocturnal rounds, kept an eye on Rome's public order, in the streets and piazzas, and also in the inns and the houses of the whores, and in the zone of monastic houses, nunneries especially. Their reports sum up some aspects of the authorities' arduous task of controlling urban space.[6] Not only do these papers give a lively picture of night life, with its crimes and illicit acts, breaches of rules under cover of darkness; they also signal a decisive formal step that often set off inquisitorial proceedings in a Roman court.

Every Roman tribunal had its troop of cops (*birri*). Although the most important force attached to the governor, who also commanded a *bargello di campagna* (chief constable of the countryside), many police operations fell to other forces. It is easy to imagine the rivalries and tensions, and the abuses and violent acts of these men, often recruited among delinquents, sometimes outlaws who, in gratitude for turning in accomplices, had been rewarded with a pardon and—for daily bread—a job among the *birri*. The governor's *bargello*, appointed by a brief of the pope himself, commanded a varying company, arrayed by rank. In the sixteenth century he had between 25 and 200; in the seventeenth, his band ranged from 120 to 300 men. This growth in numbers suggests that the forces available to control the city were becoming more numerous and stable. These men cut an unpretty figure; like low-grade wine their bad reputation matured for centuries, becoming a notorious classic by the nineteenth century, when, to modernizing critics, they distilled papal conservatism and repression. Scowling, swaggering with harquebus on shoulder, these shabby custodians of pub-

6. An examination of these reports appears in Sabrina Auricchio, "'La ronda di notte': Le Relazioni dei Birri nella Roma del Seicento," laurea thesis for l'Università di Roma "La Sapienza," 1994–1995. See also Michele Di Sivo, "'Rinnoviamo l'ordine già dato': il controllo sui birri a Roma in antico regime," in *La polizia in Italia e in Europa: Punto sugli studi e prospettive di ricerca*, ed. Livio Antonielli, 13–24 (Rubbettino: Soveria Mannelli, 2006).

lic order could hardly be further from the spanking "night watch" of Rembrandt's famous portrait, his shining mirror to rich, orderly Amsterdam, as that city hoped to see itself displayed and feted.

For all their flaws, in Rome as in Amsterdam the *bargello* and constables did make their rounds, and did turn in their reports, more or less detailed, evocative and lively. The *birri* deposed them before a notary, whose educated hand hides from us the speaker's unpolished acculturation to a city that for centuries called him "infamous" and, as we know from trials, also tarred him with "horny goat—cuckold" (*becco cornuto*) and other nasty epithets. Despite the notary's mediation, these reports, read over the long haul, suggest, behind the paper, a policeman's voice and narrative mode, distinctly his. Succinct descriptions—"just the facts, signora!"—bare data of crime and criminal, sit side by side with detailed but often garbled accounts that strive to reconstruct, often with evident difficulty, a scrambled nocturnal scene in the street or, not rarely, indoors: a bedroom, an inn, a courtesan's apartment. The spatial coordinates for these tales are the usual urban reference points: palaces of nobles and cardinals, major offices of the papal curia or city government, churches. Things grow murky at identifying suspects arrested, almost always on their say-so—"He says that his name is . . ." is a constant *bargello* refrain—or on the word of some acquaintance or real or supposed friend. Clothing often figured in reports as an essential identity clue; it suggested an origin: "dressed in the French fashion," or "with a doublet of black velvet in the Spanish style." These external signs, sometimes supplemented by the suspect's fragmentary words, conjured identity and gave an early clue to the risk he (or she) posed. Vagabonds, foreigners, gypsies (*zingari*), prostitutes, and idle young hoods all peopled a night life not easily policed.[7] The *birri* reports convey the impression of a small city, where everyone is acquainted and where outsiders and immigrants fall far oftener than others into the law's mesh.

7. Helen Langdon, *Caravaggio, a Life* (London: Pimlico, 1999), 131–53; Langdon, "Gypsies, Tricksters and Whores: The Steet Life of Caravaggio's Rome," in *Darkness and Light: Caravaggio and His World* (Melbourne: Art Gallery of New South Wales, 2003–4), 22–25; Peter Burke, *The Historical Anthropology of Early Modern Italy* (Cambridge: Cambridge University Press, 1987); Elisabeth S. Cohen, "Honor and Gender in the Streets of Early Modern Rome," *Journal of Interdisciplinary History* 22 (1992): 597–625; Cohen, "To Pray, to Talk, to Hear, to Speak: Women in Roman Streets, c. 1600," *Journal of Early Modern History* 12, no. 3–4 (2008): 289–31.

It is a city full of eyes and ears of spies, as figured in baroque art, of "friends of justice" on the take for cash for survival's sake and happy to hawk themselves to the highest bidder, the better to dodge jail and justice.[8]

There were abundant arrests for "making an unseemly uproar around the monastery," as happened to three youngsters from the Kingdom of Naples—a Palermitan blacksmith named Pietro, Francesco Cavalcante from Messina, and Cesare Melfi, a Neapolitan, who all had been singing, to a lute and "Italian guitar," outside San Silvestro.[9] They were released a few days later when a friend of theirs, also from the Kingdom, put up bail. On novice-veiling days, there were often ruckuses (rumori) in the night, and even in the day, in front of the convent of the Convertite, which housed prostitutes and other women whose sexual lives looked out of line, and who had embraced redemption or been corralled and jailed there. On 2 March 1611 Captain Marchionne reported:

Yesterday evening, at the fifth hour of the night [one hour before our midnight], in front of the nunnery of the Convertite, a man was walking back and forth in the street that runs to the Corso, making a great racket. He was hollering that the little goats have their little horns and the big goats have their gross bad horns, and he went on saying this many times, making noise in the night against the rules of the bandi, and moreover it was Lent and near a monastery, so I brought him to jail at Tor di Nona. His name is Tommaso de Biello, a Parmesan, and he also had a sword, with the permit for it.[10]

To decode this doggerel by a house for women of shady sexual conduct, note that, in Italy and the European Mediterranean, for centuries, the goat was a universal symbol of male failure to keep one's women faithful, and that, as still today, "horns" signaled cuckoldry.

Such incidents often involved young noblemen who, secure in their elite impunity, "made noise" with obscene words and songs outside churches and nunneries. Such transgressive actions struck authorities as open provocation in the face of the Council of Trent's

8. See Michael Stolleis, *Das Auge des Gesetzes. Geschichte einer Metaphor* (Munich: C. H. Beck Verlag, 2004); Adriano Prosperi, *Giustizia bendata. Percorsi storici di un'immagine* (Turin: Einaudi, 2008).

9. ASR, Tribunale Criminale del Governatore, Relazioni dei birri (17 secolo), busta 104, f. 105v.

10. ASR, Tribunale Criminale del Governatore, Relazioni dei birri (17 secolo), busta 104, f. 37r.

rules, which aimed to sunder nunneries from the city by imposing strict enclosure and mandating architectural improvements
like bricked-up windows and higher walls. Note though that, even
late in the seventeenth century, many nunnery walls remained low,
and streetward windows were sometimes still unplastered. Even
in Rome and the Papal State, resistance to enclosure rules stayed
widespread and stubborn.

Given the weaknesses of the constabulary, crises strained its capacity to cope. For the police, everyday life, with its violence, thefts,
and slanging matches, was already hard enough. An emergency—
an epidemic or political crisis, for instance—hit with little warning and the cops were often unprepared. We see ready sign of this
in the early-summer crime wave of 1656, when the bubonic plague
that had just struck Naples and Genoa arrived at Rome.[11] Theft
of life's necessities, like food, and forbidden weapons became the
"new normal"; despite the emergency, the humdrum police reports
only broke stride when the extraordinary surfaced. On 3 December 1565, the *bargello*, who proclaimed himself "a zealot for public
health," reported as follows:

Cristoforo Chillaro, in love with a young woman named Maddalena, if I
remember properly, fearing neither God nor communal welfare, entered
the house of the same woman through the place that had been sealed
with an official notice whereon was written "Public Health" [*Sanità*: this
was a plague notice quarantining an infected dwelling]. Having entered,
he kept the young woman for many days, and lest it be known that he
had gone in . . . from outside the said Maddalena had the ticket on the
door, inscribed "Public Health," reattached.[12]

Cristoforo was betrayed by a friend and by local gossip: "It began to be known, and people said that he had shut himself in with
the aforesaid young woman." Rash Cristoforo himself managed to
escape and the court tried only a false friend of his who had shown
up at the two lovers' doorstep with a fraudulent "notary of the Public Health Authority" (*della Sanità*) in hopes of robbing him. In this
instance it seems not to have been the breach of sexual and mor-

11. For the plague of 1656–1657, see "La peste a Roma (1656–1657)," ed. Irene Fosi,
in *Roma moderna e contemporanea* 1–2 (2006). For infractions during the epidemic, see
Alessandro Pastore, "Tra giustizia e politica: il governo della peste a Genova e a Roma
nel 1656–7," *Rivista storica italiana* 100 (1988): 126–54.

12. ASR, Tribunale Criminale del Governatore, Relazioni dei birri (17 secolo), busta 20.

al codes that most troubled law's guardians. At issue was stopping the plague and protecting health, in this case from an irresponsible love's dire effects.

A POLICEMAN'S LOT WAS NOT A HAPPY ONE

To believe the constables' reports, any arrest repaid a culprit's scant respect for the *bandi*. By such a high-minded claim, the police strove to justify their modus operandi, in the face of much obstruction, sometimes violent, and taunts and showers of defiant stones:

Not long ago [wrote Ipolito de Sanctis in his report of 26 January 1681], perhaps an hour after sundown [*circa 1 hora di notte*], I was at home at my house in the Vicolo di Scannabecchi [so called, but officially and today still Scanderbeg]. As I was changing my clothes, in the street I heard a noise, people shouting "Hit him! Hit him! Kill! Kill!" I stepped outside to see what the matter was and was hit by a flying stone in one leg and in the face. There came up to me the person whose name appears below, saying to me, "*Birro*, fucked billy goat" and other insults and I reached for the sword that I was carrying. Because I defended myself he fled into his house, which is not far from mine, and I went there and took him prisoner. He asked my pardon saying that he was drunk, as in fact he is, and his name is Girolamo di Paolo Ridolfi, a Roman.[13]

One could heap up such examples, at once all alike and each distinct, evidence of a narrative capacity that, even if hitched to stereotypes, still heeded the yen to demonstrate professional abilities in keeping the city's public order, without abusing weapons and without tormenting captives through extortion and abuse. But, in fact, just how one caught captives and hauled them off to jail hung on social station. When they played the social situation wrong, the *bargello* and his *birri* were not only liable to suffer derision more violent than usual, but also likely to kindle a real revolt.[14] Not only in Rome did such things happen; note some Bolognese events from the late Seicento. There, in 1673, *bargello* Mancini, though supported and defended by the cardinal legate, was killed, perhaps by Agostino Marsili, for having repeatedly offended nobles and students by

13. ASR, Tribunale Criminale del Governatore, Relazioni dei birri (17 secolo), busta 119, f. 78r.

14. Peter Blastenbrei, "La quadratura del cerchio. Il bargello di Roma nella crisi sociale tardocinquecentesca," *Dimensioni e problemi della ricerca storica* 1 (1994): 5–37; Blastenbrei, "Violence, Arms and Criminal Justice in Papal Rome, 1560–1600," *Renaissance Studies* 20, no. 1 (2006): 66–87.

high-handed, brutal behavior. He had arrested one of Marsili's servants "contemptuously."[15]

Let us go back to Rome some hundred years earlier. On 19 July 1561, the governor interrogated the *bargello*, along with other witnesses, about the capture of Captain Cencio Capizzucchi, a young soldier from an old civic noble family, who had asked to be led to jail "not tied up. . . . And, because the *bargello* wanted to tie him, he promised on his faith to come with him, as a gentleman, without the escort."[16] Free of the *bargello*, Capizzucchi took swift refuge in Piazza Sciarra. Meanwhile, news of his arrest had stirred up other nobles, who saw in the policemen's actions an affront to their rank and station. From the house of the great baron Alessandro Colonna, says a witness, "five or six men came out with pikes." Servants of Prince Paolo Giordano Orsini joined them en route, "and there were many, many others, with long-handled weapons, but I did not know them," adds the witness, ducking behind the code of prudent silence.[17] This raucous response was no exception to the rule. Hearing of Capizzucchi's arrest, Giovanni Battista Maddaloni, another solid civic noble, remarked that hoary custom ordained that men of station must escort arrested nobles to the prison, according to a ritual of caste solidarity that trumpeted defiance against the pope's justice. "So we took up our capes to go escort Captain Cencio, because, when a gentleman goes to prison, one escorts him, in case he needs a surety, or anything else." Here, Maddaloni hopes to keep from the court the noble accomplices of Cencio's eventual escape, but he also touts his solidarity with irenic Alessandro Colonna, who, he says, went into the street after the *birri* had already departed, "and he went there without arms, and said that one has to honor the forces of order, and words like that."[18] A note dated 30 May 1563, on the margin of the first page of the interrogation papers, is eloquent testimony to the contradictory and wavering position of the papacy in the face of a riotous, violent noble class: Pius IV quashed the case.[19]

15. Angelozzi, "Il tribunale criminale di Bologna," 759.

16. ASR, Tribunale Criminale del Governatore, Processi (16 secolo), busta 76, case 6, f. 271r. For Capizzucchi, see Giampiero Brunelli, *Soldati del papa. Politica militare e nobiltà nello Stato della Chiesa (1560–1644)* (Rome: Carocci, 2003), as in the index.

17. ASR, Tribunale Criminale del Governatore, Processi (16 secolo), busta 76, case 6, f. 271r.

18. ASR, Tribunale Criminale del Governatore, Processi (16 secolo), busta 76, case 6, f. 289r.

19. ASR, Tribunale Criminale del Governatore, Processi (16 secolo), busta 76, case 6, f. 268r.

The *birri* and their captain touted themselves in public as protectors of the laws, custodians of order, and bearers of the rules that disciplined individual and collective conduct. They were certainly hated and reviled for their "executions" (arrests), their bribes, and their confiscations, often of humble possessions, from those afoul of justice, especially debt's victims—and debtors were Rome's majority. Their intervention seemed an unmerited and often violent intrusion, imposing, via systematic everyday violence, an order based on alien values. Their power went down badly, especially in the countryside and the distant towns, nor were they well received in cities, where, in self-defense, people found refuge in other powers with deep urban roots: the palaces of the nobles with their privileged impunity, the churches, and the many foreign embassies enjoying diplomatic immunity (*franchigia*) and the right to grant asylum.

In July of 1627, in the Spanish Quarter of Rome at Trinità dei Monti (today famous as Piazza di Spagna), near the embassy of Spain's Catholic king, were found some foreign corpses. They were the mortal fallout of an immunity tussle that became a trial by combat between *birri* bands and embassy strong-arm men. We know this from witnesses in the long trial that followed. The showdown had troubling echoes in high politics: the Thirty Years' War, with its Italian sideshow in the Duchy of Monferrato, had pitched the papacy of Urban VIII (1623–1644), self-styled "father of all" but partisan nonetheless, as strenuous defender of Italian liberty against Spain's expansionist claims in Italy's North. Rome and its neighborhoods became a sounding board for tense politics abroad; this tension surfaced in a flood tide of violence as the papacy strove to repossess, at least symbolically, parts of the cityscape long sequestered from its magistrates' sway. In the trial, many averred that in night's deep darkness they had seen nothing. Others admitted that they had recognized some Spanish soldiers as they hustled off "the corpse of Don Gonzalo, barber of the lord Ambassador," and said they had seen a clash with *birri* who, under harquebus fire, fled "like men possessed by demons" while the Spaniards pursued them "with weapons in hand. And I saw the Spaniards fire harquebuses three more times, and they [the *birri*] fled, one man one way, and one another."[20] The witness, anxious to keep his nose clean, goes on,

---

20. ASR, Tribunale Criminale del Governatore, Processi (17 secolo), buste 225–27. The citation is to busta 226, f. 85r.

"I heard nothing said, and I was not interested to know any more about it and I heard nothing more." Under interrogation, the *bargello* offered details to prove how diligently he had striven to make his corporal respect the ambassadorial immunities. "I told him that he should leave the scene, as it was the Spanish Quarter, and that he should respect it, and go elsewhere, that the Count, his lord [the ambassador], did not want the *birri* to be in that street, and that the quarter belonged to the Spaniards." On the one hand, Roman justice recognized the zone's immunities; on the other, it would not tolerate, given the political tensions, what everybody knew: that in the count's ambassadorial palace they played every kind of prohibited game—cards, dice, *primera* (a cousin of poker)—and they sold without the proper tax "wine to all who go there." Above all, the police knew that the delinquents guilty of these many and repeated crimes were legally exiled from Rome. Above all, there was Giorgio Strozzi, a Roman,

guilty of many crimes that have won him exile. But in spite of that and in contempt of Justice he has been continually in Rome, all over town in the palaces of princes, and above all he lodges at the palace of the Lord Ambassador of Spain at Montecavallo.[21]

Episodes of this ilk were not isolated. They recurred, echoing the politics of the moment, for European affairs always had their Roman echo. Clashes with the Spaniards in the century's thirties and forties,[22] and with the French in the years of Alexander VII (1655–1667), troubled the city's peace.[23] In the sixteenth century, various popes had wrestled with ambassadorial liberties, but none had solved the problem. Although repeatedly threatened with excommunication,

21. ASR, Tribunale Criminale del Governatore, Processi (17 secolo), busta 226, f. 179r–184r. As for Montecavallo, this was not the usual place for the Spanish embassy, which was then already in Piazza di Spagna, as it is today. But the ambassadors rented other Roman palaces or stayed with nobles, and, at this time, may have been at the Colonna palace, near Montecavallo. For the story of the Spanish embassy, see Alessandra Anselmi, *Il palazzo dell'ambasciata di Spagna presso la Santa Sede* (Rome: De Luca, 2001).

22. A relation by Governor Spada gives a detailed description of the clashes of 1635. See Giovanni Battista Spada, *Racconto delle cose più considerabili che sono accorse nel governo di Roma*, ed. Maria Teresa Bonadonna Russo (Rome: Società Romana di Storia Patria, 2004).

23. Ludwig von Pastor, *History of the Popes*, vol. 31 (London: Routledge, and New York: Kegan Paul, Herder, 1957), 94–102; Blastenbrei, "La quadratura del cerchio. Il bargello di Roma nella crisi sociale tardocinquecentesca," 5–37.

the armed defenders of these immunities seldom deigned to surrender the delinquents and fugitives they harbored. The test of force went on, often shadowing shifts, far beyond Rome's borders, in the continent's political balance.

Hated but not feared, often goaded because readily scorned, the constabulary experienced papal endeavors to tighten discipline and cure abuses and corruption. Among proposals, one, at the Seicento's end, touted levying police among nobles and men of station. In a memorandum to Cardinal Pietro Ottoboni, Giuseppi Retti observed:

The behavior and the operations of such ruffians [or "curs": *canaglia*] . . . infamous persons, [who,] even though they are paid more than they need, conduct not without the city's public scandal such immoral lives that for them the title of "executor of justice" gives them total impunity and a safe conduct for any sort of evil misdeed. There is no kind of robbery or extortion not fomented and protected by them.

The zealous author then spelled out his plan: to "confer all the subordinate jobs to noble persons, mature and prudent—the posts now held by *bargelli* of the countryside and of all Rome's other tribunals" and to "set noble, prudent persons in charge of the *birri*" to the prince's certain advantage and profit.[24] The whole project, hopeless of course, did reflect the swarm of woes that for centuries beset administrators who strove to recruit the underlings, ranging from notaries to constables, who furnished justice with its public image.

The Roman model for police organization differed little from that of the state's other cities, or from the pattern elsewhere in Italy. In Bologna, for instance, the *bargello* of the Tribunal of the Torrone (the chief court) deployed forty foot soldiers for urban security and twenty-five cavalry for the countryside. Things were similar in Perugia, in Ascoli, in Fermo. Matters were more ticklish in the little towns where a shortage of men made public order precarious and undermined the court's honor and repute. As we have seen, the *birri* were hardly esteemed in Rome itself. Court records from the hinterland demonstrate the solidarity of communities, of neighbor-

24. BAV, Ottob. lat. 2349, "Riflessioni sopra gli abusi e sconcerti cagionati dalla sbirraglia con insinuazione di metodo proporzionato per estirparle." The full transcription of this document appears in Sabrina Auricchio, "La ronda di notte: Le Relazioni dei Birri nella Roma del Seicento." Laurea thesis for l'Università di Roma "La Sapienza" (1994–1995), 187–200.

hoods, and of "friends"—not otherwise described—who helped arrested persons escape, or who, hurling stones, attacked the guards, or otherwise thwarted the execution of their duties. In Rome and in the lesser cities, discontinuity haunted the land's control. Policy oscillated, moderation mixing with throes of repression and setting a harsh example, in response to political tensions and interpersonal conflicts. The fragmentary nature of the territory in both city and country, its patchwork of privileges and immunities, compounded the confusion.

To control the landscape, one had to repress the power of the nobles. In behavior and lifestyle, they always clashed with papal sovereignty and with the Counter Reformation's religious and moral models. In some zones of the Papal State, the nobility still held a position that, without exaggeration, one could describe as sovereign. It was sustained by an untamed desire for independence and by refusal to submit to Roman overlordship. Centuries of insubordination, disorder, and violence, fed by factions that, like tentacles, spanned lands and cities, undermined and baffled Rome's authority. Nevertheless, after a sixteenth-century turning point, the nobility would change profoundly.

5

Restless Nobles

COMMUNITIES AND FEUDAL LORDS
CONFRONT JUSTICE

In the middle of the sixteenth century, the pope's territories were still racked by widespread internal instability and the final, tragic stages of the Wars of Italy, by communal revolts, and by untamable noble violence. In those years, the dramatic and often brutal intervention by Rome's justice signaled its attempt to quell a pervasive habit of rebellion that threatened the political stability of a territory still neither thoroughly defined nor firmly led.[1]

The popes had their hands full, striving to defeat heresy, to reorganize Catholicism's central regime, and to master their own territories through a new, more robust machinery of governance. The nobles—the Roman barons, the great families of the newly conquered cities, and the little local aristocracies, deep-rooted on landscapes often tucked into the state's margins—were all targets of an offensive aimed to undo their class's behavior and ideology.

There was no lack of high-born rebel causes célebres, but far commoner were the minor nobles, often scions of collateral branches of great families, who persisted stubbornly in insubordination and rebellion. Theirs was the risky turmoil of a tight-knit caste, girt by privileges and immunities, fond of violence, and caught, in Italy as elsewhere, between profound political changes and their traditional military vocation tied to masterless feudal lordship. In the Papal State, two kinds of crime had noble perpetrators.

The first of these had the generic, catch-all label "excesses" (eccessi). These were acts of violence, insolent abuses of power at noble (or other) hands, judged harmful to communities. Such behavior stemmed from earlier centuries; it was fostered by the absence of sovereign power that could control a landscape. These "excesses"

---

1. Renaud Villard, "L'homme du secret du pape: un gouverneur de crise dans l'État pontifical au XVIe siècle," in *Attori sociali e istituzioni in Antico Regime*, ed. Bertrand Forclaz, a special issue of *Dimensioni e problemi di ricerca storica* 1 (2004): 15–42.

conflicted with a new ideal and function for nobles, elaborated in
the sixteenth century in hopes of taming the aristocracy and bind-
ing it to sovereigns, to pacify and control the state's lands. "Excesses" were at once banal and dangerous. Major cases surfaced early
in the papal North, and later further south. Prosecution's history here marks less a crime wave among nobles than the march of
state repression. In the Romagna, in 1535, a case arose against Francesco Theodoli, member of a restless local family destined later to
prosper in the curia. In 1538 some nobles from Tolentino were accused, and in 1549 the Gentiloni counts of Osimo, in the Adriatic Marches. In 1550 Carlo Paganelli, a nobleman of Matelica, was
charged with "prison break." The Ottoni family, dominant in Matelica, would be accused in 1565 of excesses against the inhabitants. Another charge, "abuse of power," was also common. South
of Rome, rival baron families, the Conti and the Colonna, waged
raids judged "excessive" at Piperno and Proceno. In 1545, Alfonso
Colonna was singled out for his violence against the community of
Riofreddo. The charge fell on nobles like Giuliano Cesarini, lord
of Rocca Sinibalda, in 1556 and, in 1566, on Don Ferrante Vitelli,
feudal lord of Montone.[2] Struggles between great baronial clans,
especially in the popes' coastal province of Campagna e Marittima, marked the southern boundary with the Kingdom of Naples,
whenever tension flared between the papacy and Spain. In 1562,
Bonifacio Caetani was accused of "violent invasion of a place" after he tried to seize lands of nearby communities. Meanwhile, the
standing Conti-Colonna rivalry played out via rustling, woodland
arson, and slaughtered flocks. The campaign to tame the nobility and
quell rebellions spurred repressive steps, especially at mid-century.
Though unsystematic, justice could be violent to set an example, and
could also repress whole villages that rebelled against lords and their
officials, accusing them of violence, embezzlement, and other abuses.

The second crime was banditry. It was adjudged a crime of lèse-
majesté (crimen lesae maiestatis), that is, rebellion against the pope's
sovereignty. Nobles had participated in such organized crime forever. But they piled in with renewed zest in the sixteenth centu-

2. Thomas V. Cohen, "Communal Thought, Communal Words and Communal
Rites," in *Sociability and Its Discontents: Civil Society, Social Capital, and Their Alter-
natives in Late Medieval and Early Modern Europe*, ed. Nicholas Epstein and Nicholas
Terpstra (Leiden: Brill, 2009), 24–50.

ry's second half, when a tsunami of banditry washed over the whole state.[3] Noble participation in crime, diffuse and deep-seated, has been explained as a self-conscious feudal revolt against the centralizing Papal State.[4] This theory might hold for some noble revolts in the Marches, like the one led in 1555 by Mariano Parisani.[5] But it hardly explains the ineradicable presence of Roman and provincial feudatories from, especially, Romagna, Umbria, and the Marches, throughout sixteenth-century banditry. Rather, banditry was the most extreme form of habitual anarchy and violence, protected by legal immunity and social privilege and by a local particularism still barely touched, in late century, by papal power. Nobles' violence, like that of other social classes, was neither random nor irrational; it had its patterns, and its functions, social control among them, and was well adapted to a polity where laws and institutions had short reach. As central institutions grew stronger, these archaic patterns collided with the state's new ambitions.[6] Papal monarchy was keen to bolster its bureaucratic structures and machinery of repression against the lords' high-handedness and anarchy. Nevertheless, thanks to structural weaknesses and to the lack of a social class that opposed the nobles, the Papal State was in no shape to oppose them coherently and resolutely. Nobles connived with exiles and bandits and commissioned notorious crimes. Only with Clement VIII did internal conditions favor decisive action against banditry. Moreover, economic conditions improved after the years of dearth between 1590 and 1592. Furthermore, international relations calmed down, with the end of the French Wars of Religion and the death of Philip II of Spain, so that a decisive military campaign could help damp down banditry's fires, rendering the epidemic just endemic, a mere borderlands phenomenon, more easily tamed but still justly feared.

3. For a fuller treatment of the problem, see Irene Fosi, *La società violenta. Il banditismo nello Stato pontificio nella seconda metà del Cinquecento* (Rome: Ateneo, 1985), and her essays in *Bande armate, banditi, banditismo e repressione di giustizia negli Stati europei di antico regime*, ed. Gherardo Ortalli (Rome: Jouvence, 1986).

4. Jean Delumeau, *Vie économique et sociale de Rome dans la seconde moitié du XVIe siècle*, vol. 2 (Paris: De Boccard, 1959), 542–43.

5. For the episode and for the figure of the noble from Ascoli, see Giuseppe Fabiani, *Ascoli nel Cinquecento*, vol. 1 (Ascoli Piceno: D'Auria, 1957), 321–22; Fosi, *Società violenta*, 56–58.

6. For a paradigm of noble violence see Edward Muir, *Mad Blood Stirring: Vendetta in Renaissance Italy* (Baltimore: Johns Hopkins University Press, 1998), 13–48.

In feudal lands, to the end of the sixteenth century, the law's reach was very circumscribed and tentative, the court often conducting a minor trial just for gaining information, especially when it was tracking an interfamily feud. This ritualized mayhem typical of the nobles' violence, with domestic walls and isolated villages its theater, and city palaces too, could still spark a chain of vendetta murders and blood feuds. The state's justice criminalized this old habit of private violence, and redefined it as public crime, painting it as a bad example for the whole community. So a tidal shift began. Starting with the pontificate of Pius V (1566–1572), more serried and accurate investigations, often ex officio by the governor, targeted nobles' deviant or scandalous private behavior. This shift in justice's idea and functioning derived from the spiritual climate of the Counter Reformation. Nevertheless, when facing lordly crimes on fiefs, until the century's end papal justice proved unsure of itself, inconsistent, and largely ineffectual. With the gravest crimes (*crimina atrociora*), the governor usually proceeded ex officio, that is, without the victims' initiative. He would depute a judge called an "apostolic commissary" (*commissario apostolico*), who, with his notary, *bargello*, constables, and letters patent spelling out his powers, arrived to investigate, interrogate, and inventory the castle's contents with an eye to seizing the noble's goods. The village beheld this "cavalcade," justice in person. It happened when a lord committed repeated outrages, or when the police themselves disturbed the peace by depredation and abuse.

In these cases, although the investigation's methods were generally uniform and rule-abiding, the sentences handed down by Rome's highest court seem altogether diverse and contradictory. Their variability traced to many things: the crime's nature and circumstances, the culprit's position in and outside his family, and his links with the curia, the College of Cardinals, and even the pope himself. Some bloody mid-sixteenth-century episodes in the histories of baronial families demonstrate how the pope's justice attempted to conduct an investigation, at least, into crimes committed in the feudal orbit.[7] Some appalling crimes still seemed to

---

7. For a fine example of this, note the murder by Federico Conti of his wife, Francesca Caetani. ASR, Tribunale Criminale del Governatore, Processi (16 secolo), busta 159, case 19. See Irene Fosi, "Signori e tribunali. Criminalità nobiliare e giustizia pontificia nella Roma del Cinquecento," in *Signori, patrizi, cavalieri in Italia centro-meridionale nell'Età moderna*, ed. Maria Antonietta Visceglia, 225–27 (Rome: Laterza, 1992). For the

reside in a private sphere, where a code of values, if offended, demanded violent reprisal. Had papal justice not taken such behavior as an explicit threat, it might have continued to curb its response. Later in the century, as the Counter Reformation took hold, with the ascent of energetic popes like Sixtus V, punishment of nobles' crimes became more frequent, more loudly trumpeted, and more keen to set an example. The law's hesitations and inconsistencies lived on, but condemnations became an instrument of political propaganda and a means to moralize society, via, above all, surveillance and discipline of the noble class.

ON THE NEAPOLITAN BORDER: THE CAETANI

By the onset of the seventeenth century, the Caetani had lost much of their political power and habit of lordly violence. Lords of the Duchy of Sermoneta, perched on the coastal Via Appia and on the inland Cassino road and dominating both these land links southward to the Kingdom of Naples, in earlier decades the Caetani had been party to bloody episodes, clan-based vendettas and, mostly, blatant banditry.[8] Later, having the Caetani duke of Sermoneta dwell in Rome, and a family cardinal too, helped curb their ways.

The family's story can stand as an example. At the beginning of the 1570s, like many, they shifted from the French faction to that of Spain and the Holy Roman Empire. This volte-face, changing sides in European politics and in the factional divisions that dominated the College of Cardinals, did not quell brigandage on their lands or end their long alliance with outlaw bands. Revolts, family vendettas, and ever more intolerable acts of violence and insubordination continued, especially in the Caetani di Maenza branch. This thirst for vendetta hurt the interests of another Caetani branch more tightly linked to the papal court, that of Sermoneta.

Territorial rivalry between the two branches sparked conflict. In 1555–1556, the Caetani di Maenza tried to grab Sermoneta. In those years, Paul IV, as a French ally, waged war with Spain, and

---

ritual nature of the execution of the adulterous wife, see Ottavia Niccoli, *Rinascimento anticlericale* (Rome: Laterza, 2005), 149–57.

8. For this, see Irene Fosi, "Il banditismo e i Caetani nel territorio di Sermoneta (secoli XVI–XVII)," in *Atti del Convegno "Sermoneta e i Caetani. Dinamiche politiche, sociali e culturali di un territorio tra medioevo ed età moderna,"* ed. Luigi Fiorani, 213–25 (Rome: L'Erma di Bretschneider, 1999).

with its partisans, the Colonna barons. As the Caetani were in the French faction, their feud played out in the theater of the war's last phase. In subsequent years, trials, investigations, and reports by apostolic commissaries sent by the governor into the fiefs on the Neapolitan border help sketch out the range of crimes by the Caetani of Maenza. There were blood feuds, kidnappings, impoundings for ransom, and plunderings of official couriers, all at their hands or orders. Although the governor gathered abundant evidence from suspects and the accused, who of course tended to upload all crimes onto their potent bosses, few trials bruised the Caetani themselves. The pope's frequent direct intervention produced, thanks to the family's cardinal, only a suspended penalty, a cancelled sentence, and an obliterated paper trail.

In the second half of the sixteenth century, the lesser branches of the Caetani—of Maenza and Filettino, hostile to the Caetani di Sermoneta, who were stronger and linked to the curia—engaged in notorious spates of banditry and collaborated with outlaws, jeopardizing papal bandit policies. In 1571, Cristoforo Caetani was tried for, but later absolved of, "receiving bandits." His brother Cesare, of the Filettino branch, had been tried already, in 1565, but in 1570 the pope absolved him totally. Cesare never changed his colors. Thanks to his feudal immunity and family prestige, he felt it was safe to take part again, in person, in assorted crimes by outlaws who sheltered on his estates. His troubling behavior was known in Rome; it perturbed Cardinal Nicolò Caetani, protector of the family's name and honor at the curia. In 1582, the Naples courier was robbed. Cesare's participation in the crime gave Gregory XIII the chance for an exemplary act of "rigorous justice," the confiscation of all Caetani fiefs, as "the receptacle for all the bad characters in the Kingdom [of Naples]." Although Cardinal Nicolò leaned on the pope, Cesare was locked up in Castel Sant'Angelo. He tried a daredevil escape, but the rope snapped. He was put to death in November 1583 and the Apostolic Chamber (the papal treasury) swallowed his fiefs, but did restore them post mortem. Caetani's execution would seem a sign of sterner justice toward unruly nobles had it not been so isolated amidst muddle and compromise, until Sixtus V and Clement VIII took power.

The story did not end with Cesare. In 1592, his sons, Scipione and Antonio, were condemned to death, in absentia, for having convened,

in their lands, Filettino, La Torre, Trevi, and Vallepietra, a large outlaw band and committed a string of murders to avenge their father.
Again, the Apostolic Chamber confiscated the offending fiefs. But
this time the cardinal's influence with the pope carried the day. On
20 May 1596, the papal nephew Cardinal Pietro Aldobrandini absolved the brothers of all their crimes and restored them to "home-
land, reputation, honors, and possessions."[9] Note the inconsistency
of papal policy, thanks to the pressure that a family like the Caetani, even in its decline, could put upon a pope to mitigate decisions
that might otherwise have set a strong example. Having forgotten,
or conveniently parked, their rivalry with the Sermoneta branch, the
Maenza lords often called for help to the Sermoneta cardinal, Enrico
Caetani, a prestigious diplomat and effective family champion inside
the curia.

The Caetani had enjoyed the support of the Colonna, who, for
violent ways and strategic ties with barons, came second to no family. The Colonna shared the habits and Spanish sympathies of their
Caetani neighbors. Nevertheless, when the violence of Pirro and
Prospero Caetani became intolerable, the tacit Colonna protection
lapsed. In the Sacred College, Cardinal Marcantonio Colonna began to argue for containing the crimes of his rambunctious neighbors and strove to dispel suspicions of Colonna complicity. Then,
in 1594, Don Filippo Colonna was attacked at Sezze. Almost by
miracle, he saved his skin but left much loot in bandit hands. That
was the last straw, ending all solidarity and reciprocal protection.

In politics, the Sermoneta Caetani had more heft than the
Maenza. Their several cardinals, Nicolò, Enrico, and Luigi, attest
to that. The dukes of Sermoneta had to calibrate a balance in their
relations with the curia and Rome's judicial bodies. They must
defend their prestige and feudal power, but also collaborate with
popes and tribunals. The courts' interference in the duke's own justice at Sermoneta grated. The duke, complaining of a vassal's arrest, by Rome's *bargello* of the Campagna, wrote in no uncertain
terms to his own judicial official:

I have been filled with distaste by it because I see our jurisdiction trampled. If one did not protest, vassals would dare to take recourse every day

9. Gelasio Caetani, *Domus Caietana*, vol. 2, *Il Cinquecento* (San Casciano Val di
Pesa: Stianti, 1933), 173–74; 317–18.

in these [papal] tribunals. . . . If, in the future, these tribunals ask you for the trial transcript of a person condemned by you [Caetani was writing to his own high judge (*luogotenente*), Cesare Scotucci], do not give it without my express permission. Tell whoever asks you for it that you have this order, and let them instead ask the Lord Cardinal and me.

There is no sign here of an open clash with Rome, as often in the past with the Caetani di Maenza. In the end, a kinsman should not sap the credibility of the family's cardinal, and his power to mediate and protect. Thus the compromise: on the one hand, latent protection and hidden or explicit deals with outlaws; on the other, more or less compulsory collaboration with Roman justice. This, in essence, was the line of conduct that let feudal lords conserve power and authority in their dominions.

The correspondence between the duke and his judges at Sermoneta puts in high relief the ongoing difficulty of applying coherently, in the face of the local population and of families, the norms imposed by Rome, and of repressing "the audacity of these bad men" who undermined the security and economy of a place like Sermoneta. Interpersonal violence, aggressions, and woundings filled the letters the feudal judge sent to the duke in Rome. The letters bore witness to the desire of the duke's official to appear to his master as the sure, trusted guarantor of local public order. They are also a clue to the deep, habitual everyday violence that readily exploded, with dire results. For the feudal judge, as for the papal magistrates, it was ever more urgent to control public order and to deal out harsh punishments to set an example. The judge's letters to the duke, and sometimes to the cardinal, illustrate the tangled relationships that fed banditry: family feuds, rivalries internal to the village, misery, and hunger. They also reveal the methods, with all their limits and trammels, used to put down a collective violence that, at the end of the sixteenth century, seemed to overflow the brim and become unbearable. Anyone who fought banditry knew well that the bonds of family and community, plus protection by lords, were justice's worst impediments. One thus must break those bonds and scorch the earth around the outlaws.

In this context, the feudal high judge (*luogotenente*) had a tricky perch. As a privileged representative of the Caetani and intermediary between lord and community, the judge was often a stressed interpreter of an unquiet reality, the balance-needle of complex, tricky equilibria. If his interventions were too heavy-handed, the populace read them as lordly abuse and bullying. On the other hand, to the duke's eyes, and even worse to Rome's authorities, his caution might seem like favoritism and outright complicity with criminals. In this precarious balance of powers sometimes at odds, it was far from easy to punish family complicity and to criminalize entire networks of friends and kin linked to the outlaws. The duke himself urged persecution of the bandits' social allies. While the local judge (*podestà*) of Sermoneta, to whom the policy's application fell, seemed inclined to optimism, the *luogotenente* often worried, for he suspected the troubling consequences of a sweeping, indiscriminate criminalization of the rural world, and, above all, of its families.

In Sermoneta, as in other villages, judges used spies. These were the "mortal enemies" of those living "out on the land" as bandits. They also employed ex-bandits who had deserted to the law, seduced by promises of absolution from banishment and of bounty money. But how thereafter to treat these turncoats and informants, who were still guilty of grave blood crime? A lordly pardon could compromise justice's image by undermining punishment's conceptual ground rock—severity: as example, instructive warning, and deterrent. One the other hand, punishing collaborators might cut off the precious chance to rebuild peace in sorely troubled lands. So, normally, whenever the matter arose, Caetani officials passed the decision to the Sermoneta duke, or, ever more often, to the cardinal. At the state's center, to official eyes, to impute guilt and criminalize an outlaw's nearest kin, to jail the women, raze the house, and confiscate the family goods, all this spelled seizing the terrain that fostered banditry. To local officials' eyes, on the other hand, such actions all did just the opposite. Feudal administrators well knew that such policies promised to recreate, ad infinitum, conditions that fed the very crimes they hoped to quell. Other solutions were needed.

Down through the Seicento, for the Caetani, justice and good order remained a constant dilemma. In 1607, the *luogotenente* wrote the duke: "I am up to the neck in problems and Sermoneta castle reminds me of the Torrone di Bologna [the main court and prison there]."[10] The Caetani fiefs were still a theater of endemic violence,

---

10. Archivio Caetani, Rome (henceforth AC), n. 4923. "Up to the neck: *sono colmo.*" For feudal justice, see Bertrand Forclaz, "Les tribunaux du seigneur. L'administration

made worse by pervasive conflict between local officials of justice dependent on the ducal family, subject villages torn between fidelity to the lord and fear of consequent reprisals, and papal authorities ever keener to break the rapport between Roman barons and outlaws.[11] Sermoneta's geographic position, on the border of the Kingdom of Naples, subjected the duchy to oscillations in political mood between the papacy and Spain. Having ducked lingering suspicions about their connivance with outlaws, in Rome the Caetani continued to oversee the governance of their fiefs, keeping order, assuring the rule of law, supervising their judicial officials, and even meddling in their subjects' morality. They published *bandi* with an eye to disciplining daily life and the *feste* and times of recreation, and to punish those who offended decency.[12] All told, this last policy jibed with the popes' own.

"I THINK I RECOGNIZE THE HAND OF LORD SAVELLI"

In the Cinquecento's middle years, a time crucial for forming and stabilizing papal monarchy and taming the nobility, the Inquisition was often summoned. Villages vexed by lordly abuses turned to it, the pope employed it to investigate and punish suspect behavior, and other Italian princes also used it. As we shall see, for nobles as for others, many crimes morphed into sins.

Like many other fiefs, some lands in Savelli hands were, in the sixteenth century, the scene of repeated tensions that invited Roman courts to intervene. In 1545, the governor sent a commissioner to investigate "excesses" that had taken place much earlier, just after the 1527 Sack of Rome, in the village of Torri, in the Sabina, and at Vacone during the *festa* of Sant' Egidio. There was talk of killings and a sack of the richer houses. Then the prison was taken by storm, the prisoners were freed, a convent was furiously ransacked, and a friar heaved down a well. These were violent acts of desecra-

---

de la justice dans les fiefs du Latium au XVIIe siècle," in his *Attori sociali*, 67–82; Bertrand Forclaz, *La famille Borghese et ses fiefs. L'authorité négociée dans l'Etat Pontifical d'ancien régime* (Rome: Ecole Française de Rome, 2006).

11. Thomas V. Cohen, "A Long Day in Monterotondo: The Politics of Jeopardy in a Village Rising (1558)," *Comparative Studies in Society and History* 33 (1991): 639–68; Caroline Castiglione, *Patrons and Adversaries: Nobles and Villagers in Italian Politics* (New York: Oxford University Press, 2005); Gregory Hanlon, *Human Nature in Rural Tuscany: An Early Modern History* (Basingstoke: Palgrave Macmillan, 2007).

12. AC, n. 65394.

tion, almost a ritual of inversion. The sack used a *festa* to scorn those in power and to mock religion. The grain was set afire and "infinite are the thefts and killings and although Vacone is a little village and there are few people, in spite of that, and among them there have been and are now many homicides," wrote the baffled commissary sent there.[13] He added that, in all this tumult, "I think I recognize the hand of lord Savelli." Why, here, as in other cases, did Rome intervene only after so many years—and then with a mere inquiry? When Rome did act, it was certainly the fear of new troubles, of revolts in a zone reputed to be especially turbulent, crisscrossed by bands of mercenaries; it was a receptacle of bandits and exiles who always found protection, as is clear from a later trial against Onorio Savelli. Moreover, behind actions so blatantly sacrilegious, Rome sniffed a whiff of heresy.

Against Onorio, this same shamelessly riotous, violent nobleman, Pius V unleashed an offensive to show that, henceforth, from a baron, papal power would no longer tolerate such misdeeds. But the firm step was also a chance to strike at long-precarious Savelli family finances. To sequester properties, to lodge them with the Apostolic Chamber, and then to transfer them to the pope's kin or to their allies was a standard attack on the old nobles. The whole business might be called a true, and continual, political trial. This process, repeated case after case, did set off, or accelerate, the internal transformation of the corps of nobles, causing the decadence or disappearance of some families, or at least of minor branches of the great houses, and occasioning the transfer of wealth, and feudal properties and their attendant privileges, toward families of a new nobility. These latter were often from other papal provinces—for instance the Boncompagni, Peretti, and Pamphili. Or they came from other parts of Italy, as did the Ghislieri (Pius V's own family), and the Borghese, Barberini, and Chigi. The most famous example of this political attack on the Roman nobility, and its more violent members, is Clement VIII's 1600 trial of Beatrice Cenci, ending in her and her mother's beheading, for patricide. By 1600, Beatrice's line, a new family who had risen fast in the 1550s, had come to live like nobles. But the Cenci trial was only one of many episodes, famous or obscure, of a strategy to compress and sap the authority

13. ASR, Tribunale Criminale del Governatore, Processi (16 secolo), busta 10, ff. 817r–820v.

and power of the nobles.[14] It was only in the nineteenth-century re-telling that the events in the Roman family, marked by the behead-ing of the young Beatrice, assassin of her dissolute, allegedly inces-tuous father, came to signify the ruthless politics of Clement VIII, thirsting for blood and money, and, in that same year, also send-ing to the stake the philosopher monk Giordano Bruno. In more prosaic reality, the Cenci, like other noble Roman families, had not figured out how to adjust their lifestyle to a society in transforma-tion; they knew neither how to find good friends and allies, nor how to detach themselves from outmoded violence.

❧

In 1566, Pius V resolved to intervene against unruly Onorio Savel-li. Behind his endeavor, however, lay not only desires to protect or-thodoxy and to inflict exemplary punishment on baronial scandals, but also the need to solve an in-law problem, in Onorio's marriage to Camilla Orsini, contracted without the assent of her brother, Car-dinal Giacomo, *vicario* in 1560 and close collaborator in the pope's arduous campaign to moralize Rome's society and clergy. If the lat-ter task was almost impossible, far easier was it to umpire family af-fairs. Pius V undid Onorio's wedding and then targeted his person and his goods. Contemporaries did not fail to discern the pope's true reasons. Commenting on the surface motives, a weekly Roman newsletter (*avviso*) wrote:

Signor Onorio Savelli is persecuted by the pope. They say the reason is some homicides, and having had a hand in a killing done in the time of Pius IV. He is also accused of heresy. He confesses the homicides and the killing, but asks for pardon and grace. As for the heresy, he asks for a safe-conduct, to go settle wherever His Holiness desires.[15]

While this transpired, the pope had the governor send an apos-tolic commissary to Aspra and Rignano, Onorio's fiefs, one east of the Tiber in the Sabina foothills and the other across the riv-er. They were to "take possession of the castle, make an inventory, and proceed to confiscate all the moveable and immoveable posses-sions of Signor Onorio, for many excesses and enormous crimes."[16] For more than two decades, it was well known, Onorio Savelli had

14. For the events, collective memory, and later historiography of this affair, see the essays in *I Cenci: nobiltà di sangue*, ed. Michele Di Sivo (Rome: Colombo, 2002).

15. BAV, Urb. lat. 1040, f. 207r (30 March 1566).

16. ASR, Tribunale Criminale del Governatore, Processi (16 secolo), busta 116, case 3.

practiced in his territories every sort of violence: rustling, punitive incursions into his villages, rapes. The accusation of complicity with bandits finally provoked papal intervention, tardy but now justified by the controverted marriage. Moreover, the pope's zeal for morality could dust off the accusation of heresy made years back and now spelled out formally by restive peasant vassals.

The village headmen (*massari*) were interrogated closely. Their stories summoned from memory episodes of violence, some from long ago. The told of the *charivari* and rape, commissioned by Signor Onorio, of Caterina, a widow who had resolved to remarry and moved in with her lover before the wedding.[17] The weaver Jacobo, the future husband, was abducted from his house by two villagers and by "some others, servants of Signor Onorio Savelli," stuffed into a bag and carried off. Caterina, meanwhile was led

to the castle where Signor Onorio was, while through the village they played a drum and many rough bells, kettles, pots, and pans, they way they do when someone weds a widow. I heard that they had hoisted a sheet on a pole as a sign that they were collecting young men to go to the castle and screw the said Caterina.

Now this condemnation and the scorning of the marriage project, desired and guided by Savelli himself, used the traditional *scampanata* ("belling"), a rough ritual of collective scorn widespread in the rural Sabina, but a gang rape at the lord's behest was an atrocious twist of an old usage. Still, the Roman criminal tribunal's action was not immediate. There was no lack of mitigating pressures on the curia and on the pope himself. They surface in a letter of Pius V inviting the executors to allow Lucio, Onorio's son, "to live and feed himself according to his station, as a lord who is a child . . . lest he suffer, for he complains that they have taken from him everything, but do this without prejudice to the needs of the Fisc and of the Reverend Apostolic Chamber."[18]

The governor ordered seizure, in the name of the Apostolic

17. ASR, Tribunale Criminale del Governatore, Processi (16 secolo), busta 116, case 3, ff. 645v–47r. For some forms of social control via collective derision in the region of Rome, see Martine Boiteux, "Dérision et déviance: à propos de quelques coutumes romaines," in *Le Charivari*, ed. Jacques Le Goff and Jean Claude Schmitt, 237–49 (Paris: Mouton-Ehess, 1981); Natalie Zemon Davis, "The Reasons of Misrule," in *Society and Culture in Early Modern France*, 97–103 (Stanford, Calif.: Stanford University Press, 1988).

18. ASR, Tribunale Criminale del Governatore, Processi (16 secolo), busta 116, case 3, f. 721r.

Chamber, of Rignano, Aspra, and other villages, and the replace-
ment of their officials. The community, charged with complicity
for having received Onorio while banished by Roman courts, was
therefore punished with heavy fines. But the peasant vassals ral-
lied to their lord once more, against Roman authority, by refusing
to collaborate. Their choice was savvy, for six months later, on the
pope's own behest, Onorio's son was pardoned and reinstated in his
rights and feudal goods.[19]

In the years of Pius V, the law's intervention became more energetic, stimulated by the pope's earlier career as chief inquisitor.
Nonetheless, it was as sapped as ever by internal pressures that re-
versed the final results. The Inquisition, a new and fearsome instrument, seemed flexible enough to quell rebel lords, especially when
they evinced moral shortcomings or a whiff of outright heresy. At
the time of the Savelli inquest, in June 1566, Pius warned all tribunals of the Papal State to obey the Inquisition, and send their prisoners to Rome, "even if they have been jailed for greater crimes."[20]
The prosecutor of the Inquisition reasserted the same demand
forcefully to the governor of Rome, the cardinal *vicario*, and to the
auditor (a judge) of the Apostolic Chamber.

In the case of Onorio Savelli, besides the governor's tribunal,
the Inquisition also intervened, invited by his long-suffering peasant vassals, victims of his violence. The charges, as listed, spelled
out in detail his presumed crimes against the faith. Onorio Savelli,
like other Roman barons, had participated in the German wars, for
the Holy Roman Empire, against the heretics, but was suspected of
having spread in his fiefs "the contagion of the Lutheran plague."[21]
According to the charges, during his stay in Germany and at Trent,
in the train of Cardinal Mandruzzo, "he went to the sermons and
gatherings of the Lutherans." In particular, it was said, he had dis-
puted in public "with priests and preachers and held that there was
no paradise or purgatory." He was accused of eating meat on Fri-

19. ASR, Tribunale Criminale del Governatore, Processi (16 secolo), busta 126, f.
167r (January 1568).

20. BAV, Urb. lat. 1040, ff. 302v–303r.

21. For the massive participation of the Roman nobility in the wars against the
Protestants, see Gregory Hanlon, *The Twilight of a Military Tradition: Italian Aristo-
crats and European Conflicts, 1560–1800* (London: Taylor and Francis, 1988); Giampiero
Brunelli, *Soldati del papa. Politica militare e nobiltà nello Stato della Chiesa (1560–1644)*
(Rome: Carocci, 2003).

days and urging his subjects to do likewise. Some testified that "in public, the said lord, holding the opinions of Martin Luther," had denied "the power of the pope and the sacraments and orders of the Holy Church, holding, specifically, that the sin of lechery was no sin and that a woman, without a dispensation of the Apostolic See, married to one man, could marry another." And others affirmed that he wanted to take "the sacrament [the wafer] and the holy oil for anointment and try them out on dogs," and that he had more than once denied transubstantiation, and, speaking of the mass, had said, "let's go to the common error."[22]

In a long deposition, Onorio Savelli admitted his guilt, his frequenting heretics and reading dangerous books, all "crimes" committed together with his brother-in-law, Carlotto Fausto Orsini, lord of Mugnano and Cottanello, a fellow soldier in the wars against the Lutherans in the empire's German lands.[23] It was Carlotto who had introduced him to forbidden reading in heretical texts and to the reformed ideas that went the rounds and influenced not a few noble soldiers battling the Protestants. Savelli's deposition raises the question of the diffusion, among Italian nobles and Roman barons, of Reform ideas. The Holy Office also heard the testimony of eminent prelates, like Cardinal Cristoforo Mandruzzo, Girolamo Galimberti, the bishop of Gallese (not far from Rignano), and of Roman barons like Paolo Giordano Orsini, who all exculpated the lord of Rignano. The defense presented Onorio as a good Catholic and a just judge in his fiefs, attentive and generous to those in need.[24]

The sometimes vague idea of a better, more efficacious justice, free of connivance and pressures, motivated the community's denunciations against lordly abuse. But villagers often found the Inquisition hard going. Before the tribunal, having at the outset trustingly invoked its justice, peasant vassals were besieged by theologizing questions that stumped them utterly, or sketched out as best they could inconsistent explanations, and, in the end, often retracted their allegations, muffled their accusatory tone, or actually defended their lords' doings. The fear of breaking the precarious balance of forces between lord and community seems to have pre-

22. ACDF, S.O., St. St., R. 2-m, f. 749r.
23. ACDF, S.O., St. St., R. 2-m, ff. 669r–691v.
24. ACDF, S.O., St. St., R. 2-m, ff. 628r–839v.

vailed over hopes for justice from further away.[25] But, with Savelli, even though the vassals backed down, Pius V still won. On 10 January 1568, Onorio Savelli, after severe warnings, abjured his errors solemnly and theatrically before the cardinals and the pontiff. He was constrained to pay a thousand scudi, a palpable sum but, for a lord of his station, hardly ruinous. In asking pardon he was joined by Niccolò Orsini, the count of Pitigliano, a protagonist of yet another long and controverted affair, this one involving the pope and Cosimo I, the duke of Tuscany.

A "DEVIL" AS MASTER

Niccolò Orsini, head of a branch of a large clan of barons, was dissolute and violent. His seat was Pitigliano, an imperial fief of southern Tuscany, on the border of the Papal State. In 1547, he drove off his father, Count Giovan Francesco, and, almost at the same moment, went over to the French party in the Wars of Italy and made his county a bulwark for the defense of Siena, a French ally, in the war that ended with Siena's defeat and absorption by Florence.[26] Orsini fled to France. In 1556, Paul IV, a pro-French pope, called him back and gave him a cavalry command. Shortly after, however, he jailed him for fourteen months in Castel Sant'Angelo in Rome, for "excesses" committed on papal territory, counterfeiting, and suspicion of heresy. On 17 October 1557, Giovan Francesco conceded Pitigliano to his son, meanwhile released from prison, absolved of heresy, and reconciled with both his family and the pope. The mediators of this politically important peace pact were the cardinal of Pisa, the bishop of Verona, the duke of Paliano (a kinsman of the pope), and Camillo Orsini.[27] The county of Pitigliano was still in the sights of Cosimo I, duke of Florence, who was trying to extend southward the lands of the Sienese Republic he had just conquered. In January of 1562, Alessandro Orsini, Niccolò's son and enemy, caused Pitigliano to rebel and acclaim the duke of Florence as its new overlord.[28]

25. For village-lord relations see Castiglione, *Patrons and Adversaries*.

26. ASR, Tribunale Criminale del Governatore, Processi (16 secolo), busta 11.

27. Archivio di Stato di Firenze (henceforth ASF) Mediceo del Principato, filza 2776, f. 56r.

28. *Narrattione del fatto de Pitigliano come l'ha fatto intendere il Duca di Fierenze al Re Cristianissimo*, document cited by Pietro Fanciulli, *La contea di Pitigliano e Sorano nelle carte degli Archivi Spagnoli di Simancas e Madrid e dell'Archivio di Stato di Firenze (Mediceo del Principato)*, (Pitigliano: A.T.L.A., 1991), 55.

Cosimo stepped in as guardian of the imperial fief. Had he taken full possession of the county, he would have violated the terms of the Peace of Cateau-Cambrésis and set off a new French-Imperial war in Italy. That would have been for him a scorching political setback. Spain had interests in the county, as it bordered on the Stato dei Presidi, site of its garrisons on the Tuscan coast, and Cosimo could also not ignore the marriage alliances between Niccolò Orsini and the Farnese, lords of the state of Castro, just south of Pitigliano, and eager to take Pitigliano too. Moreover, it was imprudent to alienate Pius IV, who in 1560 refused to take sides on the legal issue, and who, above all, made no claim himself to the county, and set no obstacles before the duke of Florence.

Meanwhile, Cosimo had tried other devices to acquire full authority over the county; one year earlier, he had instigated a trial against Niccolò Orsini in Florence, taking advantage of the Roman Holy Office, a new, powerful tool that the church now put at his disposal. In 1560, Rome's Inquisition became involved, at the invitation both of Cosimo I and of the "poor men" of Pitigliano, astutely played by the Medici commissioner Francesco Vinta, sent to the county by the duke. At once the duke of Florence turned to the Inquisition to repair Orsini's injuries to his own vassals. The theatricalization of Roman justice served very well the strategies of Cosimo, who, in these years, was very careful not to alienate the papacy. Thanks to the testimony of Pitigliano's inhabitants, the duke and his men succeeded in portraying Niccolò as a demonic criminal, daubed in sin and crimes (in legal thought, these two vices were growing ever closer).[29] Orsini's failings, vividly described, were then broadcast all across Europe. The imperial feudatory was defined only by his faults, his bestial conduct, the antithesis of his proper role, as if he were Cosimo's utter opposite.

In the fall of the same year (1560), in Florence, before the chancellor of the Otto di Balìa court, began the interrogations of various persons who had served Niccolò Orsini or held office in his county. After torture, their depositions paint a grim picture of the count's conduct—his abuse of power, immorality, and acts of sacrilege.[30]

---

29. Paolo Prodi, *Una storia della giustizia. Dal pluralismo dei fori al moderno dualismo tra coscienza e diritto* (Bologna: il Mulino, 2000), 265ff.
30. ACDF, S.O., St. St., R. 2-m, ff. 223r–227v.

Thirty-five charges, based on multiple, concordant depositions before the Florentine magistrates or the Medici commissioner, were
then drawn up and signed by the community's leading men. They
affirmed that Count Niccolò had "had the company and familiarity
with, and many times known carnally Jewish women, and those of
the Hebrew religion, both in the village of Pitigliano and in Sorano,
both married ones and virgins and young women." Charges two to
six laid out the dire consequences of these dissolute Jewish frequen-
tations, which had led the count to celebrate the Jewish Sabbath by
eating meat on Fridays, to dig up the bones of the dead in churches
and cast them to the four winds, and to make "every sort of baccha-
nal." Detailed accusations also covered treasons committed before
Siena fell to the Florentines—Orsini's trip to France and his support
for anti-Medicean exiles led by Piero Strozzi. Orsini was also accused of having "hanged from the walls of Sorano friars and priests
without trial, examination, or sentence and without having them
stripped of their holy orders or obtaining permission from the Apostolic See." Moreover, he was accused of having "hanged in Sorano,
and stripped of flesh, and quartered alive many persons without confession, trial, examination, or sentence, nor was he willing to let them
confess their sins."

Besides the killings and the arbitrary acts enforcing justice, vividly described in testimony destined for the Inquisition, was the
seizure of monastic property. In 1553, indeed, Niccolò Orsini "drove
from the monastery and convent of San Francesco, half a mile from
the village of Pitigliano, all the observant friars of Saint Francis,
without putting other friars, priests, or monastic clergy in; he took
the said monastery and buildings . . . and the woods for his own
use and convenience, and shut down the church and holy worship.
And he used it as his villa, for profane use, down to the present
year, with much scandal and bad example to Christian religion,
and this was and still is true." He had prohibited anyone from becoming a friar or a monk, under pain of confiscation of goods; he
had taken property from churches, from the cathedral itself, and
from pious charities, and, as the seventeenth charge affirmed, "the
said count removed the altars and the images of Jesus Christ, of the
Glorious Mother, and of the saints in some churches of Sorano,
a small town in the bishopric of Sovana, and from them he made
stalls for the horses and barrels, and used them publicly."

Other grave charges were levied against Orsini. He was said to have eaten "meat on Friday and on the Sabbath, in public, at his table, both at home and in company, and he wanted his dependents to eat it." By decree, he had extended carnival into Lent, and he had made men and women work on his lands "on the feast days and Easter, and on their eves." And there were further charges of sexual abuses, accusing Orsini of having raped and deflowered many virgin girls. If they refused to come to him he cast their mothers and other kin in jail, having his way in utterly immoral fashion, and, if ever he found a girl not to be a virgin, he would know her carnally "against nature."[31] One witness before the Otto di Balia testified concerning meat on holy days that the count "did not tell us anything because here we just ate what was prepared and there was a scarcity of fish and an abundance of young goat."[32] To cover for his complicity, the witness added, "I would rather not have served him, for I have served a devil and not a master."[33] He went on to corroborate the charges of rape and violence, and of treason in the Siena war.[34]

This long catalogue of accusations was cut to fit the Inquisition; the Florentine duke, his men, and Orsini's vassals all hoped it would liberate them from Count Niccolò's awkward presence. So, as described on paper, the county of Pitigliano became an exemplary world turned upside down, governed by a dissolute lord, and populated by Jews who shared and instigated his unbridled actions. What remedy could be better, then, than to summon the Inquisition to condemn the count and to bring the good order that only a Christian prince, faithful to both church and pope, could vouchsafe? The tormented time of the Siena war, and Niccolò's politics, blur and fade from memory. In the foreground hover the crimes against morality, the outrages to the church's power, and the frequentation of persons who, like the Jewish concubines, stood for threat to orthodoxy. All accusations aimed to instantiate a scandal that subverted and contaminated good order. Annibale Fab-

---

31. ASF, filza 2776, ff. 255r–365r: these pages contain the charges and the records of testimony of witnesses printed by Francesco Vinta and then sent to European courts to justify Cosimo's position. A manuscript version of the same interrogations is preserved with other papers in ACDF, S.O., St. St. R. 2-m, ff. 298r–304r. Other documentation is in ASF, Archivio Capponi, buste 166–168; 173; 175.

32. ASF, Mediceo del Principato, filza 2776, f. 278r.

33. ACDF, S.O., St. St. R. 2 m-c. f. 227r.

34. ASF, Mediceo del Principato, filza 2776, f. 258v.

broni, Medici *uditore* (judge), sent the duke the testimonies "about what one might call the epicurean, heretical, and tyrannical life of Count Niccolò, and, I believe, if I continued to take testimony even for an entire year, I would always find new, still unheard acts of viciousness to make this case worse."[35] Meanwhile, Francesco Vinta informed Cosimo that he had sent to print the trial "about the life of Count Nicola," with the thirty-five charges, and posted it to the Holy Office and Imperial court.[36]

A SINNER, NOT A HERETIC

Orsini's position became more delicate with the pontificate of Pius V, marked, at its outset, by papal good relations with the duke of Florence. The Ghislieri pope yearned to vaunt his severity, and Niccolò "had a great fear of this pope and in the mornings he would take the breviary and read it and on the holidays he had mass said," said a witness who, earlier, on the torture rope, had declared that Orsini, "at the time of Pope Paul [IV], for more than two years, in all that time never went to mass."[37] But the Roman Inquisition was scrupulous in procedure, and Niccolò had protection at the curia, especially among the Farnese. These two facts probably frustrated the hopes of the town, and of Cosimo and his collaborators; they had hoped to see the count accused of heresy, expelled for good from the game of politics and diplomacy, and stripped of all claims to Pitigliano. The congregation's decrees mark the case's slow progress at the Holy Office, which, in those very years, was occupied with Onorio Savelli.[38] These papers also show how dissoluteness, violence, and abuse of one's own subjects did not themselves, for the pope and the members of the congregation, merit condemnation by the Inquisition.

On 20 June 1567, the defense contested the accusations point by point. The accusers were themselves accused, and then the defense took a different tack. Niccolò Orsini's actions had indeed occasionally been violent, but sometimes they had been necessary, especially against men who, turning friar to duck justice, remained at large, roaming his fief, committing every sort of crime.[39] If Niccolò had

35. ASF, Mediceo del Principato, filza 492, f. 67r.
36. Haus-, Hof- und Staatsarchiv, Vienna, Judicialia latina nn. 399/14, 400 e 401.
37. ACDF, S.O., St. St., R. 2-m, f. 226v.
38. ACDF, *Decreta 1565–1566*.
39. ACDF, S.O., St. St., R. 2-m, f. 501r.

skipped communion, this was hardly because he scorned the Eucharist, but because he knew well that he was embroiled in hatreds and enmities; a good Christian, he dared not approach the sacrament.[40] Nor, said the defense, should the court put much stock in witnesses who, hardly theologians, alleged heretical propositions: denial of the existence of paradise, or of the validity of indulgences, or other affirmations: witnesses who attested to such things should furnish precise coordinates—how, where, and when were such things ever said? Witnesses had accused the count of owning and reading texts placed on the Index of Forbidden Books, without however naming author or title. Meanwhile, had not Niccolò Orsini affirmed that he had ordered burned, under Paul IV, "books of Boccaccio, Machiavelli, Berni and Aretino"?[41] The congregation credited the count's exculpatory declarations, declaring him no heretic, and ruled that all charges against him had been assembled by enemies and ill-wishers.[42] In this sentence, what had been the impact of the recommendations of cardinals, nobles, and Niccolò's other "friends," especially Cardinals Orsini and Caetani, busy in the orbit of the newly elected Pius V, pressing him to end the affair with full absolution?

The long inquest finally came to its definitive end at the very beginning of the pontificate of Pius V, who used the Orsini affair, along with others, especially Onorio Savelli's and that of Pietro Carnesecchi, a well-born Florentine who died condemned of heresy, to make a dramatic show of his unbending policy of moralization. At the end of February, Niccolò Orsini, still "half ill," came of his own will before the Roman Inquisition. The case of the rebellious lord seems to have tangled more and more with Carnesecchi's, as the *avvisi* (newsletters) noted.[43] On 26 April 1568 a Roma *avviso* reported that "in the congregation of the Inquisition held on Thursday before His Holiness there was discussion of ending the imputation of heresy against the lord count of Pitigliano and Onorio Savelli, and there is hope for their innocence."[44] Niccolò Or-

---

40. On the refusal to attend the sacrament of communion see David W. Sabean, *Power in the Blood: Popular Culture and Village Discourse in Early Modern Germany* (Cambridge: Cambridge University Press, 1987), esp. 37–60.

41. ACDF, S.O., St. St., R. 2-m, f. 622v.

42. ACDF, S.O., St. St., R. 2-m, ff. 620r–624v.

43. On 1 March 1567, after notices about the Orsini case, the *Avviso* added, "and, about Carnesecchi, finally, the hopes are dim." BAV, Urb. lat. 1040, f. 378v.

44. Ibid., f. 399r.

sini remained in prison for almost a year more and finally, on 10
January 1568, an *avviso* reported that "they had the abjuration of 23
persons under inquisition at the Minerva [the seat of the Inquisi-
tion] . . . count Niccolò Orsini abjured last Saturday with a canoni-
cal and general confession in the palace of the Inquisition . . . and
he is confined at the place of the Theatines [a new religious order
founded by Gian Pietro Carafa, eventually Paul IV] at the pope's
pleasure and he also has to pay 1000 scudi for pious works."[45]

Two days later, from Pitigliano, there went to Cosimo a more
detailed, somewhat different account of the trial's conclusion.[46] The
absolution permitted Niccolò to return to Pitigliano, purged of his
misdeeds and placed under the guardianship and control of the
duke of Florence. In those very years Cosimo, paying Pius's policies
a heavy tribute necessary for his principality's lasting stability, allowed Pietro Carnesecchi's trial and condemnation. The court asked
the Florentine protonotary if he knew Orsini. His denial came as no
surprise but the inquisitors gave him the lie, producing a letter of his
to Giulia Gonzaga. He had been so au courant about Cosimo's designs on Pitigliano that he had written, "That prince must be among
the elect, for everything turns out well for him."[47] Because Calvin-
ist theology stressed the salvation of the "elect," and the term had a
heretical ring, the phrase could be turned against Carnesecchi. The
matched timing and entanglement of the last phases of the two tri-

45. BAV, Urb. lat. 1049, f. 498r. Cf. Ludwig von Pastor, *History of the Popes from the
Close of the Middle Ages*, vol. 17 (London: Routledge and Kegan Paul; New York: Herder, 1951), 305 n. 1.

46. "On Saturday morning on the third day of this month, Signor Niccolò came out
of the prison of the most holy Inquisition, and he abjured in that said prison with the
doors open. At that abjuration there were present, as I have been told, three cardinals
with their families, and many others. And when that Signor, reading on his knees his
sentence and many other things written and contained in his trial, one of the said cardinals told him to consider well and pay attention to what he was reading and to control his behavior in the future. But that, if he did these things another time, he would
not have forgiveness for any thing, and so he has been sent to the Roman monastery
of the Jesuits to make a [confession] of his life with the general of the said order at the
pleasure of His Holiness. He cannot leave without express license of the said cardinals of the Holy Office, with other salutary penitences that it is the custom to impose
to similar penitents and the evening of the said Saturday he went out and was taken by
coach and all this happened with the doors open, and he was there together with the
Valentino and another person was with him in the coach and there were two on horse-
back bringing up the rear." ASF, Mediceo del Principato, filza 533, f. 265.

47. *I processi inquisitoriali di Pietro Carnesecchi (1557–1567)*, ed. Massimo Firpo e
Dario Marcatto, vol. 2 (Vatican City: Archivio Segreto Vaticano, 1999), 822–23.

als, a thing the *avvisi* noted repeatedly, and the contrasting endings, one positive and the other tragic, suggest a tight link between the cases. They concluded with an "exchange of prisoners" between the inquisitor pope and Cosimo I, in the name of *ragion di stato*. Thus, Carnesecchi's consignment to the Roman tribunal was not merely "the ruthless offer of a token in exchange for the hoped-for concession of the ducal title" but also the price for the "necessary" expansion southward of the Medici principality.[48]

In the second half of the sixteenth century, for the papacy, it became urgent to tame the nobility, especially on the frontiers to the north and south. Success would fortify them against claims by other princes, both Italian and foreign. Defining boundaries mattered when territorial power still faltered due to political pressures and to the discontinuity of the popes' non-hereditary monarchy. Niccolò Orsini's notorious judicial story was emblematic, for it had international implications. The interests of other princes in Italy and elsewhere fed the case. His fief perched on the border between the papal and Tuscan states. At issue was a political problem, but the fierce and monstrous image of the lord the case created helped further Cosimo I's designs to extend his duchy southward.

TOWARD THE SEVENTEENTH CENTURY: A TAMED NOBILITY?

In the seventeenth century, noble presence in the ranks of bandits and outlaws shrank or vanished, as it did in other states, not in Italy alone. In many states, the nobility's domestication and insertion into the system of the princely court shifted its behavior and shunted elsewhere the aristocratic violence earlier expressed through banditry.[49] This explanation works well too for the Papal State, so long as one keeps in mind the geography of banditry over the centuries and the complex, often elusive morphology of its noble class.[50] At the end

48. Arnaldo D'Addario, *Aspetti della Controriforma a Firenze* (Rome: Pubblicazione degli Archivi di Stato, 1972), 159.

49. Norbert Elias, *The Civilizing Process*, 2 vols. (Oxford: Blackwell, 1969–1982); Jonathan Dewald, *The European Nobility 1400–1800* (Cambridge: Cambridge University Press, 1996). So, for example, see Xavier Torres Sans, "El bandolerismo mediterraneo: una visión comparativa (siglos XVI–XVII)," in *Felipe II y el Mediterraneo*, coordinated by Emanuel Belenguer Cebriá, vol. 2, 397–423 (Madrid: Sociedad estatal para la commemoración de los centenarios de Felipe II y Carlos V, 2001); Francesco Manconi, ed., *Banditismi mediterranei secoli XVI–XVII* (Rome: Carocci, 2003).

50. See Maria Antonietta Visceglia, ed., *La nobiltà romana in età moderna. Profili*

of the sixteenth century, and, above all, in the seventeenth, feudal geography changed. Many ancient baronial houses sold great chunks
of their lands to rising families in the Roman court or kinfolk of the
pope. These new lords, like the Borghese, the Barberini, the Peretti,
the Pamphili, and the Chigi, and some old ones too like the Caetani
of Sermoneta, resided in Rome and administered, policed, and disciplined their fiefs from afar, via their *vicarii*. But in turn they themselves were under surveillance, under the eyes of the papal court and
the Roman magistrates. In play in their own conduct were family
honor, economic fortunes, and the chance to grow. Their values had
changed, moving ever further from those nurtured, required, justified, and defended by the anarchic violence and back-country political imperatives of the previous century.

At the same time, we should not underestimate the sharp differences among Roman baronial families; the social transformation made this particularly evident. The Colonna merit a story of
their own, above all the princely Paliano branch. Despite the loss
of some territories, sold to the Barberini, like the fief of Palestri-
na in the Alban Hills looking down on Rome, they continued to
extend their "states" (*stati*)—that is how they defined them and
the term had political meaning—in a broad swath of territory in
the papal southeast, along the border with Naples. In league with
Spain, who repaid them in honors, titles, and cash, they knew they
held real power that protected their untouchable independence
from centralizing officials—magistrates and the pope himself. The
little book *La baronia liberata* [The Barony Set Free], written in
the Seicento by a member of their house, was the latest sequel of
the neo-Ghibellinism expressed by this anciently Ghibelline (pro-
Empire and anti-papal) family, from the Cinquecento's start.[51]

---

istituzionali e pratiche sociali (Rome: Carocci, 2001), and especially the editor's remarks
on p. xviii.

51. Archivio Colonna, Monastero di Santa Scolastica, Subiaco, II, A. 12. For the
Colonna role in the politics of the early Cinquecento, see Alessandro Serio, "Pompeo
Colonna tra papato e 'grandi monarchie,' la pax romana del 1511 e i comportamenti
politici dei baroni romani," in Visceglia, ed., *La nobiltà romana*, 63–87; Alessandro Se-
rio, *Una gloriosa sconfitta I Colonna tra Papato e Impero nella prima età moderna* (1431–
1530) (Rome: Viella, 2008); Thomas Dandelet, "Between Two Courts: The Colonna
Agents in Italy and Iberia, 1555–1600," in *Your Humble Servant: Agents in Early Modern
Europe, 1500–1800*, ed. Hans Cools, Marika Keblusen, and Badeloch Noldus (Hilversum: Verloren, 2006); Thoms Dandelet and John Marino, eds., *Spain in Italy: Politics,
Society, and Religion 1500–1700* (Leiden: Brill, 2006).

Before the governor's court, trials against bandits and their accomplices became ever rarer after the 1620s. The prize legislation—
the bounty policy—adopted in sporadic fashion and applied only
in rare cases by Pius V, was applied systematically by Sixtus V. Often revised to curb the inevitable abuses, as rules issued under Urban VIII (1623–1644) and Innocent X (1644–1655) testify, it continued for the whole Seicento.[52] *Bandi* and edicts invited the capture
or destruction of entire bands or, more often, single outlaws, and
guaranteed a bounty and a "nomination"—the remission of the sentence of a banished person, to be chosen ("nominated") by the cap-
tor (or bandit killer). After the first decades of the seventeenth century, the bounties became formally different: one might call them
"personalized," as they were now attached to the capture of a given
bandit, about whose identity officialdom usually supplied fairly generic information. These changes suggest a change both in the phenomenon itself and in its perception by those in authority. It seems,
in fact, that the danger from malefactors' association—a thing
feared but still lacking juridical definition—now seemed less urgent,
even if some *bandi* still thundered "against the conventicles of persons of evil life."[53] As a consequence, drastic repression to cope with
collective violence gradually lost its edge; the bandit campaign slowly abandoned the ferocity that had marked the policies of popes like
Sixtus V and Clement VIII. Meanwhile, their supposed successes
became a mythic source of widespread propaganda.

The seventeenth century saw theoretical elaborations that defined and improved the workings of the bounty system, the confiscation of goods, and the remission of banishment.[54] There was an
unceasing effort to give the central bodies of the state, in particular the Sacra Consulta—high court for the whole Papal State, for
criminal matters *inter alia*—the power to decide, as court of last
instance, on bounties and on procedures against those who fled the
courts (*contumaci*). With time, disputes multiplied. In 1655, in a petition to the governor of Rome, Pietro de Amici and Cola Romito
da Gorga declared how

52. ASV, Misc Arm. IV–V, vol. 57.

53. ASV, Misc Arm. IV–V, vol. 57, p. 98. In Italian: "contro le conventicole di per-
sone di malaffare."

54. See Prospero Farinacci, *Consilia*, in *Opera Omnia*, vol. 7 (Antwerp: apud
J. Keeberquium, 1618), or any other edition, using the index.

in the year 1655 they delivered into the hand of the courts Eleuterio Flori and Giovanni Merangelo, public bandits, criminals, and killers. They had been infecting the countryside of Legni and Gorga, committing robberies on the road and rustling livestock, as appears in the trial carried out by the commissioner Bonaventura. . . . Not having obtained the usual nomination rights, they ask your most illustrious lordship to deign to have it conceded in conformity with the usual custom.[55]

Sometimes the consignment of the head of a banished man was the first step toward the "redemption" of a man sentenced as a criminal, his reintegration into his family and community. But how many bounties were actually ever paid? And how many frauds shook free the money? It was easy enough to exploit the uncertain signs of premodern social identity and defraud imperfect oversight.[56] One could bring in any old head, or, more often, just some enemy's, passing it off as an outlaw's. Such things did happen.

The letters between the magistrates in the periphery and the governor or the prefect of the Sacra Consulta, and the profusion of *bandi* and instructions recalling established rules and forever adapting them to shifting imperatives—all these things prove how hard it was, at the state's edge, to carry out multiple, often baffling instructions from Rome. It gradually became clear that the main reason that it was so hard to control the landscape was the penalty itself—banishment and exile. It was applied far too often, thanks to the old regime principle that guilt and punishment required no tight fit or common measure. Public order therefore depended on the capacity of provincial governors to mediate, and on the center's ability to comprehend their motives when they did so.

In the seventeenth century, banditry's repression, now a borderlands affair, seemed to be using the same systems as had been in force in the 1590s. But, in reality, something had profoundly changed, both in the typology of the phenomenon and in relations between central authority and papal subjects. Nobles' blatant and massive

55. ASR, Tribunale Criminale del Governatore, Atti vari di cancelleria, busta 131, n. 95 (1658).

56. For the difficulty of establishing criteria for identifying persons, see Valentin Groebner, "Describing the Person, Reading the Signs: Identity Papers, Vested Figures, and the Limits of Identification 1400–1600," in *Documenting Individual Identity: The Development of State Practices in the Modern World*, ed. Jane Caplan and John C. Torpey, 15–27 (Princeton, N.J.: Princeton University Press, 2001). And by the same author, *Der Schein der Person. Steckbrief, Ausweis und Kontolle im Europa des Mittelalters* (Munich: C. H. Beck Verlag, 2004).

participation in banditry vanished, but their violence went on via the use of country thugs to do misdeeds and pursue vendettas against enemy lords, and to afflict the locals in countless ways. As always, the borderlands remained the sore spot, for Rome and for provincial authorities. In the north, the nobility of Bologna seems to have been especially violent, at least among some noblemen who carried on like feudal lords, profiting from the power vacuum in the uplands where the legate's strong arm seldom reached. The cardinal legate himself, Girolamo Lomellini, described to the secretary of state how hard it was to fight Astorre Barbazza, who lived like an absolute lord on his lands on the Modenese border. He was "a man devoid of any good morality, a habitual keeper of concubines."[57]

Papal justice continued to make unsparing use of banishment and exile, the separation of the suspect from his family. The custom expressed and symbolized justice, but was a major reason why banditry persisted. The punishment was a subject of constant negotiation. The verdict could be remitted, and commuted to three years in the galleys, or, more and more often, to a fine that menaced the often shaky finances of a convict's family, but that, on the other hand, guaranteed the fisc some income, via pledges or through the aid and mediation of confraternities and charities.

❧

Despite the draconian policies and military incursions against rural crime in the waning sixteenth century, banditry did not vanish altogether. It did burn less hot and the bands shrank. It also changed, thanks to massive recruitment of outlaws for the conflicts of the seventeenth century's first half, in the Valtellina during the Thirty Years' War, and on the papal frontiers when the War of Mantua threatened. Roman nobles from all over the state, with trains of followers on their payroll, took part in all these military actions. But banditry, above all, lost its aggressive, menacing armed bands, with their many followers, ready to strike and dangerously hard to quell. Villagers' intolerance for this endemic collective violence was ever more tightly tied to their respect for conditions imposed on their communities by increasingly intense contacts with central authorities. Congregations like the Sacra Consulta and the

---

57. Giancarlo Angelozzi and Cesarina Casanova, *La nobiltà disciplinata: violenza nobiliare, procedure di giustizia e scienza cavalleresca a Bologna nel 17 secolo* (Bologna: Clueb, 2003), 35: "huomo privo d'ogni buon costume, concubinario habituato."

Buon Governo figured here. So did the grant of greater powers to local judges, to involve them in territorial control and to cut the distance between center and periphery. In the era, other Italian states followed similar policies. Their results depended on their geography, their lines of communication, and their governors' training and pay.[58] Meanwhile, the Papal State was trying to construct a thick web of controls that used a synergy of governors, bishops, and inquisitors. This web's fine mesh, as Rome well knew, was less fact than theory.

58. Marco Bellabarba, "Informazioni e fatti. Casi di storia del processo penale nell'Italia centro-settentrionale," *Storica* 20–21 (2001): 155–75.

6

Collaboration and Conflicts
Governors, Bishops, Inquisitors

From the second half of the Cinquecento, via the confessional and other devices, the Holy Office continued to extend its surveillance over illicit activities and overt or covert "bad" practices like magic, witchcraft, and divination.[1] This oversight had a tight-knit network of officials with internal synergies, or so Rome intended and hoped. In the pope's domains in Italy, between the sixteenth century and the eighteenth, the Inquisitions were nine in number: Bologna, Ferrara, Faenza, Rimini, Ancona, Fermo, Gubbio, Perugia, and Spoleto. Some of these went back to the Middle Ages; others had been set up later to ease surveillance over territories that fell to papal control in early modern times, as at Ferrara (1598), Fermo (1631), Gubbio (1632), and Spoleto (1685). Around Rome itself, in the provinces of the Patrimony (northwest of the city) and Campagna e Marittima (coastal, south, and east), in matters of faith it was the bishops who served as judges. To complicate this panorama of tangled, fragmentary, and inevitably scrappy jurisdictions, there were the ancient great abbeys, Farfa and Subiaco, independent of any bishop, where the Inquisition's vicars (vicari) repeatedly attacked the privileges of the noble abbots, who held the two houses in commenda and battened off their ample lands. The scarcity of trial records in the archives makes it arduous even to summarize the Inquisition's repressive activity in papal domains or the rest of Italy. This lack of records also makes it hard to trace its relations with the other courts at Rome and in the hinterland. Nevertheless, what trial records do survive, plus the congregations' decrees and the letters between the tribunal and officials further out,

---

1. Adriano Prosperi, *Tribunali della coscienza: Inquisitori, confessori, missionari* (Turin: Einaudi, 1996); Christopher F. Black, *Church, Religion, and Society in Early Modern Italy* (Basingstoke: Palgrave Macmillan, 2004).

all confirm a pattern. The Inquisition aspired to install an efficient machinery of control via confessors. And, far from Rome especially, it strove for better collaboration with bishops, and with officials of the state's temporal courts, both clerical and lay. This collaboration was not always smooth, as we see from letters to the Inquisition's cardinal-overseers sent by bishops complaining of inquisitors' interference. It was an affront, they felt, both to their own jurisdiction and prestige and to the local governors.

❧

In a letter to Cardinal Pompeo Arrigoni, Antonio Maria Gallo, bishop of Osimo, complained of Paolo da Cremona, an inquisitor based nearby, at Ancona. He lamented

the notable damage that the present inquisitor of this city [Osimo] is doing to the tribunal of my church in cases that pertain to the Holy Office. This happens all the time in my diocese, because he is keen—without any participation by me or my *vicario*—to go to torture, without a condemnation against the suspect, and without the least consideration of what the holy canons command. In the end, despite an appeal and protest made to him—I send your most Illustrious lordship a copy—he has had the torture rope applied to two of my diocesan clerics to show that he holds me in small regard. And for that reason, since it seems to me that by this friar my jurisdiction has been scorned, I once more notify your most Illustrious lordship, so that you deign to consider my honor and reputation and to give this fact proper remedy.[2]

The bishop denounced the affront for its social implications too; as a member of a major Osimo noble family of feudal origin, he saw in this inquisitorial intrusion a blow to his prestige in local eyes. Inquisitor Paolo da Cremona was soon replaced, in February 1608, by Eliseo Masini, author, in the early seventeenth century, of the fundamental treatise *Sacro arsenale*, which codified inquisitorial procedure, and, until November 1608, Ancona's inquisitor.[3] Masini's energetic conduct soon sparked conflicts with local bishops, especially the bishop of Recanati, who asserted that "the legal briefs [*consulti*] of the trials in his sees of Loreto and Recanati had to be drawn up in his presence, and in the presence of the congregation of scholars [*dottori*] deputed by the Holy Office for that ef-

2. ACDF, S.O., St. St., DD 2-b, f. 14r (30 December 1606).
3. For his correspondence with the Roman congregation see ACDF, S.O., St. St., DD 2-b, ff. 139r–239r.

fect." These and other daily problems required wise heads in Rome, Masini opined, "so that one can do good service to this Holy Inquisition with quiet and tranquility."[4]

In the provinces of the Papal State, the Inquisition, thanks to its superiority (imposed by Rome but not accepted meekly), was often called in to umpire legal controversies and jurisdictional disputes. A letter from the bishop of Perugia to the cardinal nephew, Francesco Barberini, a senior cardinal with enormous authority in the Congregation of the Holy Office, summarized the stages of an uxoricide trial against one Antonio Cortonese. "After he had poisoned his wife, on account of his carnal traffic with Antonia, a prostitute (for he was eager to join her in matrimony) and after the notary was sent to the site of the crime and the stricken wife was interrogated," Antonio was then accused (querelato), as was his lover, Antonia. The husband was captured; the mistress fled. The trial was sent to the bishop's court at Perugia. But, from Rome, the Sacra Consulta—as a superior tribunal competent over all the Papal State—instructed the bishop "that he should consign the prisoner to a lay tribunal." Caught between two competing courts, the bishop carried this order out, grudgingly: "And despite all that, on account of the reverence that one accords the Sacra Consulta, the consignment of the imprisoned man was done right away." But the bishop asked the cardinal nephew to reassure the Inquisition about the change of venue for the case, "with the customary prudence and justice that this Tribunal be notified of the evident prejudice done to its ecclesiastical jurisdiction, all the more so in that there could arise from this case manifest harm to the Apostolic See."[5]

The bishop, supporting his bid for church jurisdiction, remarked that the crime had offended the sacrament of matrimony. He cited exempla from the Bible, evoking Bathsheba, stolen from her husband by King David's low trickery. Marriage, he went on, had recently been undermined by the bad example of Luther and his followers but it was now staunchly defended by theologians like Bellarmine. It was a hard decision for Cardinal Francesco Barberini, unsure whether to favor the Consulta, the state's highest court, or to defend episcopal jurisdiction. The cardinal, as both Inquisition member and man of state, chose to favor the second option, for Rome aimed for constant,

4. ACDF, S.O., St. St., DD 2-b, ff. 147r and 227r (17 April 1608).
5. ACDF, S.O., St. St., L 3-f.

unconditional collaboration on the part of bishops and their officials.

For the sake of moral and social order, a double, tightly linked system, both episcopal and inquisitorial, was constrained to repress in harmony and also to collaborate with lay courts at the center and periphery. It was often hard to have fast answers from Rome, and the bishops, although aware of procedures' long delays and of the flood of letters that swamped the Roman congregation, kept on writing, to protect their own modus operandi. Girolamo Giovannelli, bishop of Sora, a town south of Rome, wrote:

It is seven months now that Friar Nardo Fatone, from Castelluccio, a professed member of the Mercedarian order, has been in my jails for having taken a wife. And I am keeping him in irons lest he flee. In recent days, he tried to strangle himself, and would have done so had my serving folk not arrived on the scene, for the jail is above the door of this palace. All he says is: "If you have to hang me, hang me! Don't make me suffer any longer." I know that this Sacred Tribunal has infinite things to do, but I have also judged that this [letter] serves as a reminder.[6]

Informing Rome and waiting for its replies and rulings stretched jail time and put off the resolution of cases. But the communication was necessary for public order. The continual exchange of letters served "the bureaucratic, administrative, and political centralization of the Roman machinery of governance."[7] It also helped build a new and altered rapport between center and periphery. The letters were not only an instrument of communication but also a means of disseminating norms and clarifying understandings about law's right conduct. What the center sent to the periphery was not abstract doctrinal definitions or rules from manuals, but "decisions that did not always refer to a common principle, but were capable of flexible adaptation to contingent situations, and of finding specific solutions."[8] As has been observed,

the inquisitorial system was thus based on written communication between the center and the periphery, on the constant updating of cases current in the peripheral seats, and on the pertinent decisions made at the top. The sum total of the different questions, the focusing on all the diverse realities on the periphery, to which one responded as uniformly

6. ACDF, S.O., St. St., Q 3-a (Sora, 25 August 1629).

7. Introduction to Pierroberto Scaramella, ed., *Le lettere della Congregazione del Sant'Ufficio ai tribunali di fede di Napoli 1563–1625* (Triest: Edizioni Università di Trieste—Istituto Italiano per gli Studi Filosofici, 2002), xvi.

8. Ibid., xxiii.

as possible, are the mark of the juridical system established by the Roman Inquisition in Italy, and the principal characteristic of its broad and flexible model for operation.[9]

To gauge the efficacy and precision of this system's workings, consider the flood of letters to Rome, with their ceaseless denunciations of judicial snafus, conflicts, and logistical problems; it was a product of coping with a wide variety of local situations.

The bishops' letters to the Holy Office, throughout the seventeenth century, continually proclaim their doubts about procedure—should one use torture, and if so how much, or which blasphemies were heresy and thus grist for the Inquisition's mill? But they also reveal conflicts over jurisdiction, not only between the episcopal courts and the Inquisition but also between all tribunals of the church and local lay courts. Trouble arose readily when the suspect was accused of a hybrid crime. The blurring of jurisdictional boundaries stemmed from the Inquisition's widening range of action. In its work, it crossed paths with other judicial powers that hesitated to defer to its asserted superiority.

In 1602, the bishop of Terracina, Fabrizio Perugini, governor of Campagna e Marittima, wrote that he had jailed in the Carmelite monastery one Nicola Antonio Grimaldi on charges of theft and necromantic writings. The congregation ruled that the man should be consigned to the local *vicario* of the Inquisition to decipher the writings on his confiscated pages. As often, at the arrest the authorities had found pages with suspicious-looking drawings and prophecies. There was a hand, sketched out, on which appeared unknown names. Such crimes, in the seventeenth and eighteenth centuries, were becoming ever more common or, perhaps, ever more often persecuted by the Inquisition. They haunted the borderlines of magic, and, perhaps, of heresy as well. Officials were unsure of the shape and consequences of such goings-on. They seemed elusive because they were perpetrated within domestic walls; but their effects could contaminate, and their repercussions, the church thought, could range broadly, touching things and persons in ways that were hard to control. Sadly, because of spotty surviving papers, we do not know with Grimaldi's trial, as with many others, how things turned out in court.[10]

9. Ibid.

10. For an orientation to the papers of the Inquisition, see John Tedeschi, *The Pros-*

Outside the pope's own lands, jurisdictional conflict between the Holy Office and local courts also flared in other Italian states. There, this competition often provoked critical comparisons of the procedures of lay tribunals, less scrupulous in their protection of witnesses and of the accused, with the Inquisition's methods. These were strenuously defended by the congregation, which cited their caution and their guarantees for suspects. In the Papal State, however, this conflict took a different shape. There the distinction between lay and ecclesiastical was largely theoretical, since many governors and all legates were churchmen. The legates and *rettori provinciali* had such broad competence, in spiritual jurisdiction too, that boundary conflicts arose readily between the state's officials and local bishops.

At Rome itself, as we have seen, the governor was a prelate. He was a bishop, and vice-chamberlain, and represented papal authority in the city. Nevertheless, he too collided with the wish, buoyed by principles enshrined at Trent, to preserve and bolster the jurisdiction of bishops' courts and the Inquisition against lay tribunals like his that dealt in other crimes, even if run by clerics. In papal territories, thanks to the nature of the power of high administrators, most of whom were churchmen, the policies of bishops often clashed with those of legates or governors, especially in the sixteenth century, before episcopal functions had been redefined and strengthened. Till then, in many places, legates still supplanted the local bishop in spiritual matters. At the beginning of the following century, however, in the legations (where there was no governor)— Bologna, Ferrara, and Romagna—and also in cities ruled by prelate governors, conflict yielded almost everywhere to collaboration.

Collaboration to build moral and social order was a shared project of *buon governo*. If deftly managed in concord with rival bodies, or against them, the project could help an ambitious bishop advance his own career. Indeed, there was no lack of institutional concord, carefully recorded in the flood of letters linking bishops to the Roman congregation. These dispatches stressed unity of purpose and willingness to fulfill the Inquisition's directives, but also flaunted the fidelity and willingness to serve demanded by curial policies and by courtly language—two things tightly linked. In the periphery, in dis-

ecution of Heresy: Collected Studies on the Inquisition in Early Modern Italy (Binghamton, N.Y.: Center for Medieval and Early Renaissance Studies, 1991).

tant, poor, unprestigious dioceses, a job well done—service, good governance, the realization of Rome's desired order and consensus— could advance a bishop's career. Bishops therefore tried to carve out a zone for their own initiatives. It could be hard: "My Cardinal d'Este," wrote the *vicario* of the bishop of Albano in 1616 to Cardinal Millini, a senior cardinal atop the Congregation of the Holy Office, "is so officious that he does not let me live, with recommendations first for one thing and then for another."[11] For sure, being at Albano, so near Rome, simplified control, making it easier for the bishop to communicate and to resolve his doubts. "The nearness of Rome and the desire that I have [is] in conformity with the obligation to be among the first to publish and to carry out any order given me," wrote Antonio Gozzadini, bishop of Civita Castellana, to Cardinal Millini, to show all requisite zeal to fulfill commands and prove himself a diligent champion of order.[12] A bishop, especially when he had inquisitorial power, as in the dioceses around Rome—in provinces of Campagna e Marittima and of the Patrimonio—could sometimes protect his towns and villages against faulty governance by bad judges. Thanks to his powers—he could excommunicate—the bishop could play the defender of his faithful and his community against Rome's officials. That happened with Alatri's bishop, Bonaventura Ortano, a conventual Franciscan friar, who in 1592 told the Inquisition, after informing the Sacra Consulta, that "Giuseppe Ridolfi from Macerata has been sent here as *podestà* [judge], who not only treated this people badly," but also, once excommunicated, "held the excommunication as a thing of naught, having already been excommunicated other times." To defend the community the bishop asked for larger powers, "as I cannot with my weak arm do what needs doing."[13]

Some bishops, even those close to Rome, complained of the disastrous mess, the disorder, the scarce observance of Rome's directives. On 22 September 1623, Alessandro Carissimi, client of Cardinal Scaglia and bishop in Castro, a small town on the malarial coastal plain ("not much of a diocese"), wrote to the cardinal of Cremona, Pietro Campori:

As I am the episcopal inquisitor, for there is no other proper tribunal, the office has fallen into mockery, for there is no longer a record, nor

11. ACDF, S.O., St. St., Q 3-a (29 October 1616).
12. ACDF, S.O., St. St., Q 3-a (20 February 1628).
13. ACDF, S.O., St. St., Q 3-a (4 August 1592).

are there edicts or orders in matters of the sort, nor is anyone required to make denunciations. They view as licit a thousand superstitions—of prayers, and signs, and sacramental herbs. There is an infinity of blasphemers. They don't know what a prohibited book is, even though I myself have some idea. . . . I supplicate your most Illustrious Lordship that you give orders to the secretary of the congregation to send me a copy of the general edicts that they decree in matters of the sort, for I would like to have them published in all the villages . . . and to advise each of the parish priests of the obligation they have to denounce, and to manage to make provision for the many inconveniences.[14]

It seems unlikely that this bishop's zeal would win him any reward. Would Castro's parish priests really have communicated all that Rome demanded? And would its other edicts really have been read and obeyed?

In the very composite structure of the Papal State, even in the far provinces there was no lack of zealous collaborators who grated on bishops' nerves. This shows up in a letter from Bishop Luca Antonio Gigli of Alatri, who in 1618 wrote to the congregation:

If the pious person who reported to the supreme Congregation of the Holy Office that in the places of my jurisdiction there are many who have the gall to blaspheme the name of God and the saints heretically—had he had proper zeal, he would have notified me, and I would have disabused him, showing him that I have never lacked diligence, having prohibited blasphemy in my synodal constitutions . . . and no one has ever been denounced for blasphemy—and it was proven true—and not been punished.[15]

To sum up the implications of this memorandum: the faithful were to be alerted and mobilized by their confessors, parish priests, and bishop to expose deviance from orthodoxy. But, as one should respect the hierarchies, their denunciations were to be vetted and passed through proper channels to prevent the flock's direct recourse to Rome.

Inquisitorial jurisdiction jostled local equilibria. Nevertheless, when civil power faltered or bad governance deserved denouncing, the Inquisition could reinforce bishops' authority. The late sixteenth century saw frequent recourse to inquisitorial officials to preserve order and guarantee good governance. In the next century,

14. ACDF, S.O., St. St., Q 3-a (14 October 1618).
15. ACDF, S.O., St. St., Q 3-a (14 September 1618).

the practice waned. By then, inquisitorial powers were better defined and limited; officials shunned trespassing, which seemed an abuse of power. Nevertheless, controversy sometimes flared.

When governance was hard, collaboration between inquisitorial *vicari* and governors grew necessary. In distant towns like Gubbio, Visso, and Norcia, on the high borderland between Umbria and the Marches, problems could be logistical.[16] It was a poor, mountainous zone of wretched roads, aswarm with outlaws and brimming with superstitions that seemed no less perilous. Collaboration aimed to discipline daily life and control the *feste* without upsetting customs centuries old. In January 1609, early in Carnival, the circuit priest Giulio Geggi wrote anxiously to Cardinal Maffeo Barberini, then bishop down the mountain, at Spoleto.

Here they have begun to go out masked and do the customary local things and the women go dancing with the masked men and with other men in the streets and particularly in four places before the doors of churches, where they are celebrating the most holy sacrament, and monasteries of nuns. And, this abuse seemed to me very improper and inconvenient, as there was no lack of other places, near these four, suitable for exercising these carnival follies. If it seems to you proper that I issue a *bando* with a given penalty for the men, and women too, ordering that in the future they should not dance before the doors of the churches where they are celebrating the most holy sacrament and monasteries of nuns, be so good as to advise me, and I will follow your orders.[17]

The zealous *vicario* soon learned that he should not make matters worse by posting decrees. On 1 February he wrote that he had managed to stop the dancing before the monasteries, but

as for going masked in this town of ours, and our mountain district, they do it on Sundays and other holidays. Only in the last week of Carnival do they do it on work days, and few do it on those days because of the great poverty, and almost everybody has some trade. They attend to working and earning their bread. And one is well aware that on Friday they do not dance nor do they go masked. Both one and the other thing are immemorial custom and this town [*patria*] has no other recreation besides what they do in these *festa* days.[18]

16. Caterina Comino, "La prefettura di Montagna come esempio di distrettuazione periferica," *Archivi per la storia* 13, nos. 1–2 (2000): 231–41.

17. BAV, Barb. lat. 8914, f. 7r.

18. BAV, Barb. lat. 8914, f. 9r.

The cleric knew perfectly well that only by respecting and protecting local customs would he succeed in having Rome's impositions and rules accepted. Further futile decrees or other repression would have rendered the consensus his regime desired even more fragile. One needed prudence and balance. To Maffeo Barberini he wrote, "I have not made a ruling of the sort." In the provinces, to avoid jurisdictional conflicts with lay authorities, prudence did not suffice and zeal did little good. The lay official in question was *prefetto* Angelo Stufa, who ran the Montagna prefecture, chasing malefactors and respecting asylum rights and immunities and privileges of sacred places. To win his collaboration, it helped to spell out the Sacra Consulta decree obliging a *prefetto* to obey the bishop's court "in everything."[19]

In other provinces too, conflicts between local state officials and bishops or their vicars abounded. In 1635, at Velletri, just south of Rome, Giuliano Viviani, the suffragan bishop, petitioned Cardinal Francesco Barberini to be transferred because of great friction with the local governor, who,

although he does not stay here continually, comes here every month and stays as long as he likes, and he persecutes me, treating me as an enemy, and he prohibits everyone from speaking to me and he wants them to treat me badly. . . . Face to face I could tell your Eminence how the grain office is working and other things that damage and impoverish the public.

Bishop Viviani prayed the cardinal to send him instead "in a hermitage, or to Salona, my bishopric, to suffer martyrdom."[20] For years he kept on writing, begging to be sent to Colle Val d'Elsa up in Tuscany, or to Teramo on the Adriatic coast. Instead, finally, in 1639, he was transferred to the diocese of Isola, in Calabria. Cardinal Barberini had forwarded his repeated requests and his denunciations of bad governance and conflict to Cardinal Marzio Ginnetti, who came from Velletri. Barberini hoped that Ginnetti, with his high rank, knowledge of the Velletri scene, and patronage of local client families, could mediate and resolve the conflicts. But Velletri was a problematic see. Bishops considered it a prison. Viviani's successor, suffragan Alessandro Sperelli, also sought transfer. He denounced

19. BAV, Barb. lat. 8914, f. 52r.

20. BAV, Barb. lat. 8925, f. 23r. Salona, near Split, now in Croatia, was across the Adriatic. Turks might have supplied the unlikely martyrdom, but the desire is mere rhetoric.

"scornings and affronts," but his stumbling block was not the governor but the Inquisition's *vicario*, who turned civil trials criminal and tried to grab jurisdiction over cases belonging to the episcopal court. "Along with other things, this has alarmed the entire clergy, and everybody, to avoid persecutions of the sort, abstains from associating with me."[21] As often, relations between inquisitors, bishops, and lay governors were ambiguous and oscillating. On the periphery, as in Rome, plural jurisdictions kept getting tangled, and officials often scrapped over privileges.

THE PATENT-HOLDERS OF THE HOLY OFFICE

In 1651, Cardinal Camillo Pamphili, nephew of Innocent X, forwarded a letter of the Sacra Consulta to the governor of Ancona. It concerned a summary of a Holy Office trial of one of its own patent-holders. The cardinal hoped "that he be put to torture, given the quality of the evidence against him."[22] Patents were papers that attached a man to the Inquisition and granted assorted legal privileges, not only the right to bear arms, and to go escorted by armed servitors, but also tax-exemptions. Cases involving patent-holders were frequent, thanks to the ample impunity of men who held such privileges. They raised problems of jurisdiction; one had to ask the Holy Office's permission to prosecute, with all the necessary caution. And relations with that body were often difficult.

In the seventeenth century, from many parts of the Papal State there came strong protests against abuses by the Inquisition's patent-holders. Voices of vexed communities and subjects reached the cardinal legates, who, hoping for a remedy, quickly forwarded them to the cardinal nephew. In 1630, as Ferrara was threatened by the War of Mantua and by the plague the Imperial troops brought with them, the consuls at Filo, a small town near Argenta in the legation of Ferrara, sent the legate a memorandum explaining how "when a supplementary tax [*colta*] was put on top of the *estimo* [tax], for paying the equipment, priests and friars and other of the richer people in the town showed up with patents from the Holy Office, claiming that they did not have to pay." The petition added:

Of the parts of the lands, the aforesaid [patent-holders] hold two thirds, so that the entire sum owing is restricted to being laid on that little [por-

21. BAV, Barb. lat., f. 29r–v.
22. BAV, Borg. lat. 729, f. 2r.

tion] that assorted particular persons possess. And then, in particular, the persons of the Holy Office should not enjoy a real exemption, for there is no formal tribunal in Argenta, but only certain patents that these people have acquired, to not have to pay, and among them are many who don't even know Latin.[23]

There had been unsuccessful efforts to correct abuses. In 1646, "in consideration of the number of familiars and officials of the Inquisition in Italy," precise rules strove to limit the number of familiars (semi-officials) and patent-holders. They also imposed tighter membership criteria, as, for example, "not to use persons who are quarrelsome, dissolute, youngsters of bad repute or those who have active enmities [formal personal quarrels], but only to enroll persons who are useful in themselves for the service and who are resident in the places in which they are signed on."[24] Familiars' rank was a bit confused. There were, in theory, three categories of patent-holders, with different privileges. Those "on salary" had a regular stipend and permission to bear arms. Others, volunteers, or marked with the cross—named *Crocesignati*, usually noblemen or merchants—were unpaid but could carry forbidden weapons (as could their servants) and enjoyed the privilege of being subject only to church courts (*privilegio del foro*). The third kind, the "simple patent-holders" (*patentati semplici*), who served the noble *Crocesignati*, had the privileges of church courts and of a permit to bear arms even when not escorting their lords.[25] In Rome some two hundred patent-holders had legal immunity from lay jurisdiction and the right to bear arms. Meanwhile, some eighteen hundred others had only the right to carry forbidden arms in the entire state.[26]

23. Irene Fosi, ed., with the collaboration of Andrea Gardi, *La Legazione di Ferrara del Cardinale Giulio Sacchetti (1627–1631)*, 2 vols. (Rome: Archivio Segreto Vaticano, 2006), 785–86.

24. ACDF, S.O., St.St., UV II, f. 287rv.

25. ACDF, S.O., St.St., LL 1-a. See also Elena Brambilla, "La polizia dei tribunali ecclesiastici e le riforme della giustizia penale," in *Corpi armati e ordine pubblico in Italia (XVI–XIX sec.)*, ed. Livio Antonielli and Claudio Donati, 73–111 (Soveria Mannelli: Rubbettino, 2003); and by the same author, "I poteri giudiziari dei tribunali ecclesiastici nell'Italia settentrionale e la loro secolarizzazione," in *Le secolarizzazioni nel Sacro Romano Impero e negli antichi stati italiani: premesse, confronti, consequenze*, ed. Claudio Donati and Helmut Flachenecker, 99–112 (Bologna: il Mulino; Berlin: Duncker & Humblodt, 2003).

26. ACDF, S.O., St.St., LL 5-c; St.St. M 2-m, ff. 345v, 358v–359r.; Peter Schmidt, "De Sancto Officio Urbis: Aspekte der Verflechtung des Heilige Offiziums mit der

The steps Rome took to reform patents sought to ease tensions with the Inquisition's assorted neighbors. Reducing privileges, setting clearer criteria for joining, and strengthening the Roman congregation's control over the peripheral Inquisition might quell, or at least hedge, the strong unease, fear mixed with resentment, about the whole tribunal, not just its privilege-holders. Rome desired above all to avoid "controversies with the governors" over bearing arms and over the mayhem arms provoked. It did not want the yen to stigmatize patent-holders and familiars to condemn the whole institution. Moreover, there were others: "officials—*vicari*, notaries, process servers, *birri*, jailers and others like them, without whom the Tribunal cannot function [and who] enjoy the advantage of the privilege of legal immunity, both active [freedom to sue] and passive [immunity from suit], in criminal and civil matters."[27] In 1646, the papacy stepped in to survey the shape of things; it ran a census of the privilege-holders and other servants of the Holy Office, in the Papal State and elsewhere. The investigation revealed the numbers and real power of these persons, mostly sons of the local nobility who used the patents to bolster their privileged status and to ward off the Inquisition. A few years later, in 1658 and 1665, Alexander VII undertook a more thorough revision of the tribunal and its tasks. He returned to the questions of privileges, notarial abuses, misuse of funds, and the corruption of local personnel.[28] He also targeted the conflicts, far from Rome, between Inquisition functionaries and local courts, and between it and central organs like the Sacra Consulta and the Buon Governo, which, since 1592, had overseen the fiscal management of villages, towns, and cities.

Nevertheless, the problems continued. From Faenza, in the second half of the seventeenth century, came this denunciation: "Some patent-holders of this sacred tribunal of the Holy Office in the town of Fabriano claim that they need not pay the *gabella* [commercial and consumption] taxes"; and already in 1681, they had claimed exemption from the wine *gabella*. At Sant'Arcangelo di Romagna, the community complained that "some people have themselves appoint-

Stadt Rom im 16. und 17. Jahrhundert," *Quellen und Forschungen aus italienischen Archiven und Bibliotheken* 82 (2001): 404–89.

27. ACDF, S.O., St.St., UV 11, ff. 287v–298r: Relatione del numero degli officiali e famigliari di ciascheduna Inquisitione dello Stato Ecclesiastico.

28. ACDF, S.O., St.St., Q 3-d, *sub voce* Patentati, ff. 633r–657v.

ed as patent-holders to escape the burden of the *gabelle*, even though they do not meet the conditions for exemption from the payment of the community's collective obligations." The complaint continued: Some persons "had themselves appointed secretary [*cancelliere foraneo*] of the Holy Office in the small town [Sant'Arcangelo], even though they are gentlemen of Rimini [ten miles east], where they reside continually and hold property."[29]

Meanwhile, there were also frequent frictions with other tribunals—with their notaries, process servers, and constabulary. At Rimini and Pesaro, the *bargello* and the Inquisition jailers declared, in a long letter to the congregation, that the treasurer of Urbino had pestered them to pay taxes to the Apostolic Chamber, and they wanted to be exempt. They petitioned to have the concession "to enjoy, like other privileged patent-holders, the privilege of clerical exemption of the Holy Office, for they are of no worse condition than similar servants of the episcopal court and the lay court of Monsignor President of Urbino, who with all their staff [*famiglia*] enjoy these exemptions." They stressed that they held the right, thanks to the

faithful service that they afford the Sacred Tribunal. And they receive no other reward than this miserable exemption and meanwhile those who serve other courts, besides the exemption, have other payments and advantages. And to deprive the patent-holders of the Holy Office of them would be as if to sap them of zeal [*disanimarli*] for the good and faithful service that at their own expense they afford the Sacred Tribunal, which needs them daily.[30]

The battle for privileges and the benefits they offered, to supplement income and conserve social position, runs through the entire Seicento. It is no accident that it became more acute toward the century's end, when Rome began to try to reform justice and to review the jurisdictions of tribunals, both at the center and beyond. But Rome also battled a rising tide of radical critiques of the Inquisition, of the church courts, and of the control of consciences. By 1700, this flood of criticism was lapping at the Roman system from several directions.

29. ACDF, S.O., St.St., EE 3-a, ff.nn., dated 1693–1701. This is a petition, dated 3 June 1693, from Sant'Arcangelo to Innocent XII, forwarded by the pope to the Inquisition.
30. ACDF, S.O., St.St., EE 3-a, ff.nn. (but before 1738).

A SLOW REFORM

At the middle of the seventeenth century, to confront attacks against inquisitorial abuses, the congregation tried to count and know its men. Its "census" for the papal domains reveals a network that was dense but full of apparently useless persons, surely enrolled only for the privileges and aura of power attaching to a "family" member, and the fear that the label inspired. To serve the tribunal seems, especially in the provinces, to have been a sure path to honor and local prestige, useful above all for immunity against accusations and against imbroglios with other church or lay courts. Conflict and recourse to Rome were therefore inevitable.

The reform of 1646 proposed that, at Ancona, there be just forty familiars of the Holy Office, twelve for the city and the rest in other zones of its local jurisdiction. Thus, one had to strip of their patents all other current holders, except the economic administrator (*depositario*) and the physician. In the eyes of the congregation, however, even after this reform, Ancona was still overloaded. There remained some specialist officials, for instance an extra notary for cases belonging to this jurisdiction, two inspectors of clothing and personal goods, a surgeon, an interpreter for languages, and a trip-agent [*foriero*]. And the inquisitor justifies this by saying that it is because it is a seaport, and every day there turn up Mohammedans, schismatics, and heretics, and there is a ghetto of the Jews, for which reason the Sacred Tribunal maintains itself in office.[31]

At Perugia the reform had intended a reduction to eight persons: the prosecutor, the notary, the lawyer for the accused, and a *bargello* with four *birri*. To these they added a bursar (*depositario*), a physician, and an accountant. It was decided to strip of their patents the surgeons and the apothecary. As for the familiars, they were to number only forty. Although, in the list sent to Rome, the number of familiars came in even lower, at just thirty-seven, it was necessary to add two lay notaries, two bursars, two administrators of the jail, two physicians and apothecaries, an agent (*fattore*), an architect, and a carpenter of the construction office (*fabrica*), these last two employed in building the new seat for the tribunal. Now, all these persons were to lose their patents as servitors of the Holy

31. ACDF, S.O., St. St., UV II, f. 294v.

Office. So they stood to lose all their privileges, with their prestige and Perugian "reputation." The reorganization desired by Rome did not prove easy. The local nobility had long found these tasks a sure way to accrue personal honor and show off power otherwise scarce in politics and, often, in the economy as well. Ridolfini, Vermiglioli, Della Penna, Della Cornia, Oddi, and Crispolti, all aristocratic Perugine families in mid-Seicento, boasted membership in the patent-holders list.[32]

Meanwhile, at Ferrara, by the new rules the inquisitor was to administer twelve *consultori* (a small body of lawyers and theologians who formed a permanent advisory council for every inquisitorial court), twenty-four familiars, two inspectors of suspect books, two notaries, a lawyer, a second lawyer for defending suspects, two physicians, a surgeon, a process server and two *birri*. The "multitude of familiars" had recently been restructured, with great difficulty. At Ferrara, the eighty-two familiars had been reduced by the inquisitor, who, "to keep the world from making a great fuss, has removed fifty-seven or fifty-eight of them and little by little will do the same with the rest, if the Sacred Congregation does not decide to do so itself. For it will be a great relief to him not to make himself more enemies, and if he removed them all he would be out of trouble."[33] At the local level one desired to avoid tensions and preferred that all be resolved at the center. And from Rome came the request that no patents be granted to any two persons from the same house and line, lest the device become a weapon to help wage family feuds with impunity. Still, the familiars were too many. Nevertheless, the *relazione* stressed that "in the four years that the inquisitor has been in Ferrara there has not been any disorder."[34] In this case as well, a structural reorganization was negotiated between center and periphery, with an eye to keeping order, and to defending a local consensus in favor of an essential device for governing consciences and other matters.

From Rome, for some time, there had come requests for clarity and regularity in practices. One desired shorter proceedings, respect for the established fines, and weekly registration of official papers. Rome forbade receiving gifts of any kind, even small ones. Concerning this prohibition, Francesco Barberini had the pope informed of

32. ACDF, S.O., St.St., UV ii, f. 301rv.   33. ACDF, S.O., St.St., UV ii, f. 289r.
34. ACDF, S.O., St.St., UV ii, f. 289r.

the discontent at both the center, among cardinals at the Inquisition's headquarters in the Minerva convent, and among local inquisitors. There was the objection that, given the poverty of many inquisitions on the periphery, the whole apparatus of repression could be funded only through "politenesses" (gentilezze) and gifts. Therefore, Cardinal Barberini suggested in the letters sent to inquisitors that one should forbid gifts only from suspects' kinfolk and that, moreover, "no inquisitor or his official, who desires to be backed or favored in his work, nor anyone who hopes or desires to enter into the service and charges of the Holy Office should be allowed to give, or to receive from any such person."[35] An intervention decades later, by Alexander VII, may be ascribed to his more elaborate project to reform the procedures of the central courts: Segnatura, Sacra Consulta, and Inquisition. Still, in the second half of the seventeenth century, the problem of the patent-holders of the Holy Office inspired a more generalized and radical attack on the institution itself, on its procedures, and on its ministers' abuses.

⚜

The legal commentator Cardinal Giovanni Battista De Luca wrote for Innocent XI (1676–1689) a memorandum, "Concerning the Use of Patent-holders and Ministers of the Holy Office in the State of the Church."[36] There he put in high relief the abuses perpetrated by such privileged persons in the pope's territories and strongly recommended eliminating them almost entirely, restricting them to the state of Milan, as a bulwark against heretics from across the Alps. His polemical tone was reminiscent of the reforms of Alexander VII disciplining the tasks of the patent-holders. He affirmed that it had long been a strategy of nobles to have themselves nominated to enjoy exemptions and privileges, like bearing arms, but also to duck taxes to the Apostolic Chamber or to towns. By these accusations he hoped to demonstrate the absurdity and uselessness of the Inquisition and its ministers in the Papal State, where the pope's own authority should suffice to ward off heresy. In reply, all batteries firing, came a hot defense of the institution, now under siege on jurisdictional grounds. De Luca's refutor, Cardinal Francesco Albizzi, reviewed the entire history of the Holy Office, with particular attention to Spain, where, he claimed, the nobles

35. ACDF, S.O., St. St., UV II, f. 287v.
36. Copy of the relazione del cardinal De Luca in BAV, Ottob. lat. 1113.

"think it a great honor to be made familiars of the Holy Office and they prize more highly the habit of the Cross of the Holy Inquisition than they do the collar of the [Golden] Fleece."[37]

Cardinal Albizzi also stressed the necessity of the tribunal and its men to the Papal State, both in the capital, where "there is a greater number of misbelievers, all the more dangerous because they are hidden, so that the inquisitors must remain there with a plentiful army," and in the countryside, where this crucial army will be called on to combat "heretical blasphemy, works of sorcery equally heretical, witchcraft and magic." All this was demonstrated by swift work in the Kingdom of Naples. Moreover, said he, it would be indecent to see clerics gird themselves alone to repress all the dangerous insubordinations that threatened public peace, consciences, and good order. Ministers and familiars were indispensable, just like all the executors of justice who served other Roman courts. As for the accusations leveled at the nobility, they were unfounded. On the contrary, given the precarious economy of papal territories, it was good that the patent-holders were chosen among persons of means, able to sustain the costs of their collaboration with the institution in exchange for privileges that were not in fact burdensome to communities. Albizzi's plea was a stereotyped defense, founded on a shopworn revisiting of the past, unsuited to a late-Seicento climate that, even in the Papal State, anticipated reforms. But this defense was fated to meet mistrust and hostility. Really now, had serving the Inquisition actually become, for the urban aristocracy, a fine, sure way to gain honor, defend privilege, and wield power? Was it really worth more, as Albizzi claimed, than the famous Golden Fleece and other high honors bestowed by the court at Madrid?

The problem was resolved neither by polemics between curials nor by the reforms of Innocent XI. There were further investigations, in 1706 and again in 1743. By then, in the Papal State, there were 9 Inquisition tribunals, and 291 vicariates with a total of 2,814 patent-holders among them, with or without servitors. To this one had to add 200 patent-holders present in Rome, plus 523 Jews with a patent issued by cardinals or by other curial officials in the entire state (Rome included).[38] Given the size of Rome's Jewish communi-

37. ACDF, S.O., St. St., UV 11, f. 280v.
38. ACDF, S.O., St. St., M 2-m: Notizie e decisioni del S. Offizio raccolte da Mons.

ty, a good half of adult men held patents, issued by church officials or the city government; how these patents came about and what ends they served for Rome's Jews is a matter still little understood. In mid-century, Benedict XIV, who was intolerant of Jews, tried to reign the practice in, but to little avail.

Roman Jews obtained these patents from the capitoline courts. In 1745, Benedict XIV sent a circular letter to the members of the Holy Office "to obviate the disorders that frequently derive from the multiplicity of patents with which the Jews try to elude the force of the laws and the vigilance of superiors." He ordered a verification of the patents and their holders, to attach them to the names of their holders, under penalty, if one did not present oneself to the Holy Office, of imprisonment and three hoists on the *strappado* (torture rope). The pope's order must not have achieved the desired result, for the next year the assessor of the Holy Office, Monsignor Guglielmi, was still urging the conservators of Rome not to concede patents to the Jews.[39] This attempt to limit the privileges enjoyed by the patent-holders inside the Roman Jewish community can be read as one more proof of the growing rigidity of the policies of Benedict XIV toward the Jews, as has been shown by recent scholarship.[40]

By the middle of the eighteenth century, the need for focused, decisive intervention had become urgent. The intellectual and political panorama was shifting. To save something of the institution, one

Guglielmi assessore del S. Offizio dal 1743 al 1753.ff. 345r–364r. At ff. 345r–356v there appears a catalogue of all the patent-holders of the Holy Office in the state, Rome included, in the 1730s and 1740s. The list includes a "Nota degli ebrei di Roma e Stato che hanno patenti di cardinali o di altri personaggi." The figures for the Jews are as follows: Rome: 180 patented by cardinals, 108 by others; Ferrara: 40 and 35, by the same measure; Cento (attached to the Bologna Inquisition): 5; Ancona: 62 and 9; Urbino: 12 patented by cardinals; Lugo (Ferrara Inquisition): 27 and 13; Pesaro: 32 patented by cardinals; (other towns following); yielding the total: 523 patented Jews.

In 1736 the population (the "souls") of the Papal State was 2,081,117, and, given that the Jews in the whole territory numbered about 20,000, it follows that (as Guglielmi writes) "the Jews are at least two hundred times of better condition than the patent-holders of the Holy Office." See also Elena Brambilla, "I poteri giudiziari dei tribunali ecclesiastici nell'Italia settentrionale e la loro secolarizzazione," in Claudio Donati and Helmut Flachenecker, eds., *Le secolarizzazioni nel Sacro Romano Impero e negli antichi Stati italiani: premesse, confronti, conseguenze* (Bologna: il Mulino; Berlin: Duncker & Humblodt, 2003)," 99–101.

39. ACDF, S.O., St. St., M 2-m, f.142r.
40. ACDF, S.O., St. St., M 2-m, f.142r.

could no longer just close one's eyes. It was necessary to mobilize the bishops in this reorganization, forgetting old conflicts over jurisdiction, grudges, and questions of honor and prestige. At play, in fact, was the pope's authority in his own lands. From Rome, therefore, in 1743 there went a letter to the bishops, part inquiry, part instruction, asking them "to remove, as far as possible, any disorder or abuse that can arise, from too great a number or from the condition of the patent-holders and finally from the exorbitant expansion of their privileges in the State of the Church."[41] There was a request to reduce the number of *vicarie* (vicariates), and merge them where possible, and to verify where in fact the *vicari* resided. If it was indeed necessary to have the Inquisition present, its task could fall to the parish clergy. And at the end came a recommendation that the *cancellieri* (secretaries) be professional notaries and that all the lawyers hold doctorates. The responses to the letter's survey were diverse. Some bishops furnished precise answers to Rome's questions. Still, some confusion surfaced in their answers when it came to spelling out the identity, preparation, and social station of patent-holders. The replies used expressions like "he calls himself *dottore*" or "he says he is a good notary" to describe men who had for years been working for the tribunal. Public reputation defined identity. For the authorities in Rome it was hard to restrict to five the patent-holders (*vicario*, prosecutor, advocate for suspects, chancellor, and process server), and to cut to three the patent-holders who worked in each *vicaria*. The reformers had to reckon with how hard it was to renounce privileges if one had long been serving the Inquisition on account of the income, the legitimization of armed violence (thanks to weapons permits), and the social distinction. The culling of privileges, with the bishops' help, aimed to renew and strengthen episcopal authority and to assure tight collaboration with Rome, averting jurisdictional conflicts. The bishops were supposed to be aware of rules laid down by the congregation, and to keep a copy of its edicts and orders,

so these bishops should keep an eye on the inquisitors to make sure that they observe them. And in case of a violation they should inform the Sacred Congregation about what they have on their conscience. Finally, one should write to the inquisitor not to interfere in the civil and criminal cases of these patent-holders.[42]

41. ACDF, S.O., St. St., HH 2-e.   42. ACDF, unnumbered folio.

So, as we have seen in this chapter, in the course of two centuries, the Inquisition by its very successes laid the groundwork for its eventual decline. Its powers and its privileges stirred up resistance that left it open, in a changing moral and intellectual climate, to a campaign, at the center, to rein it in. By the eighteenth century, the Inquisition's intemperance, abuses, and crimes were to be judged, freely, by lay or ecclesiastical courts. The separation of tasks, the distinction between competences, and the reduction of privileges were a necessary first step for overcoming the confusion between sin and crime, that, in practice, would continue to mark papal justice.

In the course of the eighteenth century, thanks to the attempt to limit abuses and to redefine the tasks of the Inquisition, the Roman congregation had to try harder to collaborate with bishops who, till then, had more often seemed to its eyes rivals or obstacles to supremacy. Although, to date, there have been no comprehensive studies on the eighteenth-century Inquisition, some research on aspects of its history have revealed that the activities of the Roman tribunal intensified, as it combated energetically crimes of blasphemy, irreligion, offenses to religious practice, free masonry and libertinism, superstition, and, of course, the spreading of Enlightenment ideas. But, in the Papal State, first the pressure of ideas and of reforming policies, and then the whirlwind of revolution made their effects felt only briefly, especially in the two years of the Roman Republic (1798–1799). The recognition of other confessions, and the great judicial reforms marked, in Europe in general and in many Italian states, the end of church courts and the demise of their central role in the system of the law. At the Roman curia there was resistance. During the Restoration, the "restored" tribunal of the faith lost the prestige and power it had earlier possessed. Still, in the Papal State, it remained not only the highest organ for controlling the faith, but also a tribunal in direct contact with civil powers. So, in the pope's domains, except for the brief republican interlude of 1798–1799, the separation between reason and religion, and between state and church, current elsewhere in Europe, never came about before, in 1871, the Kingdom of Italy seized the pope's domains.

7

Sins and Crimes

GOING SOBERLY, WITH CIRCUMSPECTION

I have been holding those women, Pontiana and Leontia, in jail for their love magic and witchcraft—a matter of deaths, abortions, inflictions of illness, breakings of peace pacts, and impediments of sexual intercourse—and for their adoration of demons and carnal commerce with them (and also with many banished men under capital sentence) and for their other enormous excesses, as you have already seen in their abjuration before Monsignore Cefalotto. This morning they were put to death and burned. Now that it is done, justice has been served, as I hope will be understood by Our Lord [the pope] and by your Most Illustrious Lordship.[1]

So wrote Bartolomeo Vanni, the *vicario* of Velletri's inquisitor, on 11 March 1587. The year given is not without significance. It might help explain the harsh repression of these two women accused not only of witchcraft, itself a crime of no small gravity, but also of sexual relations with banished men under sentence of death. In 1587 the Papal State was utterly swamped by a great wave of banditry destined to last more than a decade longer. The state's inability to break the family ties and bonds of faction and solidarity between the rural world and its outlaws led local authorities, both civil and ecclesiastical, to persecute even presumed witches far more violently than was usual in Italy, where the witch hunt was usually milder and more prudent than in France or Germany. But, still, attitudes toward witches were softening, albeit at differing rates and with different reasons at periphery and center.

Indeed, especially at Rome itself, from the late sixteenth century the Inquisition treated sorcery and witchcraft with caution, circumspection, and growing skepticism.[2] Even before the circula-

---

1. ACDF, S.O., St. St., Q 3-a (11 March 1587).
2. For witchcraft, see Giovanni Romeo, *Inquisitori, esorcisti, streghe nell'Italia della Controriforma* (Florence: Sansoni, 1990); Oskar Di Simplicio, *Autunno della stregoneria. Maleficio e magia nell'Italia moderna* (Bologna: il Mulino, 2005). For a general European picture, see among other works: Wolfgang Behringer, *Witches and Witch-Hunts: A Global History* (Cambridge: Polity Press, 2004); Walter Stephens, *Demon Lovers:*

tion of the cautious *Instruction for Carrying Out Trials in Cases of Sorcery, Conjuring, and Witchcraft,* the congregation called repeatedly for prudence. Perhaps the *Instruction* itself was provoked by the spectacle of officials with too much zeal or too little learning. The famous anonymous document, probably written by Desiderio Scaglia and first printed in 1625, had been in circulation since the end of the sixteenth century; it officially condemned the excesses of witchcraft trials and offered precise rules for correct procedure.[3]

From the 1580s on, the official papers—decrees, minutes of the congregations, and correspondence between the Roman Inquisition and bishops and *vicari* across the Papal State—all call continually for caution and prudence. Rome recommended moderation in examining denunciations for sorcery, witchcraft, and divination. Women's accusations against presumed witches seem seldom to have been taken seriously, and the formula "it was decreed that nothing should be done" often closes off a transcript's few lines. Moderation and circumspection were supposed to guide the inquest to verify an accusation. The court sought other witnesses, especially when denunciations came from within a household, for it knew well that an accusation of witchcraft could bespeak domestic tensions and hatreds. Often an Inquisition case concluded with referral to another Roman tribunal, such as the *vicario's* or the governor's, or, in the hinterland, to an episcopal court, with all evidence of crimes against the faith expunged. For crimes that did not impugn Catholic dogma, such as infanticide and poisoning, secular tribunals had jurisdiction, not the Inquisition. Practical doctrine held that exile less often suited witchcraft than it did other crimes, since "it is better to keep such persons in a place where they are known, to keep them under observation, for going away gives them the opportunity to do worse harm."[4]

Witchcraft, Sex, and the Crisis of Belief (Chicago: University of Chicago Press, 2002); *Encyclopedia of Witchcraft: The Western Tradition,* ed. Richard M. Golden, 4 vols. (Oxford: ABC/Clio, 2006); Edward Bever, *The Realities of Witchcraft and Popular Magic in Early Modern Europe: Culture, Cognition and Everyday Life* (Basingstoke: Palgrave Macmillan, 2008).

3. John Tedeschi, *The Prosecution of Heresy: Collected Studies on the Inquisition in Early Modern Italy* (Binghamton, N.Y.: Medieval and Renaissance Texts and Studies, 1991); Tedeschi, "Inquisitorial Law and the Witch," in *Early Modern European Witchcraft: Center and Peripheries,* ed. Bengt Ankarloo and Gustav Henningsen, 83–118 (Oxford: Clarendon Press, 1993).

4. ACDF, S.O., St. St., Q 3-d, f. 267r.

The eyes of the community, public *fama* (a legal term for social and moral reputation), and informing certainly helped justice to control and repress superstitions and witchcraft. But judges had to be careful to know who were "enemies" and what running quarrels were afoot—lest accusations spring from economic interest, or personal or familial tensions. In 1624, the bishop of Alatri, Francesco Campanari, announced that he had released from jail, as Rome had commanded their timely liberation, "Martia, Vitoria, and Temperanza, under investigation for witchcraft, and had them instructed by the confessor, in accord with the orders of your Most Illustrious Lordship [the Cardinal]."[5] A few weeks earlier, Bishop Campanari had sketched for his superiors an unctuous panorama of his church to prove both his zeal and his moderation. Indeed, he declared his satisfaction because, in the diocese, which he had run for the past four years, "there had been only a single case of blasphemy, for which they gave the delinquent, as public punishment, the stocks with a gag, and now there was the case of the asserted witches."[6] As for the future, he was, he wrote, buoyantly optimistic; he had confidence in the aid and collaboration of Rome, which had sent his province every pertinent instruction, and he reasserted his total engagement, seeing to it that "continually we will remind the inhabitants, aside from all the efforts that I will undertake, that such misdeeds will not take place, and, if they do, we will take steps, in conformity with the counsel of Your Most Illustrious Lordship." All in all, he was certain, he averred, that that cascade of letters to and from Rome would let him maintain order in his shearling flock. Whether harsh or moderate, the bishop seems to have been keen to please his superiors; their circumspection, with witches, could easily become his own.

The Inquisition's unceasing appeal to prudence and moderation, a commonplace back then, helps today to dispel hoary images of the tribunal's bloodthirstiness, but, in its own time, it had a pragmatic goal—the protection of the public from its own less competent protectors. It was a necessary move against all the abuses that, on the periphery, unscrupulous *vicari* and violent "executors of justice" heaped on the unlucky heads of those who fell into the machinery of justice of the entire church. These abuses, said

5. ACDF, S.O., St. St., Q 3-a, unpaginated (1 July 1624).
6. ACDF, S.O., St. St., Q 3-a, f. 26rv (7 June 1624).

the letters from Rome, were due not only to misbegotten zeal, but also to ignorance, administrative incompetence, corruption, and thirst for vendetta. Still, the mail from Rome was contradictory; it wavered between calls to caution and the yen to ascertain, by any means possible, if alleged crimes of witchcraft and magic had actually occurred. The wavering also evinces the mixed disbelief and belief in witchcraft among the inquisitors themselves, who were keen to verify if

there might be any imaginings and fantasies caused by the indisposition [i.e., the illness of the accused] and . . . nevertheless, on account of some diabolical illusion, for the case is very grave and of the utmost importance, and it is possible that the aforesaid crimes are true and real, and so it is necessary to follow a precise course and to proceed maturely and with great circumspection in order to have full knowledge of the truth about the matter.

So, clearly, as this wavering passage shows, prudent skepticism had its limits; witchcraft still was real. This letter is what, on 1 August 1590, the Roman congregation wrote the inquisitor of Faenza concerning Porzia and Maria's case.[7] Similar phrases also appeared in letters, sent from Rome in August of 1588 to the *podestà* of Otricoli, a lay law official who had jailed a woman named Brigida who had confessed to "having given her soul and her body to the Devil." Taking the charges seriously, the letter instructed him to transfer the case to the bishop of Narni, "for it was a matter for ecclesiastical jurisdiction."[8]

From the letters Rome sent out to distant officials of justice from 1580 to 1600, it is very clear that in the entire state there was a hard battle afoot to defend the right of the Holy Office to judge such cases. In those two decades, the nature of the times made witchcraft a lively issue. In the Papal States, they were hard years. Banditry had spread so far and wide as to assume traits of a real war, aggravated by an international scene troubled by the Wars of Religion and the militantly Catholic policies of Philip II. There were serried food crises threatening survival in both country and town, provoking epidemics and vexing provisioning and public order. The famines that regularly afflicted ancien régime society, with their waves of mortality, especially among children, fostered a cli-

7. ACDF, S.O., St. St., Q 3-d, f. 267r.
8. ACDF, S.O., St. St., Q 3-d, f. 29r–v.

mate of fear that pushed people to discern in everyday misfortunes the hidden hand of malignant powers that were easily personified. The climate favored magical practices, already endemic in the culture, not just among peasants, but also in all urban social classes. But the anxious mood also favored accusations against real and supposed witches. So it behooved the courts to move with caution.

A letter invited the governor of Benevento—a papal enclave inside the Kingdom of Naples reputed to be infected with witches[9]— to consign to the archbishop one Maddalena, "and other witch-women . . . because such crimes are the affair of the ecclesiastical courts and of the Holy Office for apostasy, where all the witches ordinarily go, and not a crime that belongs to the temporal court."[10] These orders came from the pope himself: it was 21 January 1589, and Sixtus V, who had published the bull *Coeli et terrae* against astrologers, was also keen to persecute illicit magic, divination, and witchcraft.[11] A few weeks later, further instructions on how to proceed against Maddalena and the others also went to the archbishop of Benevento. The task of the judges was to be

to learn from this Maddalena clearly and distinctly the given name, family name, village, age, and house, and the place of abjuration [of holiness] of each person afflicted by witchcraft, and the time, date, month, year and hour that she did these deeds of witchcraft, and how she did them. And then take care, concerning those that she confesses to have died, to know if in fact they are really alive or dead, and learn the time when they died, and of what disease they died. And, concerning those she says are not dead, take care to find out if, in the times she attests to, they had any sickness, and learn what medicines they used to bring back their health.[12]

The papal advice went on: use methods "as will seem necessary" to obtain "the pure, mere, simple truth." The use of torture to obtain a confession was left to the discretion of the local ecclesiastical judge. Maddalena's story is just one among many still in the records; it hints at the prudent mode of intervention that would

9. For relations between Rome and the Counter Reformation Benevento church, see Maria Anna Noto, *Tra sovrano pontefice e Regno di Napoli. Riforma cattolica e Controriforma a Benevento* (Manduria: Lacaita, 2003).

10. ADCF, S.O., St. St., Q 3-d, f. 269v.

11. On this subject see Ugo Baldini, "The Roman Inquisition's Condemnation of Astrology: Antecedents, Reasons and Consequences," in *Church, Censorship and Culture in Early Modern Italy*, ed. Gigliola Fragnito, 79–110 (Cambridge: Cambridge University Press, 2001).

12. ACDF, S.O., St. St., Q 3-d, f. 269v.

become the rule, if only by fits and starts, under diverse and complex local conditions.

Controversies about the precise nature and proper judicial forum of certain crimes would long embroil the *consultori* of the Holy Office, the bishops, the cardinal nephew, and even the pope himself, especially in cases of sorcery, prophecy, and witchcraft. The frequent admonition to discern whether an accusation implied crimes against the faith—Christian apostasy via a pact with the devil—guided the center's inquisitorial procedure and shaped its repeated alerts and preachments to inquisitors and *vicari* across the pope's domains. The Inquisition eschewed hasty accusations and unwarranted harm to prisoners. Sometimes, however, the cautions did not suffice. At Gubbio, in 1633, while being whipped in public, a supposed witch was stoned by an angry populace. It must not have been an isolated case, for, in 1641, the ruling went out that women suspected of witchcraft, when carried to Rome, should wear neither the penitent's *abitello* costume nor other shameful marks, lest they be "assaulted by the onrushing populace and lower orders."[13] With the witches themselves, the courts usually resorted to admonitions alone, as in 1631, when Giulia de Bonis, a Roman, was jailed with other women for alleged acts of witchcraft. After a severe warning, all were released, but they were obliged, under threat of sterner punishment, to present themselves to the Holy Office whenever summoned.[14] Also, in 1657, the bishop of Foligno, Antonio Montecatini, a nobleman from Ferrara, informed Rome that he had launched a trial against some superstitious activities for curing assorted ailments. From Rome came repeated requests to verify that there were no traces of heresy, and to free the suspects with severe admonitions and salutary acts of penance.

Cases involving witchcraft often invited other grave accusations for "horrible" crimes like infanticide, which fell under the jurisdiction of secular courts.[15] Still, the very tangle of procedures for assorted crimes urged caution and discretion. For instance, the Ro-

13. ACDF, S.O., St. St., I 2-d, f. 241r.

14. ACDF, S.O., St. St., H 6-f, ff.nn. (16 January 1631).

15. ACDF, S.O., St. St., Q 3-d, f. 272r. For a fine study of the ramifications of an infanticide case, see Adriano Prosperi, *Dare l'anima. Storia di un infanticidio* (Turin: Einaudi, 2005); see also Joanne M. Ferraro, *Nefarious Crimes, Contested Justice: Illicit Sex and Infanticide in the Republic of Venice, 1557–1789* (Baltimore: Johns Hopkins University Press, 2008).

man congregation warned the inquisitor of Faenza to be very careful when sharing official papers with lay courts:

> In sentences for witchcraft you can leave out the infanticides, but one must never release either the transcripts or the sentences of secular judges.[16]

The trials themselves, preceded always by a careful assay of the evidence, seemed to stretch ever longer. For efficiency's sake, even bishops, though their courts were fairly well developed, were urged to use all means at hand to define the crimes, guard the evidence, and keep close watch on witnesses and suspects.

FORTUNE TELLING AND IMPOSTURES

> Consorting with peasants from my parish and other villages, I have found that they have many superstitions, some of them ugly ones reeking of heresy, but I believe that most of them do so out of simplicity of mind and intend no wrong. When I try, with many examples, to persuade them to give them up, they answer me that their forebears have always observed such customs and that they help cure the ills to which they are applied. I do not write down these superstitions, for they are so very many. . . . I thought that it would be of enormous help if your most Illustrious Lordship wrote me a letter . . . and I am certain that if I can show them a vigorous, firm order from our most Illustrious Lordship, I will be able to uproot this mess [simili porcarie]. It is only zeal for the honor of God that moves me to do this.[17]

So wrote the parish priest of San Ginesio, Cosimo Passari, to Cardinal Giovanni Garzia Millini, the senior cardinal with the highest authority in the Congregation of the Holy Office. He understood perfectly the dilemma of prosecuting, or tolerating, or somehow just keeping an eye on suspect practices, superstitions that for peasants forged a powerful link to the culture of their elders, and to their own traditions. Messages to Rome from parish priests and bishops were troubled, aware as they were of the nearly impossible path of persuasion and acculturation of their own faithful. A bit different were the words of the bishop of Anagni to Cardinal Prospero Arrigoni, who lamented:

> This Roman Campagna sins greatly in this sort of superstitions. I believe it is on account of ignorance, for the men and women were quick to point

---

16. ACDF, S.O., St. St., Q 3-d, ff. 267r–272v.
17. ACDF, S.O., St. St., Q 3-a (25 January 1619).

out these vanities of theirs and denounced those who perform them, on the occasion of an edict on this matter announced in my church.[18]

Even in the Papal State, controlling magic and superstitions, and disciplining the clergy, were the most difficult problems to confront the Holy Office. Often the two issues presented bishops and inquisitors with a single, inextricable tangle. Priests, friars, and nuns were often protagonists in trials for conjuring, accused of concocting love potions or medicines for immunity from enemies and wartime gunfire, or, ever more often, charged with boasting they held the secret for finding hidden treasure. These accusations unveil practices much sought after in a poor society under threat of war. Meanwhile, for soldiers of fortune, war could also be a way to make a living: it sufficed to protect oneself and pull through unscathed.

In 1711, there arrived at the Holy Office in Rome the copy of a trial held in Todi by the Inquisition's *vicario*. It was against Caterina Fabbri, a nun at a convent there, the Santissima Annunziata. She had been denounced by a blacksmith, Michele Quirini, who "when he had to go to the Romagna as a soldier of Our Lord [the pope]" was advised by other women to turn to his cousin, the nun, to acquire "a transcript [a charm of holy words] to wear, because it had power against weapons." This was not the first time that the convent had bestowed on supplicants "conjuring transcripts against weapons." The *vicario* cast into the fire all "written charms" (*brevetti sortilegi*) found there, and enjoined the nuns "under precept, in the future to abstain, under penalty of privation of the veil and formal imprisonment." This sorcery had not been the initiative of just one nun. So the inquisitor's admonition addressed the other sisters too, on account of some "unworthy piece of work" invented "by the teacher, Sister Candida Gregori, denounced ten months ago."[19]

To fall in love, or to make another person take the tumble, looked like one sure way to clinch a good marriage and sure affection, or so one hoped, and even better, to assure parenthood, with its desirable economic stability. And if, to top it off, one then found a treasure too! The everyday problems of a precarious life would at last be solved. For many, at the hand of charlatans, con men, heal-

18. ACDF, S.O., St.St., Q 3-a, Anagni (14 May 1612).

19. BAV, microfilm Trinity College Dublin (henceforth MF, for microfilm), held at the Vatican Library, 25 (Ms 1248), ff. 135r–140r.

ers, and holy folk, there opened fair visions of unforeseen wealth. But the doors of the Inquisition swung open too, to swallow up these shady practitioners and all their "devilry." In 1694, at Urbania, near Urbino, a Giuseppe Rambaldoni was denounced via a "blind" (unsigned) memorandum, for possessing "a book of a thousand superstitions that he used, with words and signs of the cross, to make signs on children who suffer worms [usually just severe diarrhea], and a thousand other sorceries."[20] From Rome, the congregation commissioned an investigation, not so much of Rambaldoni—who had meanwhile already appeared of his own accord before the inquisitor, handing over the book with the mysterious magic formulae and paying a solid surety of two hundred scudi—as of the authors of that "blind memorandum," to find out whether they were just the usual "enemies" or disappointed accomplices. The bishop, who held inquisitorial powers, was invited to put Rambaldoni to torture. But in November, Rambaldoni's family, in a petition, declared that, "in light of its poverty, it cannot carry on without him." The suspect had withstood torture for a quarter hour without confessing further crimes. After his abjuration *de levi* [of the less weighty sort of charge], and with a sharp admonition and a warning to abstain from similar operations, under a penalty to be adjudged by the same Congregation," after about a year in prison he was set free.

This case and the many others in inquisitorial records from the seventeenth and eighteenth centuries reveal a tireless battle against magic, medical practices tinged with superstition, and popular beliefs, all things that supplemented, distorted, or rivaled official religion's own use of supernatural powers to work providential good. It was a hard fight, one that the congregation perhaps knew it could never win, against a traditional culture rooted not only in the countryside, but also in cities, on every social level. The frequent spontaneous denunciations from those who found traces of suspect material testify to a widespread uneasiness, marked by fears of accusations of complicity and, no less often, of possible contamination by sorcery's paraphernalia.

In Rome in 1636, years before the Urbania episode, Gaspare

20. BAV, MF 26 (Ms 1252), f. 162r. On the use of anonymous denunciations and their function in starting judicial investigations, see Paolo Preto, *"Persona per hora secreta." Accusa e delazione nella Republica di Venezia* (Milan: il Saggiatore, 2003).

Bonelli, originally from the Sabina district northeast of town and attached to the notarial practice of Valentino Valentini, hastened to denounce a butcher, Caterino Armellino. The butcher was in jail for having, in a brawl, gravely wounded a workman. As notary Bonelli inventoried Armellino's goods, impounded by the court, he discovered, he reported, that "among the other goods were found diverse writings and papers which, because it seemed they were matters for the Holy Office, I have brought to show."[21] It was "a little book, a demi-folio with women's names, another demi-folio that begins, 'I conjure thee'"; a piece of paper "with secrets and symbols"; another "little piece [of paper] with certain leaves of herbs"; a secret remedy "lest women corrupt you; and a piece of paper with, inside it, a lock of woman's hair with a ribbon." With the suspect materials were various prayers and litanies; the notary averred that he had not inventoried them. The case for the defense maintained that these writings could not have belonged to the butcher, who was illiterate. The fragmentary papers of the trial break off sharply, and do not show if justice took its course or if a settlement quashed the case. It is likely that this affair, similar to many others, ended up before the *vicario*, who probably threatened the butcher with salutary penance, deterring him from using or collecting compromising traces of dangerous superstitions.

SPEECH OFFENSIVE TO RELIGION

"Why am I not the Lord God, for I would make the world go round?" Leonardo di Bartolomeo, a peasant in Colle Baldo, in Umbria, asked himself this in the fall of 1701 "because his olive trees seemed to him to have yielded little." Simone, who later reported those words in court, then chided him, but Leonardo's imprecations did not stop there. He went on, affirming, "I do not care if I go to Paradise, because I don't care if my soul goes to the Devil, because where I go I will not be alone."[22] So reported Simone di Francesco, who, in 1705, denounced Leonardo to the inquisitor of Perugia. The lapse between deed and denunciation made the inquisitors suspect that in the meantime "enmities" might have induced Simone to bring Leonardo's case to them. The affair would last years and verge on tragedy. Leonardo's defense was entrusted to legal aid, via a "law-

21. BAV, MF 25 (Ms 1248), f. 272r.
22. BAV, MF 26 (Ms 1249), f. 361r.

yer for defendants," who argued, alleging many witnesses, that the defendant's imprecations contained no trace of heresy. True, he was "a habitual blasphemer," but he had "always blasphemed when angry and . . . is always drunk," as he himself affirmed in his interrogations. In the judicial treatises of the time, these were extenuating circumstances, but they did nothing, according to doctrine, to exempt such cases from inquisitorial purview.[23] Leonardo had already been admonished and then been jailed by Perugia's Inquisition for two months; so there was hope of clemency.

But it was not to be. In January 1710 came official notice of condemnation, "in conformity with the orders of this congregation, given on 3 December 1709—to prison for three years." Perugia's inquisitor, Paolo Ottaviani, nevertheless requested "clemency" on account of "his dementia that makes it necessary to keep him in solitary lest he endanger his own or others' lives." The sentence was pronounced in the presence of the archpriest of Perugia's cathedral, who had Leonardo put in solitary, obligating him to confess and take communion "on the principal holidays" and to recite the rosary and do other devotions daily. Solitary confinement had laid waste his mind. "It has altered the thought processes [la fantasia]," said a medical report, requested in 1711 and aimed to secure his release and consignment to his family. Leonardo was "melancholy" and, said the report, "he has become maniacal, but he has also hurled himself from a loggia more than forty feet high. He broke neither bones nor anything else, but rendered himself more deluded."[24] His escape from harm aroused suspicions: perhaps the devil had protected him, or had his manifest insanity shielded him from bodily harm? We do not know how the affair ended: whether the moderation of the local inquisitor, seconded by the joint expertise of physician and defendants' lawyer, prevailed, or whether orders from Rome stiffened the desire to punish a hardened blasphemer. The lesson of this sad story is that the fight against blasphemy ran through the whole period, commingling with the repression of heresy and with the tough campaign to correct the scandalous behavior of many, even of peasants who sometimes swore when meager harvests threatened their survival.

23. Carlo Carena, Tractatus de modo procedendi in causis S. Officii, 163–65 (Cremona: M. A. Belpierum, 1636).
24. BAV, MF 36 (Ms 1259), f. 376v.

Blasphemy, in fact, could be read as a noisy expression of implicit violence, often accompanied by sacrilegious gestures. It is therefore scandalous, said the moralists, a desecrating spectacle for whoever sees and hears it: via eyes and ears it strikes the soul and wounds God. But it is not only an offense against God: it is a sign of violence, of bad character, of danger to society. Blasphemers are often fathers and mothers addicted to gambling, drunkards, spendthrifts, haunters of cheap taverns. The blasphemer, said such preachments, is, all told, the antithesis of the good paterfamilias, keystone of Christian society and social and moral order.

A telling case, certainly not unique, is the tale of Bartolomeo Ceccarone of Viterbo, "a Jew turned Christian," denounced in 1698 to the *vicario* of the Holy Office by his wife, at her confessor's urgings. The woman tells how she was forced to take from the rooms of her own house images of saints—Mary Magdalen, Saint Filippo Neri, and the Virgin—lest her husband offend them with blasphemies and spittle. But in these moments of anger, said his wife, he also claimed that "the Jews go to Paradise and the others go to the devil's house . . . and that he intended to go make a Jew of the son of the denouncer [i.e., the wife]." And finally, when threatened with denunciation to the Inquisition, he answered, "Fuck off the Holy Office."[25] The inquest was entrusted to the *generale* of the Benedictine order that ruled the abbey of Farfa. Bartolomeo's fellow townsmen were interrogated, and he turned out to have no particular enemies there. The court questioned Jewish merchants in Rome who had known him as a boy and others who, one said, had encountered him at the Viterbo fairs. All denied having heard him utter blasphemous things or seen him make sacrilegious gestures. The sole depositions against him came from within his family, especially from his mother-in-law, who may never have accepted her daughter's love match with a convert who, perhaps, had a violent tongue, and who probably was still marginal in the community.[26] The defense, waged by the lawyer for defendants, cited familial en-

---

25. BAV, MF 26 (Ms 1255), f. 82r–v.

26. There seem to have been no tensions with the wife, according to the Jewish witnesses, for "they have been married for twenty months . . . and I know that they married for love. . . . It is true [the testimony's summary continues] that some times, when it was time to prepare the meal, and Angela was not as quick as she should be, the said Bartolomeo said to her, 'may you break your neck' and other imprecations." BAV, MF 26 (Ms 1255), f. 99v. The expression is very common, and merely figurative.

mities and asked indulgence for a man "recently come to the Holy
Faith."[27] In May 1698, Bartolomeo was put in solitary in the Inquisition prison, but the *vicario* asked Rome to have him transferred
to the jail of Viterbo's governor. He was threatening to kill himself and "making a ruckus." All in all, he was uncontrollable. The
man wrote, or had written for him, a petition to speed up the trial
and, in March 1699, after almost a year of defense trial, the congregation ruled that he be set free and that his behavior, his words,
and his domestic violence be put under observation.[28] The wife's
evidence had been uncorroborated, and perhaps contentious, and
condemnation by the Inquisition would do little to improve Bartolomeo's position in his own wider community. Already looked
at askance, thanks to the conversion, spontaneous or forced, now
he would have to live under the Inquistion's mark as well. But the
court's intervention also penetrated domestic space. The congregation, thanks to its prudence and to the long stretch of time that undermined the suspect's mind, had penetrated a labyrinth of family
relationships, laden with tensions and hatreds, that sought resolution in a court verdict. The Inquisition, striving to dike and prosecute blasphemy, peered ever more often inside families.

Moral reformers strove for chaste and decorous language, just
about everywhere. Letters to Rome by bishops and inquisitors denounce grave and habitual blasphemy even among clergy, especially
in the countryside. From Cagli, in the Marches, in 1607, they wrote
that the practice of blasphemy "is the rule among the regulars,
but also among the secular and parish priests with so much scandal among the good," and they reproved the scandalous comportment of one Andrea Druda, a canon of the cathedral.[29] The repression of blasphemy was also tied to the attempt to control and limit
all the sociable, boisterous occasions that gave rise to the practice:
games of cards and dice, and the frequenting of wine shops and taverns, bordellos, and prostitutes' private houses. Crowded work-
places also fell under the inquisitor's sights, and streets and ports.
Games had long been accused of provoking disorder and sin. Their
visibility on the street's stage and in public spaces accentuated such
places' danger and contamination. The Augustinian Angelo Rocca
published, in 1616, a Latin work, translated the next year into Ital-

27. BAV, MF 26 (Ms 1255), f. 88r.   28. BAV, MF 26 (Ms 1255), f. 184r.
29. ACDF, S.O., St. St., DD 2-b, f. 2r–v.

ian, that in its frontispiece expounded the church's plan to extirpate "abominable games." It was necessary to purge the streets, the squares, the riverbanks, not to mention the taverns and the wine shops, of those dangerous, noisy players. Under the lens of justice, and of preachers and moralists, in those same years, fell the poor and vagabonds. According to Rocca, the safe alternative was chess, silent and thoughtful, but unlikely to catch on with plebeians.[30]

The legal treatises also tended to hand to inquisitors' jurisdiction all matters of blasphemy, whether heretical or not. That last distinction, not an obvious one, invited diverse interpretations. One defined as heretical any blasphemy that contained errors concerning the faith, that is, when the blasphemous words asserted opinions that clashed with dogma. The jurists were quick to offer examples.[31] At Rome, Julius III (1550–1555) had ruled that cases of blasphemy should be reserved for the Inquisition, limiting the jurisdiction of the Roman tribunals, who could proceed only where authorized by the statutes.[32] In fact, the statutes stipulated that anyone who uttered in blasphemous manner the name of God, of Christ, or of the Virgin, if noble, should be subject to the considerable fine of twenty-five gold ducats. And, if he sinned again, the fine should double; on a third occasion, he should pay one hundred ducats, suffer ignomiy, and be sent into exile. A plebeian's treatment was different: if, as likely, he could not pay the heavy fine, with hands and feet bound and bare-headed, he was to be carried to the Capitol's place of shame and put in the stocks. A second time, he should be whipped through the streets, and on the third occasion, his tongue should be pierced and he should be sent to the galleys. Whoever blasphemed against mere saints paid lighter penalties, according to his station and to the judge's discretion.[33] Rome's were not the only statutes to lay out a range of sanctions for blasphemers. Indeed, all cities, and the smallest villages, even those under feudal administration, could turn to their statutes to punish

30. Angelo Rocca, *Trattato per la salute dell'anime e per la conservatone della robba, e del denaro contra i giuochi di carte e dadi* (Rome: G. Facciotto, 1617). For the moral polemic around games, see Alessandro Arcangeli, *Passatempi rinascimentali: storia culturale del divertimento in Europa (secoli XV–XVII)* (Rome: Carocci, 2004), 91–96.

31. Carena, *Tractatus de modo precedendi*, 155–59.

32. *Bullarum diplomatum et privilegiorum Sanctorum Romanorum Pontificum Taurinensis Editio*, VI, 478–81 (Turin: Dalmazzo, 1850).

33. Giovanni Battista Fenzonio, *Adnotationes in Statuta, sive ius municipale Romanae Urbis* (Rome: Camera Apostolica, 1636), 589–90.

this widespread, ineradicable practice; as with most offenses, actual sentences were often far lighter than those on the official schedule.

Against blasphemers, the Holy Office was not the only agency. It was utterly beyond the reach of justice to extirpate the custom. From the late sixteenth century to the eighteenth, the Sacra Consulta, the highest court, also intervened. Some of its decrees ordained that one should extend to those who offended saints the same penalties set out for "the profaners of the holiest names of God, Jesus Christ, and the Most Blessed Virgin": the stocks, the whip, the galley, banishment, mutilation of the tongue, "according to the quality of the crime and of the delinquent."[34]

By the middle of the eighteenth century, the futility of intervention had become clear. The Holy Office called for collaboration with the other tribunals of the state, above all those of Rome,

to promulgate another, similar edict concerning the other blasphemies that they call "simple" and to proceed with special rigor not only against blasphemers, but also against some sacrileges as well, for they take impious amusement in cursing what is most holy and abusing the venerable names of God, of Jesus Christ, and his most precious blood, and this criminal habit then opens a path to more atrocious blasphemies.[35]

Even though Benedict XIV (1740–1758) conceded new powers to the Inquisition. letting it punish the crimes of "simple blasphemy without the sound and form of a trial and in some cases without the defense," the "accursed vice" still flourished. What most preoccupied justice, and not only church courts, was the damage that this vice inflicted on Rome's image, to the "most notable scandal of foreigners who come to visit some of the sanctuaries of this same city." Confessors' collaboration had waned; they no longer denounced the penitents, not to mention the tavern hosts and innkeepers, who eyed their profits only. There was a proposal to use "the most secret spies" of the Inquisition to verify, finally, if the very "executors" of the tribunals themselves "are not habitually infected by the same vice." By the middle of the eighteenth century the old collaboration between confessors and inquisitors seemed to falter, at least in the matter of a sin that could never be stemmed.

The Inquisition did not confine its interests to the "vile plebs."

34. ACDF, S.O., St. St., D 6-e.
35. ACDF, S.O., St. St., D 6-e.

In Rome, as in other cities, dangerous ideas had infiltrated the elites, especially the nobles. One observed that

although among nobles and respectable [*civili*] persons, blasphemy does not usually rule, it is not out of bounds to suspect and fear that in their conversations, whether public, in cafés and similar places, or private, in their palaces and houses, one might hear propositions that are quite opposed to the purity of the Catholic faith and to evangelical morality.[36]

The proposed remedies were always the same: to seek the collaboration of confessors and to unleash spies. But, in Rome and elsewhere, control of the feared "libertine conversations" would prove difficult. The crime could be committed inside domestic walls, in the palaces of the nobility, in the salons, expressions of a society where the aristocracy was open to "libertine" ideas and impulses that had infiltrated from afar and for some while circulated in the pope's own city.

36. ACDF, S.O., St. St., D 6-e.

8

Inside the Family

At Rome and in the Papal State, the control of the family, of spousal relations, of violence and transgressions perpetrated inside domestic walls, and also of familial relations with society, fell to multiple and varied institutions. Ecclesiastical and "lay" tribunals—the distinction here is merely relative—plus bishops, inquisitors, parish priests, and confraternities all kept their eye on society's basic cell. Via open repression and charitable aid, all aimed to discipline behavior and punish transgressions that clashed with the family model imposed and sacralized by the Council of Trent. Family life also fell under the inquisitive, not always benevolent, eyes of neighbors, kinfolk, friends, and enemies. It was thus difficult to hide crimes, transgressive conduct, and illicit relationships. Noises, cries, and violent deeds reached the street and alerted the perennially attentive ears of neighbors and spies, often ready to denounce to authorities and courts, sometimes for grudge or envy, anything that upset good order.

THE POLYGAMOUS

From the late sixteenth century, with the decree *Tametsi*, the Council of Trent reaffirmed the sacramentality of matrimony, and polygamy became a crime open to prosecution by the Inquisition rather than by diocesan courts.[1] A rich corpus of legal thought had long argued that bigamy might involve heresy (*factum haereticale*). In the Reformation, that legal position was propagated and given weight in reaction to the example of radical heretics who denied the sacramental nature of matrimony. In a world where divorce was almost impossible and where men and women sometimes moved many miles for work, serial polygamy was a rather common crime. But churchmen feared it because it destabilized the model of mat-

1. On this subject, see Silvana Seidel Menchi and Diego Quaglioni, eds., *Trasgressioni. Seduzione, concubinato, adulterio, bigamia (XIV–XVIII secolo)* (Bologna: il Mulino, 2004).

rimony codified by the church and undermined orderly social coexistence and relations of mutual support and aid. Certainly, at least in the seventeenth and eighteenth centuries, it was above all this aspect and its moral and social fallout, rather than the whiff of heresy, that aroused the Inquisition's attention and repression. Penalties for the crime were harsh, and remained so through the entire eighteenth century. The procedure began with an abjuration, *de levi* or *de vehementi*. The abjuration *de vehementi*, the more serious form, was almost always performed publicly, signifying that if the offender were ever again found guilty of the same offense he would be declared a relapsed heretic and be liable to capital punishment. Abjuration *de levi*, less serious, usually was performed privately, thus saving the defendant the embarrassment of a public ceremony, and did not mandate capital punishment for relapses. For polygamy, the normal punishment for men was five years in the galleys; they could row up to seven for false witness and ten for changed identity. For the women, who were never sent to the galleys, after abjuration the jail doors opened. In 1637, Urban VIII codified these new harsher punishments, aiming to repress a crime that seemed widespread and ineradicable. This "controverted" *costituzione barberiniana* (Urban was by family a Barberini)—even the inquisitorial papers used this label—seems never to have been put into practice. A memorandum defending a man named Francesco Innocenzi makes that observation. Francesco, a servant of Conte Capizzucchi, had denounced himself for his polygamy and change of identity, accomplished with the help of "false witnesses."[2]

In the course of the seventeenth and eighteenth centuries there were frequent cases concerning marriages to foreigners, male or female, from "the lands of the heretics." They had come to Rome or other papal cities, often in the train of co-nationals, in search of work or on the lookout for a new life. They had converted to Catholicism, assuming a new identity, confessional as well as social. Often they had left a first spouse in the lands "across the mountains," along with a past that the conversion was supposed to cancel. A new marriage might seem to sanction firmly a new choice of life, but, in Catholic law, even a marriage blessed in a heretical church was still legal and the original spouse still had a valid claim.

2. ACDF, S.O., St. St., M 5-b.

Suspicion of foreigners, and the difficulty of tracking the identity of converts, prompted the watchful attention of parish priests, confessors, and inquisitors. With passing years, the inquests into prior matrimonial conditions, traditionally thorough, grew even longer. Also, immigrants from other parts of Italy were accused of the same crime, linked to male mobility in search of employ, or to flight from the law on account of crimes, in hopes of a new life far from one's community of origin. The difficulties of knowing foreigners' identity and life were clear, nor was it easy to ascertain the identity even of those who arrived from nearer zones. There was a requirement for tickets (*cedole*) or other papers from the bishop of the see of origin; one grilled parish priests to vet the morals of persons suspected of bigamy or concubinage. In these cases, informing and personal vendetta were very helpful to the inquisitors' hunt for irregular unions. The solidarity of allies was too often fragile, and the word got out as to who, by trickery or by tacit connivance with the new partner, had contracted a second marriage while not yet single. For many, such a marriage was a solution, breaking the chains of a mistaken marriage or liberating a woman, often a single mother, from the lonely grip of abandonment.

In 1748, in Rome, Giulia Bombardi appeared spontaneously before the Holy Office to denounce herself for having married Lorenzo Fari, a corporal of the cardinal *vicario*'s *birri*. Thanks to false witnesses, she had made a case for the death of her first husband. Then the witnesses, fearful or vengeful, had betrayed the couple, and the corporal had denounced himself to the Inquisition. The man had first tried to defend himself, asserting that he had seen the woman's husband die. But both of them were forced to abjure *de vehementi* and to accept punishment by the tribunal: to her fell "penances for salvation" and to him three years rowing.[3]

Polygamy, like other crimes—we have seen it already for blasphemy and will again for sodomy—was very often uncovered thanks to family quarrels and vendettas, some careless confidence with workmates, informing by "enemies," or mere chance. In 1723, for example, the galley slave Giovanni Francesco Gerini, whose real name was Giuseppe Josaphat Boroni, a converted Jew—this last aggravating fact may have rendered his identity less definite and therefore dangerous—proffered to a crewmate an imprudent con-

3. ACDF, S.O., St. St., M 5-a.

fession. He admitted his polygamy, having denied it in his Inquisition trial six years earlier. His polygamy, and false identity, earned him a new condemnation to ten more years of rowing. Trickery and falsehood had aggravated his legal position, and, even though he petitioned, saying, I have "repented of this great error of mine," the sentence was not reduced.[4] It was usually confessors who reported to the Holy Office irregular marriages, had others denounce them, or urged self-accusation. In the case in question, it had been the penitencer of Saint Peter's

who inspired me to come ask the pardon of this Holy Tribunal, as I am now doing, for I am resolved to leave this second, illegitimate wife and save my soul. . . . As soon as I had married the said Anna, I knew I had done an illicit thing but from fear of punishment I never took the risk of coming to denounce myself and to abandon the said Anna. Finally, with the aid of God, I have resolved to do this.

Even in the self-accusatory rhetoric of the confession, we can discern the tangle of personal, social, and, with this convert, religious motives that impelled a man to contract a new marriage.

Especially for women, a new wedding and the false declaration of a first husband's death, thanks to the solidarity of friends and kinfolk, might be the only way to break a marital tie that had grown too oppressive, or to forge a new existence alongside another man, after a husband had left home without any word of where he had gone. Sometimes it soon turned out that the new consort of a woman under investigation had killed the first husband. Appearance before the Inquisition, in any case, even if it often ended without condemnation, left a blemish on honor and reputation, a stigma that resurfaced swiftly in interrogations before other Roman judges if, once more, as often happened, one fell afoul of justice. To have a record was dangerous, an aggravating circumstance. Still, not always did women affirm that they had married believing that the first husband had died. There were other motives too, not always concealed from the inquisitor, especially if "love" had urged the new alliance. When a spouse's bad faith was evident, clemency was unlikely.[5]

---

4. ACDF, S.O., St. St., M 5-a.

5. On this subject, see Kim Siebenhüner, "'M'ha mosso l'amore' Bigami e inquisitori nella documentazione del Sant'Uffizio romano (secolo XVII)," in Seidel Menchi and Quaglioni, eds., *Trasgressioni*, 503–33.

In 1655, Vittoria de Ripi from Sermoneta, south of Rome, accused herself before the Roman Inquisition of marrying Carlo
Monaldo, though aware that her first husband was still alive. She
was accused of corrupting witnesses and the trial produced false
documents, irregularly drafted by the *vicario*'s court, attesting to
her now-unmarried state. With her second husband she was locked
away in the Inquisition's jail. Carlo was tortured and then released
as if innocent and duped. Vittoria, after an abjuration *de vehementi*,
was instead condemned to prison at the court's discretion.[6]

In the seventeenth and eighteenth centuries, the Inquisition's
campaign against polygamy was not inspired by the specter of heretical models from across the Alps or by the need to stem contamination from other Mediterranean cultures.[7] Motives were more
local. The crime was widespread; throughout early modern times
it was persecuted in Rome and in the Papal State, but with scant
success, for polygamy was rooted in a tangle of motives, personal,
economic, and social; for emotional and practical reasons, it was a
crime that often paid. A second match made sub rosa might serve
a man or woman well. But, as a sin against the sacrament of marriage, it also bound community and family to a chain of *omertà*,
falsehood, and strategic fraud that unsettled moral and social order, unveiled identity's slipperiness, and undercut a family model
the church sacralized and championed.

"THE FATHER IS THE MASTER"

Domestic walls were not impenetrable. The eyes and ears of
neighbors were quick to gather gestures, noises, cries: a house and
its rooms blended with the street, smudging distinctions between
public and private. Over what happened in houses, in families, in
fragmented domestic units, often bereft of one or two parents, the
authorities—lay and, especially, ecclesiastic—were vigilant. At
Rome, the governor, the *vicario*, and the Holy Office were all swift
to gather denunciations and launch inquiries. Other zones of the
Papal State mobilized inquisitors, *vicari*, bishops, and, especially, confessors. Court papers witness widespread domestic violence,
deep-rooted and hard to squelch; lay and church judiciaries strove

6. ACDF, S.O., St. St., M 5-a, no folio number and ff. 453r–464v.
7. Kim Siebenhüner, *Bigamie und Inquisition in Italien 1600–1750* (Paderborn:
F. Schöningh, 2006), 195–202.

to intervene, protect, and punish, and, in general, kept a watchful
eye out for it.

Mothers and daughters, and women in general, many of them
very young, placed trust in justice. Knowing that with church authorities they could find a hearing, they denounced husbands and
fathers who for years had perpetrated sexual abuse and violence
of every kind. Mothers and daughters offered up to judicial torture, for proof's sake, their own bodies, already repeatedly violated,
threatened, and beaten. Diffident and yet prudent, they denounced
and paraded sufferings, exposing themselves to the judgment not
only of the tribunals but also of the world around them. Testimony
thus both defended and besmirched their honor.

Crimes of *forum mixtum* (lay and church at once), if denounced
to the bishop's tribunal, were prosecuted by the Inquisition when it
transpired or one suspected that the culprit had abused religion to
justify and sustain his crimes, in apparent contempt of faith, morality, and justice.

Scolastica Lamberti, age twenty, denounced to the inquisitor of
Perugia her own father, Marc'Antonio, a widower, age forty-two,
because

when she treated with him in a friendly fashion he wanted to have impure touchings and kisses. . . . And, very often, when she said that it was
a sin, the aforesaid [father] told her that the Father is the master [*il Pa-
dre è padrone*] and can do what he wants with his daughters, and that he
could do no less.[8]

The young woman's denunciation also revealed attempted violence
against her sister; both the serving woman and the grandmother
knew about it. The trial's summary reveals a women's world rebelling against the bullying family head, a Venetian tinsmith long resident in Perugia. The inquisitor's inquest sifted family ties to vet the
"character and *fama* [reputation] of the aforesaid women," to see if
they had been inspired by grudge and vendetta. Word in the street
[*publica vox*] confirmed with sworn witnesses what the parish priest
had certified: they were "of the best reputation [*ottima fama*]," God-
fearing, and of honest conduct, and without quarrel with the suspect. After the congregation discussed the case, the man was jailed
awaiting trial at the Perugia Holy Office, "to avoid greater evil that

8. ACDF, S.O. St. St., M 5-p (Perugia, 1731).

he could do with his daughters." He, meanwhile, continued to protest his innocence, asserting that the charges were "all falsehoods used against him by people of evil disposition to cause his fall" and fingering as the source of his troubles his domestic relationships, soured by the hostility of his mother-in-law and serving woman. He also cited his scant support from folk who perhaps still saw him as a foreigner. In the defense, the advocate for suspects [*avvocato dei rei*] used these themes abundantly. The evidence, he argued, was so "defective and weak" that it did not even merit legal torture, much less a condemnation. The witnesses, he said, were "very suspect, because they are women, and they are all the more suspect because they are deposing against their own parent." Marc'Antonio was ruled to be in no condition to be put to torture, but the inquisitorial tribunal, after a vote of the Roman congregation, sentenced him to three years in prison. And, to guarantee the safety of the daughters, at his release either the inquisitor or the bishop was to monitor his behavior and report back often to the congregation.

This is only one example of the strenuous endeavor by diverse ecclesiastical organizations to control and correct family life and to serve as wardens and guarantors of order. Often, they succeeded in damming the daily violence perpetrated against society's weakest members. If one melds the fragmentary papers of the Inquisition with documents from lay and episcopal courts, they suggest a hypothesis: in the eighteenth century, denunciations for family violence seem more frequent than in the past. They suggest more effective action by both lay and church justice.

When it came to incest and other crimes within domestic walls, like sodomy and polygamy, that undermined the integrity of the family model, the court checked for crimes against dogma. Acts themselves might be condemned by other courts and punished in accord with statutes. But, one asked, had the suspect also believed that the deeds were no sin or even defended this heretical opinion before others, contaminating minds and spreading scandal? The sources offer a skewed image of society; the protagonists and victims belong almost always to the lowest orders. Nobles and patricians came to terms with justice, even before church courts, in far quieter ways; with them even the Inquisition was prudent, careful to exercise its surveillance and its discipline without besmirching the social prestige of malefactors.

THE "UNSPEAKABLE VICE" OF SODOM

The "unspeakable vice" (*vizio nefando* in Italian; *vitium nefandum* in Latin)—sodomy—was persecuted explicitly by statutes and by lay and ecclesiastical tribunals. In the eyes of the law, of moral theology, and of vernacular culture, sodomy—anal penetration, be it of man or woman—was an action and not at all a way of life; early modern Italy did not conceive of homosexuality as an orientation, nature, or style of being. Rather, sodomy, to codes and laws, was a violation of a natural order that mandated sex through proper organs only. At the same time, like gambling, for instance, the activity seemed somewhat addictive, and it had its devotees, who for taste or need—lacking access to female partners, or for prudence, fearing pregnancy—resorted to anal sex. For some elites in some places, a homosexual phase before marriage marked the path to male maturity; meanwhile, less advantaged young men might rent out their bodies to social betters.[9]

Sodomy, when it crossed the law, was yet one more crime that, in Rome and the Papal State, stirred up the Inquisition only when there was proof or suspicion of "false dogma," that is, when the presumed malefactor had justified his behavior, to his victims or his partners or to others, claiming it was no sin. Meanwhile, the lay tribunals, the governor's for instance, intervened if the sodomy involved violence, disorder, wounds, or other disruptions of public peace and order. It is clear, as the rich papers of the Roman court reveal, that between common culture's perception of these practices as merely normal transgressions and the severity of official punishments on the books the gulf was wide. In trials by the governor's court, denunciations by the "victim's" kinfolk most often sparked the inquest, while, with the Inquisition, it was usually the confessors who, by subtle questioning, winkled out illicit sexual practices and then denounced the practitioners to the bishop's court, or urged self-denunciation. When penitents affirmed that they believed sodomy was no sin, they awakened suspicion of heresy.

9. On this subject see: Kent Gerard and Gerd Hekma, eds., *The Pursuit of Sodomy: Male Homosexuality in Renaissance and Enlightenment Europe* (New York: Haworth Press, 1989); Michael Rocke, *Forbidden Friendship: Homosexuality and Male Culture in Renaissance Florence* (New York: Oxford University Press, 1996); Guido Ruggiero, *Machiavelli in Love: Sex, Self and Society in Italian Renaissance* (Baltimore: Johns Hopkins University Press, 2007).

Unlike in Spain, the Roman Inquisition had no jurisdiction over the crime itself. It was judged in episcopal and lay courts. In November of 1729, having misunderstood the jurisdictions of the complex of papal courts, a Spanish merchant, José Rodriguez, denounced himself to the Inquisition for an act of sodomy committed at Cadiz a full eighteen years before. Running over the years of his youth in memory, he recounted:

In the city of Cadiz, serving as a soldier of my king, finding myself far from my wife, and overwhelmed by vehement desire, I fell into the unnamable sin with a certain Antonio Otero, sergeant of the regiment of infantry of Malaga.

It had not been an isolated act, as he himself declared, for "two or three times we sodomized one another. Then I went to the Spanish Indies, where I arrived at the age of nineteen and took up residence in Cartagena." And, he admitted, he continued to practice sodomy.[10] José's self-denunciation, although it revealed a streak of violence amidst sexual practices then common among soldiers, which tribunals defined as "unspeakable," moved the Inquisition to respond in its usual way. Accordingly, as its decree affirms, the court did not condemn the Spaniard; instead, it sent him back to the *vicario*, "imposing great saving penances on him."[11] Even when cases did go to the Inquisition, whether via self-denunciation or denunciations by partners and witnesses, caution marked every moment of the inquest. This attitude was strongly recommended by the treatises on legal practice: they noted that "in these crimes of sodomy imposture and calumny are easy, and one must proceed with full maturity and circumspection."[12]

In Ferrara, in 1753, the peasant and musician Antonio Negri was accused of sodomy because "he believed it was not a sin." When he had been convinced of the contrary, and, above all, when the inquisitors themselves had been convinced of the sincerity of his affirmations, in light of his "lack of culture [*rudità*] and ignorance," he was released with salutary penances and admonitions, as per the usual practice. But one year later, he was back once more

---

10. ACDF, S.O., St. St., M 5-p., ff. 339r–340v (10 and 20 November 1729).

11. ACDF, S.O., St. St., I 2-d, f. 458r.

12. On false accusations in cases of sodomy, see, among others, Gian Domenico Raynaldi, *Observationes criminales, civiles et mixtae*, bk. 2, ch. 21, 305–39 (Rome: Corbelletti, 1690).

before the tribunal for "unspeakable acts." But this time there was more to the story. Pretending to be a "sub-inquisitor," he had absolved his "lads," admonishing each of them not to

confess such things, for he had the faculty of absolving him [i.e., the ex-partner, now a denouncer]. And every time the denouncer went to confess, before he went to the confessor, the aforesaid Negri enjoined him to do the penitence for those things, telling him that he should recite five Paternosters, five Ave Marias, and five Gloria Patri's at the wounds of our Lord, and then told him that he should not speak about this thing with anyone, not even with the confessor. And if he did talk about it, he would suffer excommunication. For that reason this man [the partner] believed that to do these things was no sin and that he did not have to go to confession.

Negri had fed other young men such fables, and they now testified against him before the inquisitor. To the court, he was a dangerous usurper of inquisitorial powers, an imposter who gave absolution, making the sign of the cross. "And he uttered some words that I did not understand," all depositions agreed. What made the man's legal position worse was the "bad opinion" that the others said they had of him, not only for practices they denounced as unspeakable, but also because, they said, "they thought of him as a man who stole hens and could not abide him." These latter accusations had nothing to do with crimes that concerned the Inquisition, but a poor society read such thievery as subverting everyday survival; it heaped yet more faults onto Negri's already shaky reputation. To defend himself, Negri denied arrogating to himself the power to absolve, but claimed to have spoken "that way, with my head in the clouds [con la testa in aria], without a thought to what I was saying. . . . I have said and done such things because of my carelessness and ignorance, without giving thought, and therefore I ask mercy of the Sacred Tribunal," as his final deposition puts it. Pretending to be mad, or at least bewildered and half-witted, was a stratagem well known to the inquisitors. Heretics and suspects for other crimes were known to do this to escape torture or capital punishment.[13] As for his sodomy, Negri affirmed that he could

<hr/>

13. Lisa Roscioni, *Il governo della follia. Ospedali, medici e pazzi nell'età moderna* (Milan: Mondadori, 2003), 183–91. For the feigned madness of Tommaso Campanella, see Luigi Firpo, *I processi di Tommaso Campanella*, ed. Eugenio Canone (Rome: Salerno Editore, 1998); Germana Ernst, *Tommaso Campanella. Il libro e il corpo della natura* (Rome: Laterza, 2002).

not refrain from it, and "even though I had heard from the confessors that such things were a sin, still this [teaching] could never enter my heart."[14] The peasant musician, "rude and ignorant," as the advocate for defendants defined him in his brief, got little grace from the tribunal: he was put in jail and, after a *de formali* abjuration, was condemned to five years in the galleys. The judges also went out of their way to reprove the advocate for the defendant for having sustained the proposition that "pollution procured by one's own hands is not a heretical proposition, is not a sin, but is just an error." This last was a dangerous doctrine, a sign of moral laxity that could undermine surveillance of adolescent behavior, not only in the family but also at places where future priests were trained.

The papers of the Inquisition also show extraordinary attention to "inappropriate" sexual behavior within marriage. Persuaded by their confessors to approach the Holy Office, many women declared that they had been forced by their husbands to practice sodomy. To excuse themselves, however, they claimed that they were convinced "that it was a great sin" and that they had tried in every way to persuade their stubborn husbands of the fact, but had given in under the threat of blows or the knife. The inquisitors' caution was clear. These could be accusations motivated by the desire to break intolerable bonds, to break matrimonial chains marked by daily violence. They could also be the fruit of hatred and private enmity, of domestic vendetta. Unspeakable acts were denounced in Rome, in 1725, by Grazia Pugliese, age nineteen, washerwoman, against her husband, Paolo Corni, a mounted escort of Duke Caffarelli, a Roman nobleman. The husband was accused of "heretical dogma." He had abused her repeatedly, with the argument that "unspeakable acts between a husband and his wife are not sins."[15] It had been the neighbors who pushed the wife to the Inquisition, and before the court the bad reputation of the husband—a violent, blasphemous adulterer—seemed to support her case. The inquisitor inquired into her "bad credulity in the past" and in the present, but above all into the violence that might have impelled the woman to denounce her husband. When the confessor had confirmed that such practices were "a very grave sin," she had tried, she said, to convince her husband, but

14. ACDF, S.O., St. St., M 5-p (Ferrara, 1755).
15. ACDF, S.O., St. St., M 5-p (Rome, 1725).

he remained silent, but afterwards he treated me harshly a thousand ways, cudgeling me and insulting me and stopping bringing me food. When I told some persons what happened to me they told me to come to this tribunal.[16]

This denunciation seems sustained by a collective consensus that wished to liberate the young wife from the violence of a man of ill repute, disliked by others as well. The tribunal appears as the sole instrument available; with its power it was sure to provide the relief that community and kinfolk had first striven to achieve by their own efforts. Nevertheless, from the congregation no immediate condemnation emerged. The man and his behavior were put under observation, as were his daily life, his relations with his milieu, and his enmities.

When *vicari* in the distant towns received denunciations from women obliged by confessors to unmask the "unspeakable things" perpetrated by stubbornly abusive husbands, they were not always zealous. The court's caution, skepticism, and continual referrals back could dishearten even the most tenacious wives. So victims might appeal straight to Rome, to the Holy Office itself, to assure a hearing and obtain at last that hoped-for justice, or at least a little protection.

That is what happened to twenty-two-year-old Rosa Bassi from Palombara, in the Sabine Mountains north of Tivoli, who approached the Inquisition in May of 1729.[17] The path offered hope, but shame as well. Going to the law was a rebellion in the eyes of kin and community, but a wife was buoyed by her man's bad repute. It was often true that the denunciations of harassed wives were justified and corroborated by the bad public reputations of their consorts. Usually, after the congregation's decree, the man was put under watch. But how often did such decisions really quell the violence?

And then there were the men who, to legitimize practices "against nature," in the face of female ingenuousness and ignorance maintained that "marriage is like that."[18] It was sometimes a device for contraception, as mothers, friends, confessors, and inquisitors alerted by marriages that produced too few children sometimes suspect-

16. ACDF, S.O., St. St., M 5-p (Rome, 1725).
17. ACDF, S.O., St. St., M 5-p (Rome, 1722).
18. ACDF, S.O., St. St., M 5-p (Rome, 1722).

ed. The "malice of men" grasped for any means to duck ecclesiastical censure, constraining the wife to keep switching confessors, or attributing to imaginary clerics legitimation for what they imposed upon their wives, or locking the woman up at home and browbeating her into silence with repeated threats.[19] That is what happened to Cecilia Dorotea, married for four years to the gilder Giulio Maccari. In 1688 the woman's mother, Elisabetta Troiani, denounced to the Holy Office "the bad inclination of this man." Elisabetta had already gone to the cardinal *vicario*, who had jailed the husband; she then decided to proceed against her son-in-law by going straight to the Inquisition.[20] Conjugal life was under the attentive eyes of city courts, a tight net of them in Rome, but it was also sustained by the equally attentive vigilance of family, neighborhood, and street.

19. On this theme see Raul Merzario, *Anastasia, ovvero la malizia degli uomini. Relazioni sociali e controllo delle nascite in un villaggio ticinese* (Rome: Laterza, 1992).

20. ACDF, S.O., St. St., M 5-p (Rome 1688).

9

Disciplining the Clergy

A few nights ago [Monsignore] brought with him from Rapolano some young Sienese—two young women who have their mother in Siena, and put the younger one in a nunnery of the city. The other young woman is a widow and they say that it is certain that she is pregnant by Monsignore.

With these words, on 4 February 1568, Siena's captain of justice furnished a short but telling notice of a suspected abduction said to have been perpetrated by Cardinal Ippolito Del Monte, the dissolute adoptive nephew of Julius III (1550–1555).[1] A few decades later, would such carryings-on be a mere memory, a relic of a scandalous past? Did such behavior grow less conspicuous, better hidden, and usually relegated to marginal zones in the country or up in the mountains? Certainly, as we have seen already, via a few examples, control by the judicial apparatus, both of state and of church, differed markedly between center and periphery, and city and country. Even on Rome's own outskirts—in the deserted lands of the Campagna Romana and on the slopes of nearby hills and mountains—the care of souls, even in the seventeenth and eighteenth centuries, still rested in hands of men who fell far short of the Council of Trent's ideals. The Roman curia recognized the gravity of the problems of clerical immorality and ignorance. Popes like Paul IV and Pius V intervened, sometimes very harshly, against delinquent clerics, especially those tarred with sodomy, simony (purchase of office), and concubinage.[2] The faithful, however, viewed such irregular behavior, some of it downright criminal, in a different, less censorious light.[3] For the Roman congregation, ecclesiastical crime and scandalous behavior compromised the campaign to bring harmony to communal life and disturbed the regulated oversight of individual and collective life entrusted to the par-

1. See Pietro Messina, "Del Monte Ippolito," in *Dizionario Biografico degli Italiani*, vol. 38, 138–41 (Rome: Istituto dell'Enciclopedia Italiana, 1990).

2. *Bullarum diplomatum et privilegiorum Sanctorum Romanorum Pontificum Taurinensis Editio*, vol. 7 (Turin: Dalmazzo, 1862), 702–03, 734.

3. See Oskar Di Simplicio, *Storia di un Anticristo. Avidità, amore e morte nella Toscana medicea* (Siena: Il Leccio, 1996).

ish priest. The control of clergy drew on much of the energy of the Roman congregations, bishops, and religious orders, and, despite frictions, pulled lay and ecclesiastical justice into joint action.[4]

From the end of the 1500s, and through the whole seventeenth century, the Holy Office intervened firmly to police deviant behavior among regular and secular clergy. But in this campaign of extirpation—of un-Tridentine moral conduct, of piety tinged with superstition and magic, of ignorance of dogma that prompted well-deserved suspicion of heresy—the Holy Office did not act alone. The many congregations founded or reformed in 1588 by Sixtus V aimed to make the whole clergy more adept at spiritual governance. But, for the pope's own territories, that also meant making them more adroit at temporal rule, at *buon governo*. Training for a church career helped make them "ministers" who were fit to be sent to the assorted parts of the state as worthy spokesmen for Rome, to forge consensus at the edges. Tribunals, whether "lay" (but full of clergy) or ecclesiastical, focused their energies on correcting, punishing, and educating a clergy destined, in the pope's own state, for rule over more than souls alone.

"WITH GRAVE SCANDAL TO THE PEOPLE"

A scan of the decrees and surviving trial papers shows beyond all doubt how the conduct of the clergy, and especially of some religious orders, like the Capuchins, lay at the heart of Holy Office concerns, in the Papal State and all Italy. Though the capital itself did not lack its sad spectacles of clerical immorality or undisciplined monastic houses, and it had no shortage of reports of everyday disorder by secular and regular churchmen, Rome was easier to control. The provinces, on the other hand, the countryside, the marginal zones, seemed from the outset far more troublesome. Nevertheless, the wave of banditry that at the sixteenth century's end set many regions on their ear, actually created favorable conditions for disciplining a clergy often accused of abetting and succoring outlaws. So it was not rare to see village monks and priests or country mendicant clergy charged with "receiving and consorting with banished men." These charges then would bring the accused before the Holy Office, where, often, they were also tried for assorted other crimes. So, for instance,

4. On the discipline of clergy, see Wietse De Boer, *The Conquest of the Soul: Confession, Discipline, and Public Order in Counter-Reformation Milan* (Leiden: Brill, 2001).

Fra' Felice from Mogliano, in the diocese of Fermo, was brought to the Holy Office for having preached, "and for shamelessly having dared [cite] those words of Saint Paul," that Christ, having risen up to Heaven, "would have taken a fantastical form, without giving any other explanation." But, mainly, as was noted in a letter to the cardinals of the congregation, he had been jailed as "very much a backer of banished men, and . . . indeed he has been exiled from the state of Our Lord [the pope] without having had any penance at all."[5]

Banditry was not the only problem. The parish priest Angelo Nardino di Capradosso was jailed in 1592 for "reception and company of banished men," but when his house was searched, in the holy oil jars were found "a piece of burnt bone, two pieces of white stone that they say are magnets, and a little stone wrapped up in a piece of paper, and one does not know what it is. In the pouch were diverse keys, wrapped up, and iron hooks for locks." Interrogated, Nardino denied knowing the nature and function of these finds, so, perplexed, the bishop of Ascoli, the Dominican Girolamo Berneri, wrote the bishop of Cervia, Alfonso Visconti, congregation member, for instructions on how to proceed with the priest.[6]

Letters to the Roman congregation most often concerned members of the religious orders. In 1610 from Anguillara, just north of Rome, came a denunciation of the local Observant Franciscans, who "give people the water that washed their feet, and say that it is good for curing animals of disease."[7] Bishops' letters abound with calls to the faithful to denounce scandalous churchmen. Members of the mendicant orders, thought bishops, could be vectors of discontent that could degenerate, disturb order, and undercut the friars' own reputation and the authority they stood for. But the bishops acted cautiously, and sometimes far too slowly. At other times, as we have seen, the congregation's inquests were set off by denunciations by judges, governors, or local officials: clerical delinquency and scandalous living was always seen by laity as an element of disorder. But all this outcry did not lead straightaway to generalized moralization or to conformity with the Council of Trent's directives and ideals. There remained profound differences, above all in the countryside, in rural monasteries and parishes. Rome strove in vain to overcome them.

---

5. ACDF, S.O., St. St., DD1-e, f. 25r. 6. ACDF, S.O., St. St., DD1-e, f. 41r.
7. ACDF, S.O., St. St., DD1-e, f. 41v.

The Holy Office was not the only body to concern itself with the shabby morality of clergy. The "criminal, very bad life, with grave scandal to the people" conducted by some priest or other might prod a town's representatives to go straight to authorities at the center, in Rome, so different from the diocesan bishop, who to local eyes seemed either hand in glove with the rascals, or incapable of brisk steps to dump bad apples once and for all. A case, at the sixteenth century's end, troubled Trevignano, a lakeside fishing village under the feudal jurisdiction of Virginio Orsini, lord of Bracciano. The parish priest, Antonio Benedetto Antino, perpetrator of diverse crimes, had already been condemned, in 1596, by Orazio Moroni, bishop of Sutri and Nepi, towns a few miles north. The punishments in no way redeemed the man, who, returning to Trevignano, once more sowed scandal. In 1598, Duke Virginio Orsini, bypassing his own feudal courts, let the priors of his village turn directly to the tribunal of the governor of Rome, "as he [the parish priest] is not subject to the tribunal of his Excellency, as he is a cleric." So the priors drew up a detailed memorandum for the governor, cataloguing Antonio's "bad, and execrable life." The delinquent cleric

on account of his enormous crimes has been tried several times by the *vicario* of the bishop of Sutri at the instance of persons of the town [Trevignano]. And he has never been punished because he has always kept the *vicari* his friends, with gifts and blandishments. In the end, the community, unable to support his very bad living, had recourse to Rome and succeeded in arranging for a commissary to go to Trevignano against the cleric, against whom many legal complaints were brought, especially about an abortion, brigandage, impeding marriages, and other scandals.

A woman accomplice in his crimes was jailed in Sutri, and then, "via a little torture, was freed," while the cleric himself was in theory to have been confined to Rome, and obliged to serve at the hospitals of the Lateran and the Consolazione. But Antonio never did this duty, for, as the priors noted,

he has always been in Trevignano where, worse than ever, he has had, and now has, an immoral, and very bad life, with grave scandal to the people, continually having brawls first with one and then with another, and committing thefts, and beating in public women who refuse to consent to his desires.[8]

8. ASR, Tribunale Criminale del Governatore, Processi (16 secolo), busta 309, ff. 852r–914r.

Father Antonio had also filched the revenues of the charities and bawled out Orsini's own men. Virginio Orsini himself, perhaps lest he compromise his own image, and fearing accusations of complicity, let the community turn to the governor of Rome. It was a significant act; it aligned the Roman baron with the moralizing actions of Clement VIII, a pope keen to repress transgressive behavior by nobles, as shown by the famous affairs of Beatrice Cenci and Troilo Savelli, both executed for crimes despite their high station. And Clement was also eager to keep a closer eye on communities and lands in feudal hands. But, as at Trevignano, synergy between papal and baronial interests could help make good the drawbacks of shaky episcopal power, too tied to the landscape, where lay and ecclesiastical jurists, corrupt or inept, were far from Trent's ideals.

CLERICAL CRIMES OF SEXUAL PASSION

It was a delicate matter, investigated cautiously but harshly punished, when clergy were accused, or just suspected, of "attempted sodomy with many boys." In court papers, the Inquisition's or others', clerics secular or regular were far from rare among those charged with "unspeakable crimes" and sexual abuse. Their presence bears witness to the conundrums of clerical discipline, to which the post-Tridentine church directed strenuous efforts. The church, in the end, would disappoint its flocks' expectations of two figures crucial for good social order: the parish priest, and the schoolmaster who taught the local children. In the early modern centuries, popular attitudes toward illicit behavior by churchmen varied, according to time and place and, of course, to the gravity of the acts. Unfortunately for historians, the manuscript record of trials before the Roman congregation is summary and fairly short, running only from the late seventeenth century to the early eighteenth. As a consequence, the surviving papers cannot support any argument that such crimes were at that time more or less often denounced or prosecuted than in the past. The lack of uniformity of the Holy Office archive—it is fragmentary, thanks to the papers' own tempestuous history—makes conclusions perilous, as, indeed, does the very nature of criminal court records. We should guard against careless modernization, or simplification, of the problem. The church, in confronting its own sexual morality, had to keep in mind the living conditions—the material, intellectual, and spiritual poverty—

of many men who took up a church career. Certainly, the denunciations, trials, and other papers left by agencies of justice give no
grounds for arguing that such crimes, any more than any others, set
the whole tone of the religious orders and secular clergy. Moreover,
such behavior clearly was not limited to the clergy alone.

Moreover, the tribunal's chief intent was to extirpate deviations
from orthodoxy, still unchecked in many dioceses, in a clergy still
far from the Tridentine ideal. Deviations from doctrine surfaced in
striking, scandalous fashion when clergy allegedly justified as licit their abusive and illicit sexual acts. If the accusations can be believed, these assertions made for a dangerous double pollution, of
both actions and of dogma. Vices could escape the bounds of monastery and parish, if touted and defended as "non-sins" by their authors, who, with impunity, flaunted their disregard for the disciplined morality wished by Rome. So, it was for heretical assertions
that the inquisitor condemned Angelo Maria Sangiorgi, a Calced
Carmelite and prior of his order's house at Lugo, in Romagna. The
inquisitor of Faenza, a nearby town, accused him of false dogma
for maintaining that his acts "were not any sin at all . . . and that
such things we need not confess."[9] The same thing happened to a
priest unworthy of his parish, in another part of the Papal State. In
1739 the bishop of Albano, south of Rome, received a denunciation
from Caterina and Cecilia, both thirteen, orphans in Nettuno, and
housemaids for the priest Tommaso Rota. He had abused them repeatedly. The charge was defloration "with heretical dogma" (cum
dogma hereticali). He had told them, says the trial, reinterpreting
a less philosophical conversation alleged in adolescent words now
lost, "that immoral dealings [le cose dishoneste] between men and
women should not be forbidden, because they are in harmony with
nature."[10]

Sometimes the tribunal stepped in early, to prevent such crimes,
lest the sacrality and honor of parishes and monasteries be harmed.
At Perugia, in 1691, the court undertook to verify two adolescents'
denunciations "of sodomitic touching" launched against a priest of
Gubbio, Filippo Costa. In this case, the assertions of the priest, said
to have argued for the sinlessness of his actions, helped propel the
trial. Though the consultori, to prove the priest's heretical ideas on

9. ACDF, S.O., St. St., M 5-p (Faenza, 1726).
10. ACDF, S.O., St. St.. M 5-p (Albano, 1739).

the subject, decided to subject him to "light" torture, the priest ma-
neuvered to duck the ordeal. His petition was accepted. In his plea,
he presented himself as "an old man of sixty years, ill with gout in
feet and hands, and subject to many infirmities, particularly with
paralysis." Having escaped torture, he answered correctly ("Catholi-
cally") the judges' questions designed to probe his orthodoxy. Nevertheless, threatened again with torture arranged by the *consultori*,
he was forced to confess to the charges and sentenced to five years
in prison.[11]

It was also young persons who denounced Carmelites at the
monastery of the Blessed Virgin Mary of Macerata, where they had
once studied and played. But their charges of sodomy also brought
to light other things. The prior of the house, Alberto Zanetti, was
said to have insulted the pope repeatedly before the confraternity
brothers—"bugger of a pope" (*papa buzarone*, an expression with
a double sense, literal or just dismissive, much like that in modern
English) were the alleged words. He had also, said the charges, be-
moaned the liturgy's excessive length, good only for filling booksellers' pockets ("these friars have made these long parts and these
additions just to give profits to the booksellers, and every day they
keep adding to these *buzorate* [knaveries]." Moreover he had tak-
en no pains to hide his impatience with monastic discipline, and
asserted that a man's only amusement was to dedicate himself to,
in the court's words, unspeakable practices. These accusations were
grave, but hardly proven. As often, the summary of the trial re-
ferred to law texts that urged circumspection and called for certain
proofs, "conclusive ones, especially when treating of persons of religion, who have in their favor a presumption against crime."[12] The
defense argued that the young witnesses "might be presumed to
have been suborned and seduced." Nevertheless, the tribunal came
down hard, condemning prior Alberto and two other brothers to
seven years in prison, without hope of a pardon or reduction of the
sentence (*absque spe gratiae*, without hope of grace).

As we have seen here, the Inquisition was rigid in prosecuting
sexual crimes, but its attention and sentences were designed to punish heresy more than sex. The tribunal strove to forestall the scandal
that could arise from culprits' affirmations to their victims, lest they

11. ACDF, S.O., St. St., M 5-p (Perugia and Gubbio, 1691).
12. ACDF, S.O., St. St., M 5-p (Ancona and Ferrara, 1722).

be communicated to others and broadcast beyond church premises. It was thus opportune, at Rome, to mount spectacular public abjurations—formal retractions of error. "That way they will all be mortified and punished for the enormity of their misdeeds, and likewise they can serve as an example, and to inspire fear in the others." That is just what happened on 24 June 1648, at Rome's chief Dominican church, Santa Maria sopra Minerva, where some nuns and friars from the diocese of Faenza abjured. They had been seduced by the "impious and pestiferous doctrine" of the priest Giovanni Battista Violano of Faenza, who, as the prosecutor phrased it, was said to have argued "that kisses and immoral touching under pretext of spirituality were not sins."[13]

SPEAKING WITH PRUDENCE

Unreflecting or erroneous declarations from the mouths of ecclesiastics, too frank to pardon on grounds of ignorance, frivolity, or light error of faith, and the Inquisition's anxiously rigid response turn up again in events at Pesaro in 1691. Cristina Giunti, age thirty-five, a wife exasperated by her husband's continual betrayals and violent abuse, turned to Alessandro Avio, the local bishop, requesting separation "of board and bed" (quoad thorum et mensam), as, in such cases, canon law provided.[14] Marital trials were long and contentious; one job of a bishop was to try to make peace between the spouses to avoid the separation. Summoning the woman to Pesaro's cathedral, the prelate made light of the husband's adulteries, affirming before witnesses: "It is nothing. . . . I don't want you instructing me what is a sin and what is not a sin." Shocked and embittered, the woman turned to her own confessor, who urged her to denounce the bishop to the inquisitor. But she found the inquisitor slow to act. The vicario of the Holy Office even tried to dissuade her and justified the bishop's utterances, saying that to his mind they should be interpreted "as well-meaning" (in buon senso). Here, the collaboration between confessor and inquisitor, which usually made for efficacious surveillance of orthodoxy and good church practices, bogged down when they faced the bishop, given the harm

13. ACDF, S.O., St. St., M 4-l (Roma 1648).

14. On separation and divorce, see Silvana Seidel Menchi and Diego Quaglioni, eds., Coniugi nemici. La separazione in Italia dal XII al XVIII secolo (Bologna: il Mulino, 2000).

an accusation might do his person and his office. So Cristina Giunti's future, and her unhappy marriage, were in the clutches of Pesaro's delicate power relations and of social and political connivances that foiled her action.

The woman, daughter of a civil solicitor (*procuratore*) in the city, chagrined by the uncertainty and the roadblocks, decided to carry the case forward on her own. In a firm, sure hand, she drew up a petition describing her husband's excesses and stressing her disappointment with the words of the bishop, according to whom "adultery was nothing and it has become familiar." The Inquisition's *vicario* sent the Roman congregation a detailed memorandum, presenting the petitioner as "a virtuous, retiring woman" of good reputation, and married to a man who had always "conducted a relaxed life in matters of the senses." The *vicario* stressed the bishop's words, and also noted the woman's rejoinder, to the effect "that it [adultery] came about because of the indulgence of the authorities, who let such crimes go unpunished; if you punished one, many would reform their behavior."[15] The woman's accusation was pointed. It expressed her deep disillusionment with justice, and in particular ecclesiastical justice, which, according to canon law, was in theory "essentially egalitarian when it came to the adultery of the husband and of the wife."[16] She did not conceal her disappointment in the bishop, who had derided her before so many witnesses, wounding her pride, she claimed, and her reputation, already sorely taxed by the immoral conduct of a violent and criminal husband. At Rome, the congregation decided to entrust to the bishop of Fano, Taddeo Luigi dal Verme, an inquest into both the facts of the case and the moral character (*qualità*) of the persons involved. This investigation then proceeded with the greatest secrecy and discretion. It found against what it saw as the uncontestable errors and superficial conduct of the bishop, who, at the express wishes of the pope, was then constrained to eat his words before the witnesses who had heard them. He also had to swallow the inquisitor's admonition: in the future, he should speak more prudently (*magis considerate loquatur*).

15. ACDF, S.O., St. St., M-p (Pesaro, 1691).

16. Andrea Marchisello, "'Alieni thori violatio': l'adulterio come delitto carnale in Prospero Farinacci (1544–1618)," in Silvana Seidel Menchi and Diego Quaglioni, eds., *Trasgressioni: seduzione, concubinato, adulterio, bigamia (XIV–XVIII secolo)* (Bologna: il Mulino, 2004), 153.

Note how, in the pope's domains, when disciplining the clergy and controlling their morality, intellectual training, and orthodoxy, the Inquisition did not at all confine itself to sexual deviance.

NUNNERIES AND MONASTERIES

The control of nunneries and monasteries not only regulated the internal spiritual life of the religious who lived there; it also looked to public order, to keep an eye on the evolving close relations between these holy places and their surrounding world. Religious houses were meeting places between the inmates, both the nuns themselves and the girls schooled there, and their families. Despite Trent's decrees mandating confinement and seclusion, convents remained places of intense sociability, especially those that housed daughters of aristocratic families, but also the humbler houses that sheltered girls forced into the monastic life by poverty. These houses too remained an important pole for family life and for the whole community, who resorted to them for social contacts, services, and prayers.

One also went to the monastery to make confession, and, in the seventeenth and eighteenth centuries, there were still many denunciations of confessors who solicited "foul deeds" (turpia) from women who came to them. In 1639, Lucia Stefanelli complained to the vicario of the Holy Office of Rimini how,

when I went to confess, along with Maria Giorgetti, a married woman [that last expression, inserted above the line, would be crucial to the denunciation], to Santa Maria at Fano, to Fra' Ludovico, Observant Franciscan, whose last name and home town I do not know, after the confession the friar began to say dirty words to her [Maria]. Among other things, [he said], "If you came to my room I would kiss you, you would touch me and I would touch you." And he urged her not to say anything [about it].[17]

The vicario wrote a detailed report to Cardinal Francesco Barberini, secretary of the congregation; he sought clear instructions. The two women who lodged the claim were, he said, "of seamless reputation." Moreover, further evidence had now come from other women, hitherto cowed to silence because anxious for their moral reputations, but, rallying, they had now revealed Fra' Ludovico's

17. BAV, MF 25 (Ms 1248), f. 191r.

persistent solicitations. He had argued, the reports alleged, that sexual favors, "one time only, to one person, are no sin."[18]

The denunciation of confessors' abuses, and of their inadequacy to the fundamental task they owed Catholic doctrine, was no new thing. In the Papal State as elsewhere, the congregation's efforts sometimes seemed in vain, so difficult was surveillance.[19] In this Fano case, as in many others denounced to the Holy Office, the incriminated confessor more resembled a character from some Boccaccio story than the image of a disciplined clergyman sculpted by the reforming zeal of activist churchmen like Borromeo or Paleotti. The inquisitorial panorama was still peopled, even into the seventeenth and eighteenth centuries, by figures like Fra' Ludovico, utterly impervious to Tridentine discipline.

In 1638 Rome received the précis of a trial against Fra' Francesco Maria Morigi of Ravenna. His dossier contained originals of compromising documents, including his letters to a nun from Carpi,

all amorous, as is the custom from a lover to a lover, with the usual terms that a lover uses. In one of them one sees that the friar tried to persuade the nun to let him go to her at the third hour of the night, but she answered that it was not possible, for, when the Ave Maria [evening bell] rings they lock the doors of the nunnery with two keys. One of which, the one for entry, the Abbess keeps, and the other, the one to go out, the manager keeps.

But the story did not finish there. The deplorable reputation of the friar was widely known. His amorous relations with the nun, and perhaps with other women, said the report, were an object of local scorn. Moreover, in the gossip, Fra' Francesco was also accused of sodomy. The currency of this last rumor was easily demonstrated by the obscene poem that Giacomo da Lodi, *vicario* of Rimini's Inquisition, diligently filed with the other trial papers.[20]

The Inquisition faced other troubles in Rimini. In 1634, the *vicario* sent in a file denouncing the jailbreak of a Fra' Francesco, an Observant Franciscan who had been accused, with some accomplices, of posing as a holy treasure finder. In his report, the *vicario* also complained, probably self-servingly, that he found the Rimini office in bad working order. If things were working badly, he implied, the fault was hardly his.

18. BAV, MF 25 (Ms 1248), v. 198r.   19. De Boer, *Conquest of the Soul*, 27–31.
20. BAV, MF 25 (Ms 1248), f. 209r.

In the chancery here are some trials which were begun and not finished by my predecessor, and I cannot tell if he has written and sent the summaries to the Sacred Congregation; for this reason I do not dare put my hand to them and prosecute them.[21]

One wrote to Rome for instruction and counsel, and, ceaselessly requested, in return, good order, punctuality, and precision in filing all the paperwork. Time passed, trials dragged on, and confused procedures did little to help settle arguments, nor did they help burnish the image of justice and its executors. The continual flow of papers reveals the congregation's centralizing impulse, and its desire to control, to impose consistency, and to make decisions stick. But the correspondence is also a mark of how procedures dragged, and of the how hard it was to master the machinery and to patch, in that wide net cast over the world, the gaping holes that often frustrated Rome's severe instructions.

There was attentive investigation of the morality in nunneries; the inquisitors vetted friendships that might veer toward impure acts. But, as with sodomy, in these matters investigations moved very gingerly, in case accusations perhaps sprang from ill will, rancor, and all the jealousies that the enclosing walls of convents both compressed and amplified. A girl might denounce herself, and then drag in other pupils, alleging that they had said that "immoral touching was not a sin," because, according to her story, a confessor had told them so.[22] If, in the long interrogations, the young women gave "Catholic" answers and emitted no whiff of heresy, such investigations usually ended up just imposing penances and placing the girls under observation. Usually, in fact, there was no trace at all of heretical ideas. Rather, what emerged was widespread ignorance. Costante Alessandrelli, *vicario* of Gubbio, summed up in his own learned words, as if quoting her, what he had been told concerning convent sexuality from a senior nun at San Luca, at Fabriano: "I neither know nor have heard what the Holy Mother Church teaches about this, nor the law of nature."[23]

The control of religious orders did not confine itself to the hard job of making individual deviants moral. It also investigated suspect devotional practices that spread readily inside the nunnery

21. BAV, MF 25 (Ms 1248), f. 295r.
22. ACDF, S.O., St. St., M-p, f. 508r–v (Gubbio, 1738).
23. ACDF, S.O., St. St. M-p, f. 508v.

walls, among faithful who were both devout and ignorant. Female houses received particular attention, both at Rome and in the provinces. Because Trent had not shattered the old ties between a nunnery and its city, at the behest of nuns' kin and friends there survived the traditional free-lance pragmatic, applied religion. It was now suspect, to the Inquisition's eye, whenever it was unofficial; prayers, love potions, and natural medicines against the ills of men and beasts sallied ceaselessly from convents, spreading the fame of nun-healers. The inquisition's *vicari* investigated them with scant success.

Sometimes ties between families and their own nuns proved dangerous to both. Kinfolk themselves in 1706 denounced Suor Orsola of Carpineto, for telling them that she had "two friars who had their hands on her head, and these were the most holy Madonna with all the saints of Paradise, and that this Orsola was one step lower than the most blessed Virgin." When members of her own family called her hardly "prudent" for saying such brazen things, she was said to have lashed out, claiming that she had at her beck and call roughnecks who could fend off any enemies. The recklessness of the nun put her whole family in danger and threatened the monastic house too. Orsola's holy megalomania looks mentally unbalanced, but perhaps it was just the repressed self-assertion of a woman shut away too young.

THREE VERY CREDULOUS YOUNG NUNS

The bad reputation of early modern monastic life has been softened or disproved by recent research which has corrected the stereotype harkening back to Sister Gertrude, the semi-fictitious unwilling and catastrophic "Nun of Monza" in Manzoni's famous novel *The Betrothed*.[24] Still, especially in the hinterland, even into the eighteenth century there were frequent inquests, often long-running, into the moral deviance and bizarre behavior of enclosed nuns who

---

24. For the vast and recent literature on nuns, see, for example, Gabriella Zarri and Gianna Pomata, eds., *I monasteri femminili come centri di cultura fra Rinascimento e Barocco* (Rome: Edizioni di Storia e Letteratura, 2005); Gabriella Zarri, *Recinti. Donne, clausura e matrimonio nella prima età moderna* (Bologna: il Mulino, 2000); Mary Laven, *Virgins of Venice: Enclosed Lives and Broken Vows in the Renaissance Convent* (London: Viking, 2002); Renée Baernstein, *A Convent Tale: A Century of Sisterhood in Spanish Milan* (London: Routledge, 2002); Moshe Sluhovsky, "The Devil in the Convent," *American Historical Review* 107 (2002): 1379–1411.

had been denounced by their confessors. The *omertà* of the other nuns and the house's fear of any scandal and bad reputation that might hurt recruitment trammeled the inquiries. The inquests usually ended with only penances for the nuns involved. The officials called in on such cases seem often to have understood the unhappiness that could arise in young girls, deprived of their families' affection and support, who had often been placed in monastic life too young, and unwilling. That is what happened, in 1706, in the Sabina hills northeast of Rome.

Eugenio Fanelli, confessor to the convent of Rocca Antica, a small Sabina town, as was normal practice for clergy in such affairs, had gone to the congregation for permission to investigate three nuns who

had agreed against their will to live in the convent and for that reason had desired to obtain the secret [device] to [let them] go out, while invisible. And they therefore forged a relationship with Lorenzo Gherardi, son of the administrator of these nuns, to get him to go talk to a sorcerer.

The nuns had refrained from making the sign of the cross "and from any other good Christian act" in anticipation of the sorcerer, who they hoped would furnish them with the secret for leaving the convent. They intended "by diabolical art to seem dead, to fly like the angels, and to have a ring with a spirit who could be compelled to kill all the other nuns."[25] All three eventually repented and confessed. From Rome the officials urged "diligence and caution." Eugenio Fanelli was up to handling the situation: a member of the Mercedarian Order for the Redemption of Slaves he knew how to confront complicated situations adroitly. He informed the Inquisition in detail, answering Cardinal Gaspare Carpegna, who had first sent him the warrant to conduct the trial. Caution, indeed! He wrote, "If I had been able to repair it without a fuss and in accord with the convent's decorum . . . with the Mother Abbess kept informed," it would have been possible to avert useless scandals. It all, he said,

was done by three young maids who entered the said convent unwillingly, and even less willingly became nuns for lack of a real explorer of consciences who could get to the heart of their desires. And the young women, while they were not happy to be at the convent, looked for some person who could get them out of *clausura* while they were invisible, but

25. BAV, MF 26 (Ms 1251), ff. 140r–157v.

their shade would remain visible in the convent. This they sought also so as to go find their lovers.

Desperate, the girls had turned to their surrounding community. They sought out men, rather than women, perhaps because they trusted in the alleged male capacity to keep secrets better. But, perhaps playing a practical joke that exploited the girls' naiveté, the men found some young men and a young woman of this place, who were better at drying out the purses of the nuns than they were at using or discovering any diabolical art. Meanwhile, so far as I could learn, they [the girls' accomplices] are good Christians.[26]

Fanelli wrote that he knew of "other rascally things" done by the three young women. He promised to reveal all to the Roman congregation by word of mouth, but wanted the whole case resolved with penances, with a minimum of fuss, not to compromise the nunnery in local eyes. He had sought the help of a physician in Rocca Antica, who had found the girls "ill with a running fever, especially Suor Giacinta, who suffers a distillation of the head in the spiritual parts that threatens her with imminent ruin." Moreover the other two, Suor Aurora and Suor Agata, turned out to be suffering such bad tertian fevers (malaria) that they ran the risk of dying.

While, at Rome, officials granted formal permission to set up the trial, the nuns penned in wobbly hand remorseful letters to their confessor, who had understood their story. Sister Giacinta Miconi, age twenty-two, wrote begging for "pity, mercy, charity, Most Eminent, do not abandon us, or deny the pardon and the grace requested, since I have repented of what I did." Her two "delinquent" companions joined her petition. The confessor received permission from Rome to hold the whole trial inside the convent, even though the "crimes" were known in the village and elsewhere. Fanelli wrote, indeed, that he had made all three girls abjure, in the presence of the vicar abbess and one older, discreet nun. They were given heavy penances. For three years the young women were to converse with no one, but only to answer, if spoken to, "may Jesus Christ be praised," and for two years they were to steer clear of the windows and grates to the world outside. They were required to follow a rigid routine of private discipline, and on Fridays with bared heads they were to recite the penitential *Miserere* with the other nuns. They were no

26. BAV, MF 26 (Ms 1251), ff. 155r–156v.

longer to have adjoining cells. Isolation and silence modeled the inquisitors' decision, for had the confessor not fingered as the root of this disorder ready communication, thanks to "the easy access that they had to the windows, the grates, the wheel [for passing messages through *clausura*'s wall], and the continual conversations, as well as the frequent traffic among them"?[27]

The Council of Trent had imposed *clausura*, the closing of windows, the raising of perimeter walls to segregate the nunneries and to block their contacts with the profane world—with the city and the street, but also with families and with feelings—ties that permitted nuns to live less desperately their often involuntary enclosure. From the end of the sixteenth century, zealous apostolic visitors had inspected the sees of half of Italy to see the new rules applied. More than a few other cases besides this one make clear that, even in the eighteenth century, this effort remained only partly successful.

RUMORS OF AN EXTRAVAGANT PLOT

From the late sixteenth century on, in all the inquisitorial inquests in the Papal State, there ran a fear that strange materials found in suspects' houses might be traces of diabolical practices used to harm one's neighbors, to undermine proper sexual conduct, or to cause sterility, kill animals, and blast the harvest. The question of heretical ideas rarely arose. On the other hand, heresy became an issue when churchmen interpreted the Scriptures too liberally, or when hardened blasphemers outraged religion. Moreover, whenever superstitions and magical practices targeted the pontiff and his household, or some cardinal, fear spurred inquisitors and bishops to harsher investigation. In the seventeenth century, especially when a crisis was afoot and politics grew tense, fear of plots repeatedly shook both the pope and his court.[28]

On 13 February 1649, Gaspare Cecchinelli, bishop of Corneto (today Tarquinia), where in 1627 a penitence house for clerics sentenced to the galleys had risen, wrote to Secretary of State Giacomo

---

27. BAV, MF 26 (Ms 1251), f. 234r. On silence as a punishment, see Roberto Mancini, *I guardiani della voce: lo statuto della parola e il silenzio nell'Occidente medievale e moderno* (Rome: Carocci, 2002).

28. See "Congiure e complotti," special issue edited by Marina Caffiero and Maria Antonietta Visceglia, *Roma moderna e contemporanea* 11, nos. 1/2 (2003).

Panciroli. He denounced the discovery of "a machination against the persons of His Holiness, and Cardinal Vincenzo Domenico Macu-lano, and Donna Olimpia," this last the pope's powerful sister-in-law. This "machination" had been denounced by the clerical convicts at Corneto, perhaps due to internal rivalries, or perhaps because they feared worse punishment. The letter itself is sparse, but the sender suggested it be passed to canon Antonio Brunetti, "my confidant, for greater security." We do not know what Brunetti said; the lines by the bishop of Corneto betray a climate of fear and suspicion. Posted with the letter came an interrogation of a witness, the Monte Cassi-no monk Carlo Spinola, also a prisoner at Corneto, and a fat set of Spinola's notes. The monk's long deposition and the jumble of notes seemed to finger a fellow Genoese, a prisoner named Valerio Rivaro-la. The papers lay out a fantastical world, peopled by demons, mag-ic, and philters, over which Rivarola was said to rule, as if he were some monastic Prospero. The papers said that to his companion and denouncer Rivarola had "boasted that he could set an entire people murmuring, and he had done so in divers courts of princes where he has been. And he says that when he leaves prison he wants to turn all Italy topsy-turvy."[29] His grandiose undertakings and projects did not stop there: he allegedly claimed that

he had poisoned three whole monasteries of his order and that everybody died except two brothers. . . . However many magicians, astrologers, and heretics there are, he says that he knows them all and that he converses with them freely. He is friends with the first rank of banished men alive today; . . . all persons banished from the State of the Church are his ad-herents.

There were also accounts of his sexual exploits, usually with nuns. But his particular field of mastery was magic. He prepared phil-ters of every sort, "he recites spells, he makes medals, he writes on leaves of ivy, he makes rings with unknown names side by side": all told, his magical arts could deal with any calamity whatsoever and satisfy any desire. Alongside these proofs of a vast knowledge of magical practices and remedies, the informer denounced as a "curi-osity" some very compromising declarations.

He has also boasted . . . to have ridden demons in the form of horses, and to have flown on them through the air, into the most secret rooms, where

29. ACDF, S.O., St. St., UV 12, ff. 48r–55v.

he has chosen to desire to go, and by that means committed crimes of every sort.

Rivarola said he could make himself invisible, a thing better done by night than day; it was useful "to recite a spell, to be surrounded by a cloud that does not let him be seen by anybody."[30] These fantasies were less dangerous than the fellow's theology.

Rivarola had already been before the Inquisition. There he had met the Dominican cardinal Vincenzo Maculano, against whom he wanted revenge, by causing his death, along with that of Innocent X and of the powerful *"papessa"* Donna Olimpia. He had made figurines of his chosen victims, keeping them hidden under a tile; he had allegedly shown them to his compatriot Spinola, who then denounced him. Condemned by the Inquisition for his magical practices and superstitions, he was forbidden to keep the instruments of the trade. At Corneto, however, he had pressed on, delving deeper into studies in magic; "he works at formulating secret materials to cause birth to go awry [to miscarry or abort]." Recently, he had passed his "secret" to an Augustinian friar from Tolfa, near Corneto, and received "coin and a little wine as payment." But, said the denunciation, his outrages did not stop there:

He teaches secrets for success at gambling and against weapons, and has given them to some soldiers. He jokes about the faith. He interprets holy scripture in sinister ways. He consults false doctrine daily, and teaches it to foolish persons and to ministers of this prison. He denies the authority of the Supreme Pontiff, calling him Antichrist, and he calls the cardinals "glutton-priests-of-Jove" [*epuloni*] and ministers of Satan. He names the Holy Office The Friars' Cash Racket [*mangerie*] and calls it the most subtle invention for the pope to take sure and universal command over the world and to make himself a monarch. . . . He says that the Supreme Pontiff cannot be called a true Prince, but just a Tyrant. He says he wants to show Christian princes the vanity of the faith, [and of] obedience to the pope, and he wants to provoke them to make war on him to destroy him or at least to restrict him to the jurisdiction of the territory of Rome and no more.[31]

If his denouncer is to be believed, Rivarola denied the sacraments, marriage especially, and preached sexual freedom. His "heresy" was the very one imputed, almost a century earlier, to unruly,

---

30. ACDF, S.O., St. St., UV 12, ff. 48r–55v. Here, the citation is to f. 50r.
31. ACDF, S.O., St. St., UV 12, f. 52r.

scandalous nobles like Onorio Savelli and Niccolò Orsini. The times had changed. Now, the fear of a plot against the pope, his powerful sister-in-law, and other persons of the curia seemed more urgent than any fear of heresy, superstitious ideas, and magical practices. The bishop, having heard out all the testimony against Rivarola, spoke for the will of Innocent X. He ordered the rector of the Corneto prison to put the monk in a cell, set apart from the other prisoners, his feet and hands in irons, until the pope could ascertain whether the accusations were well founded, above all where they concerned the plot against him and his sister-in-law. Perhaps, though we have no evidence, Corneto's bishop saw through to Valerio Rivarola's true nature, just an unhinged fabulator.[32]

To authorities' eyes the Rivarola case, perhaps because it raised the possibility, however remote, of a plot against the pope and his family, seemed dangerous: it was far from the only case of an odd vision of the universe that the inquisitors would confront. In their interrogations, they often encountered extravagant cosmologies with no Creator, or worlds with no pope or priests or anything else whatsoever to trammel men's liberties—especially their sexual freedoms.

What happened, in the end, to these persons, sometimes just hapless, sometimes half-lunatic, when they stumbled into the net of the seventeenth- or eighteenth-century Inquisition? Not all, it seems, shared the dire fate of Menocchio, the famous miller from Friuli.[33] Were they perhaps condemned to galleys as blasphemers? The absence of documentation for the actual trials prohibits following each case out to the end. Still, one can hypothesize a different evaluation, and different punishment, of these crimes. True, there was no lack of example-setting executions; still, clearly, they became more rare, replaced by longer penal detention or other kinds of seclusion. That is what happened, more generally, in the

32. In 1706, in Rome, an abbot with the same last name, Filippo Rivarola, was put to death. He was accused of "having kept in his possession pasquinades [publicly posted satirical writings] directed against the pope, of having spoken scornfully against him, and of having negotiated with heretics to put Rome to the sack." For an account of his execution, see Alessandro Ademollo, *Le giustizie a Roma dal 1674 al 1739 e dal 1796 al 1840* (Rome: Forzani, 1881), 125–33.

33. Carlo Ginzburg, *The Cheese and the Worms: The Cosmos of a Sixteenth-Century Miller* (Baltimore: Johns Hopkins University Press, 1992; Turin: 1980); Andrea Del Col, *Domenico Scandella Known as Menocchio: His Trials before the Inquisition (1583–1599)* (Binghamton, N.Y.: Medieval and Renaissance Texts and Studies, 1996).

seventeenth century, in an effort to remove from society the mad, the idle, the poor, and the vagabond.[34]

TO SEPARATE DELINQUENT CLERGY: THE CORNETO PRISON WORKHOUSE

The frame for Valerio Rivarola's story, with his true or imagined plots, was the Ergastolo [Prison Workhouse] of Corneto. On 20 July 1627, at the wishes of Cardinal Francesco Barberini, the pope's nephew, was founded the "Pious House of Penitence of Corneto," better known as the Corneto Ergastolo, a place of confinement for delinquent clergy. Its mission was to reconcile the privileges and punishments of men marked by sometimes atrocious crimes but who were also consecrated clergymen. A sentence to the galleys exposed a man to "public scorn." Therefore, it seemed good to separate the churchmen from "the vile slaves" (ciurma) of the galleys and from other prisoners, while waiting to send them to the papal fleet. They might also be sentenced to an imprisonment called opus publicum (public work), milder than the galleys and more supple, although it still set men to work in chains, lest they escape. Most clerics who washed up at Corneto were destined to such forced labor.

The Pious House found its first lodgings in Corneto's Palazzo Vitelleschi. In 1640, it was remodeled completely as a jail with cells around a central courtyard. Religious duties, though limited, served to remind the convicts of their priestly condition, to which, having served the sentence, they would return. In fact, life inside the Pious House seems not to have been too solitary, nor was its inmates' behavior tightly controlled; our description of the movements and activities of Valerio Rivarola and his associates suggest as much. Contact with the world outside went on; it was continual, and even rich. But the majority of delinquent churchmen were excluded from this privileged place; they were confined in common prisons, with other convicts, or, if lucky, were jailed either in the houses of their own religious order, or at Rome in some other "pious house" assigned the task. Even decades after the foundation of the Corneto prison, there

34. Pieter Spierenburg, *The Prison Experience: Disciplinary Institutions and Their Inmates in Early Modern Europe* (New Brunswick, N.J.: Rutgers University Press, 1991); Lisa Roscioni, *Il governo della follia. Ospedali, medici e pazzi nell'età moderna.*(Milan: Mondadori, 2003), 117–213.

were still many petitions from priests jailed in Rome's looming New Prisons [Carceri Nuove], today a grim penitentiary museum by the Tiber. The petitioners asked to be released from their punishment, and "to be liberated from the inferno of the prison." It was, for anyone who had received the priesthood's indelible anointment, an even greater degradation than the Corneto workhouse.

The Civitavecchia galleys moored in the city's port were assigned, especially in the sixteenth and seventeenth centuries, to patrol the Italian coast against Turkish and North African piracy. To their benches trooped convicts condemned by all the tribunals of the Papal State: ecclesiastical, lay, and baronial. They arrived at Civita Castellana, not far inland, under armed escort. It was far from easy; the roads were hard, in winter almost impassible, and all year long coordination inevitably was slipshod. The governor's *bargello* and *birri* took charge of the condemned when they arrived and led them to Civitavecchia. This continual shifting of men left disorder and full chaos in its wake.[35] Rumbling down the roads of towns and villages, the wagons laden with desperate men who shouted, cursed, and begged for help often caused an uproar and disturbed local peace. It was not rare to hear of real attacks by inhabitants to free the prisoners. "Resistance to the court" was a frequent charge against family members and friends, and also against villagers accused of liberating convicts from the forces of order, interrupting a journey that offered little hope of return. It was hard to survive the galley life. Sentences might run three, five, or ten years, sometimes even for life. But they rarely surpassed three years. What could spring a man free was a gracious gesture by the pope, or by a confraternity that held the privilege. In Rome, as in many cities, there was no lack of confraternities endowed with this power to mediate, which could package sovereign grace and liberate a person condemned to death or to the galleys. Such privileges were links in the thick net connecting the sovereign to his subjects.[36]

To the authorities, leading the condemned down city streets

---

35. Roberto Benedetti, "Tribunali e giustizia a Roma nel Settecento attraverso la fonte delle liste di traduzione alla galera (1749–1759)," *Roma moderna e contemporanea* 12 (2004): 507–38.

36. For this, see Cecilia Nubola, "Liberazioni per privilegio. Confraternite e grazia nella prima età moderna (secoli XVI–XVIII)," in *Chiesa e mondo moderno. Scritti in onore di Paolo Prodi*, ed. Adriano Prosperi, Pierangelo Schiera, Gabriella Zarri (Bologna: il Mulino, 2007), 235–56.

was part of terror's pedagogy, the admonitory and educative function of punishment. But the risks were great. And justice, with its
rather fragile apparatus, was not always able to bear the brunt of
incidents. In the middle of the eighteenth century, with the slow
but irreversible rise of a new culture of justice, and to avoid disorder, convict transport shifted to night time. The mise-en-scène was
less theatrical, but far less risky. To make good order easier, the
state gave up the spectacle.

As for the clergy, the discipline they faced was seldom so harsh
as what befell the less fortunate lay subjects of the pope's justice.
Their station protected them somewhat. Justice did sometimes afflict their bodies, confining them within prison or convent walls.
But old regime discipline, above all, targeted the mind and spirit.

Buon Governo
Between Utopia and Reality

LAMENTING AN IMAGINED GOLDEN AGE

Roman congregations, using every device at hand, aimed at forging something more than irreproachable ministers of God well adapted to Trent's severe discipline and ready for their ordained labors. Churchmen, in the early modern age, were also to be the blood and sinews of temporal governance; in Rome, it was they who held power and went out to far places to represent the state. They were therefore the messengers and witnesses of the double authority upholding papal monarchy, an authority defined and defended in those years by every means at hand. Clergy, then, were first of all the bearers of justice, and the shapers of the *buon governo* that Rome fostered, and championed in its propaganda.

At the start of the seventeenth century, one of the countless written instructions for prelates destined "to go and govern" set out a precise breviary of tasks—go represent the authority of Rome and, with prudence, court the support of local elites, and do not let "any good work go without reward, nor any crime without punishment."[1] The document praised the obedience and disciplined conduct of the state's subjects, calling these qualities the foundation of good governance and of the common good. The instruction then propounded a usage now long current: a continual exchange of letters with Rome, to know, correct, and adapt to local conditions the center's instructions. These aimed at "the maintenance of public things and the good of private persons . . . the magistrate's good

---

1. ASV, Fondo Bolognetti, vol. 156, ff. 73–86v: *Istruzioni per un prelato che sia mandato in governo.* On this document, see Peter Rietbergen, "Pausen, Prelaten, Bureaucraten, Aspekten van de geschiedenis van het Pausschap en de Pauselijke Staat in de 17e Eeuw" (Academic thesis, University of Nijmegen, 1983), 138–58; Irene Fosi, "Il governo della giustizia nello Stato Ecclesiastico fra centro e periferia (secoli XVI–XVII)," in *Offices et Papauté (XIVe–XVIIe). Charges, hommes, destins,* ed. Armand Jamme and Olivier Poncet, 216–21 (Rome: Ecole Française de Rome, 2005).

governance, to carry out his duty." As in kindred texts—instructions, memorials, or pamphlets—the document's pages brimmed with useful advice on setting up "good justice," to build a consensus that upheld the center's power and, thanks to subjects' obedience and the elite's support, assured the general good.

To know well one's own judicial actions meant also to organize, file, and conserve their records. So one had to keep orderly books of denunciations, misdeeds, and court proceedings. It was also important, the instructions said, to keep up to date one's notes on banished men and fugitives, recording "all the discussions at the end of trials and judicial inquiries, and every other matter that touches on the interests of the community itself." Meanwhile, the *bargello* and his *birri* were to keep a careful eye on public order, said the tract, "especially on Saturday evening, and on the eve of every holiday," when brawls and disorders due to wine and weapons most often broke out. *Buon governo* also required a watch on the streets, and the prisons and their prisoners, registering "the quality of their treatment," and eyeing cautiously informants and spies, "who, as persons of low repute, tell a thousand lies, and do the bad deed themselves and then cast the blame on some other person." The instructions also suggested keeping a convenient account of "blind memorials," those anonymous denunciations that, though spurred by rancor, helped catch and punish authors of major crimes.

There emerges from this document, and from others of the sort, so common in those years, the image of a totalizing power capable of dominating, instinctively or rationally, every facet of justice's everyday regime. But this vision of a complex but smooth-working judicial cloud castle was downright utopian. It was doomed to collide with reality, with all its fragmentation—its many jurisdictions, riddled with the particularism, privileges, and structural drawbacks germane back then to all machinery of state. But the utopian vision did serve propaganda, which retailed images and writings that celebrated both sovereign power and the fruits of good governance. The text we track here ended with a well-worn metaphor from medicine: "It is a physician's job to try all other medications before reaching for the iron and the fire. So the governor, too, bringing his subjects back from doing wrong, should first try any path other than harshness." The medical analogy was venerable: it had roots in the antique parallel of microcosm and macrocosm, of man and world, now reformulated and enriched by Christian ethics and enlivened by Trent's thinking. The local administrator was thus a physician, and the sovereign became the benign paterfamilias. These figures appeared both in formal treatises and in simple instructions like these here, which circulated in manuscript or print and broadcast concepts and behaviors that set models for government and life.

One task of any man who governed was thus to create, conserve, and defend a rigidly ordered society. The same objectives were imparted to the bishops by Roman congregations, and broadcast in instructions for apostolic visitors before their inspection tours, and in nomination briefs for legates.[2] To make sense of the early modern Papal State, note that in these writings there was no separating the temporal and the spiritual. As in other states as well, there were, in the later sixteenth century, appeals to officials, judges, and financial officers, and to apostolic visitors back from inspecting bishoprics, to hew to a moral code inspired by righteous moderation, balance, and charity. Political writings of all sorts mirrored a culture of governance shot through with Renaissance Christian thinking, an art of temperate Neo-Stoic ruling suffused with Gospel precepts and enriched with norms from Trent; throughout the whole seventeenth century this mix of norms set the model for the best conduct of governance, of maintaining order, and, above all, of justice. These precepts were repetitious, endlessly propounding commonplaces. But the many texts and instructions, the letters to legates, nuncios, and governors, express the arduous march toward a new culture of governance, founded on a service ethic, and on the suitability and competence of officials, that legitimated authority. The new culture blended universalizing Christian principles with particularistic ideals of honor based on nobles' values, and so looked beyond mere personal bonds and ties of clientele. These seventeenth-century writings attest to the ongoing formation of bureaucratic consciousness, and to a culture of governance that found its touchstone in the administration of justice, in the most totalizing sense—the control of daily life. In that epoch, this process marked the history of other states too, outside as well as inside Italy.

2. For some examples from the legations of Ferrara and Bologna, see Andrea Gardi, *Lo stato in provincia. L'amministrazione della Legazione di Bologna durante il regno di Sisto V (1585–1590)* (Bologna: Istituto per la Storia di Bologna, 1994); Irene Fosi, *All'ombra dei Barberini. Fedeltà e servizio nella Roma barocca* (Rome: Bulzoni, 1997), 95–121.

"REFORM" IN THE SEVENTEENTH CENTURY

In 1612, Paul V issued a constitution called *Universi agri domini-ci*. It confirms the persistent and inevitable obstacles to closing the gap between the ideals and the realities of governance. Structural shortcomings were many; first of all, cash was scarce, as were well-trained, decently paid lower functionaries. All this comes clear in Paul's directives for reforming justice's personnel.[3]

Justice's problems were not confined to the back country. Paul's constitution also targeted the officials of Rome's own courts—governor, auditor of the Camera, and Rota. The whole corps, said the document, needed remodeling and retraining to meet the needs of justice. But they were a privileged body, well aware of their powers, which shaped their lives. Even for a sovereign, they were thus hard to control, even if he tried to redefine their task, especially whenever they usurped the roles, the functions, and even the robes of others, to line their own pockets. The professions and other occupations, back then, still had unsteady boundaries.[4] Throughout the second half of the sixteenth century, at Rome and elsewhere, lawyers, prosecutors, and notaries had provoked papal attempts to redefine their tasks. The state desired to bring cases to the courts, rather than leave them to private settlement, a traditional practice then still common.[5] The space Paul's constitution devoted to the reform of law's functionaries suggests how pervasive was the practice and how strongly the state had now come to feel that private justice was a public problem. But above all it testifies to how the pope perceived its solution as a first, inevitable step toward a form of justice that firmed up his own power. Paul's legislation targeted the functions and roles of assorted figures, from the notaries down to the *bargello*; the farther down officials perched on the ladder of prestige and office, the more contact they had with the state's own subjects. The pope's strategy, above all, was to stress incorruptibility;

3. For Paul V's reforms, see Irene Fosi, "Tribunali, giustizia e società nella Roma del Cinquecento e Seicento," special issue edited by Irene Fosi, *Roma moderna e contemporanea* 5, no. 1 (1997): 7–184.

4. Alessandro Pastore, in the introduction to *Avvocati, medici, ingegnieri. Alle origini delle professioni moderne*, ed. Maria Luisa Betri and Alessandro Pastore, 14–15 (Bologna: Clueb, 1997).

5. For Bologna, see Claudia Evangelisti, "Gli 'operai delle liti': funzione e status sociale dei procuratori legali a Bologna nella prima età moderna," in Betri and Pastore, eds., *Avvocati, medici, ingegnieri*, 131–44.

officials satisfied with their salaries would abstain from taking gifts or extorting payment of any kind. The pope's aim was ordered, natural justice, unsullied by the machinations and procedural games that lined pockets. The pope's regulations laid bare justice's commonest abuses and defects, hitherto repeatedly assailed in vain.

The pope's assorted regulations raise a question: was corruption widely perceived as illicit, and punishable, or did it just seem to officeholders of the ancien régime to be the perfectly normal way to get things done, and not only in the courts.[6] In reality, what people called avarice, and the easy corruption so often denounced, resulted from a deep-seated ambiguity about the meaning of service, throughout early modern times. To serve, back then, meant to establish an open-ended, very personal relationship, on the model of mutual generosity expressed in a very wide variety of offerings, both material and emotional. Thus, if pay was low, as it often was, ministers did their jobs anyway, expecting that their efforts would still be repaid, via gifts, or, as they were called, "the uncertain things" (incerti), but, above all, via the honor and prestige that came commingled with such goods and services. And high pay hardly helped. Corruption therefore had broad borderlands, and the exact profile of the "common good" remained subjective.

Certainly, when papal authorities, from the late sixteenth century down to around 1700, tried to remodel justice and its ministers, they acted in the name of Counter Reformation religious and moral claims that saw bad governance, corruption, abuse, and the misuse of funds as moral disorders, and therefore as sins. The popes knew that corruption was there, and condemned it, especially when it overstepped a boundary and became intolerable, subverting good governance and justice, and besmirching the image of sovereignty and judicial equity. That does not mean that papal remedies worked; the machinery of state was too weak; surveillance faltered, and compromising deals still flourished.

The reforms of Paul V, fruit of consultation with eminent jurists, redesigned radically the conduct of trials themselves. They stressed equity and good procedure. They left it to the judges to assess and sort out the abundant routine social violence. To punish

---

6. On corruption, see Jean-Claude Waquet, *Corruption: Ethics and Power in Florence, 1600–1770* (University Park: Pennsylvania State University Press, 1991; original edition, Paris: Fayard, 1984).

it all would choke the overburdened courts. So, to Paul, the judge, picking his way, was to be the source of certainty, the prudent, sure-footed reinterpreter of the rules, immune to personal rancor and to pressures. His decisions were to be coherent, and concordant with those of the heads of his tribunal, especially whenever his actions violated general laws or statutes. The judge was to use torture sparingly, only when the crimes were "atrocious," and not to influence the testimony of witnesses by taking advantage of their inexperience or shaky legal standing. Nor should a judge push parties to a hasty settlement, in hopes of easy gain through quick court fees. Whatever the crime, the suspect must be informed of damaging evidence, and receive a copy of the transcript with all names removed, at no cost if poor, so as to be able to consult with lawyers who, themselves, were allowed to see the originals, names and all. The torture of the *veglia*, painful hours standing, should be applied only in the worst of crimes (*in delictis atrocissimis*), after a vote by the criminal congregation. Nor could the accused suffer other tortures that same day. Nor should judges insult suspects or witnesses, calling them names. All such things served competence, discretion, and prudence, to make justice efficient, swift, and fair, a faithful translation of the sovereign will.

The same principles inspired the rules for the judges in civil cases; as with criminal trials, the reforms restated the need to clean up corruption and the abuses that stemmed from the confusion of roles between judges and lawyers, and from the familiarity and kinship that too often connected judges, lawyers, and notaries, groups at once social and professional who tended to defend their privileges. The reform also attacked the disorder of the archives of assorted courts, which hobbled the supervision of their operations. The need to keep order was all the more urgent when commissaries of the Roman courts went out into the country on "cavalcade," to interrogate witnesses, take evidence, set up trials, and inventory confiscated goods. This last task was an opportunity for legal looting; locals denounced it repeatedly, resenting the court's violent interference in the life and balance of their villages. Commissaries' morality was supposed to guarantee equity in the hinterland; they were to represent sovereignty, equity's very source.

Through all the pages of Paul's court reform ran the theme of education. He targeted justice's workforce. It is this pedagogical intent that justifies calling Paul's constitution a reform, more than its actual impact on how things were done. The political context mattered. The Interdict conflict with Venice was raging; it was a time of fierce polemics, stirred up in France especially and widely circulated in Italy by the writing of Cardinal Bellarmine in defense of the pope's *potestas indirecta* (his authority in other states).[7] Papal monarchy was using the very best polemists to defend its *potestas* in these years. Accordingly, Rome was eager to appear in renewed, well-ordered command of justice. Iconography, too, celebrated the theme.[8]

But in the very years when Paul V was laying out his court reform and depicting the new moral ideal for judges, Rome itself offered examples that were hardly edifying. These were neither rare nor new. Some prominent lawmen, it was well known, engaged in corrupt practices, arranged cozy trials and sentences, and filled their pockets. Prospero Farinacci, author of fat, encyclopedic tomes on criminal law, did such things more than once.[9] Thanks to his learned reputation, Farinacci's case stood out, but was not alone. For years, the governor's court had intervened, decisively and firmly, against officials guilty of "excesses" in town governance, or of "thievery and bullying" in running community finances. The court often strayed beyond its jurisdictional boundary, the forty miles of the District, to weigh in on notorious cases of maladministration, dealing out exemplary punishments with real political consequences. Roman justice intervened against lay magistrates and churchmen who governed cities. So, for instance, in 1545 a trial was launched against the cardinal

7. On the relations between Venice and Rome and the problem of the Interdict, see William J. Bouwsma, *Venice and the Defense of Republican Liberty: Renaissance Values in the Age of the Counter-Reform* (Berkeley and Los Angeles: University of California Press, 1968); Filippo De Vivo, "Dall'imposizione del silenzio alla *Guerra delle scritture.* Le pubblicazioni ufficiali durante l'interdetto del 1606–1607," *Studi Veneziani* 41 (2002): 179–213; De Vivo, *Information and Communication in Venice: Rethinking Early Modern Politics* (Oxford: Oxford University Press, 2007); Sylvio Hermann De Franceschi, *Raison d'état et raison d'église. La France et l'Interdit vénitien (1606–1607): aspects diplomatiques et doctrinaux* (Paris: H. Champion, 2009).

8. Steven F. Ostrow, *Art and Spirituality in Counter-Reformation Rome* (Cambridge: Cambridge University Press, 1996); Antonio Menniti Ippolito, *I papi al Quirinale. Il sovrano pontefice e la ricerca di una residenza* (Rome: Viella, 2004).

9. Niccolò Del Re, "Prospero Farinacci giureconsulto romano (1544–1618), *Archivio della Società Romana di Storia Patria* 98 (1975): 135–220. The article by Aldo Mazzacane in *Dizionario biografico degli Italiani*, vol. 45, 1–5 (Rome: Istituto dell'Enciclopedia Italiana, 1995), records some of the more notorious incidences of Farinacci's corruption.

of San Giorgio, legate of the Romagna, accused by representatives
of Ravenna of taking wood and hay from the city, and of allowing
the henchmen of Cesare Rasponi, the head of a noble party who held
sway locally, to carry

offensive weapons in the city, and wheel-lock harquebuses under their
capes and on the saddle bow when they ride for pleasure in this city. Besides that, the captain has allowed all the foreigners who come to visit
him to carry arms around the city, and this is done with great danger and
scandal to the city of Ravenna. . . . And he puts out decrees that one cannot play forbidden games, under the gravest punishments, and then sells
gaming rights in the entire province, and besides the evil that arises on
account the gaming, worse are the blasphemies that they say.[10]

In 1572, Decio Fiorenzi, ex-lieutenant [judge] of Perugia, was tried
for embezzlement. In 1596, the same accusation was leveled against
Giulio Giacometti from Recanati.[11] As the seventeenth century went
on, although they become less common, direct interventions of the
governor's court against abuse of power and fiscal misdeeds never
ceased. And they found, in the Sacra Consulta at Rome, an increasingly powerful and attentive backer.

THE SACRA CONSULTA

Founded in 1559, and given a new mission in 1588, the Sacra
Consulta was by the late seventeenth century an important and effective support for papal sovereignty.[12] It was composed of five cardinals, one of whom, almost always the cardinal nephew, served as
prefect, and it also had a secretary and prelates called the *ponenti
di Consulta* who drew up cases. It fell to the Consulta, among other things, to appraise the legitimacy of trials by peripheral courts
in cities ruled by governors. But it had also to pronounce on appeals of judgments rendered in feudal courts. On the other hand,
it very rarely intervened in the judicial activities of the legations;
there it dealt only in appeals. In the political and administrative
geography of the Papal State, the Consulta exercised considerable

10. ASV, Misc. Arm. II, vol. 80, ff. 249v–250r. For Rasponi's faction in the sixteenth
century, see Cesarina Casanova, *Gentiluomini ecclesiastici. Ceti e mobilità sociale nelle Legazioni pontificie (secc. XVI–XVIII)* (Bologna: Clueb, 1999), 29–74.
11. ASR, Tribunale Criminale del Governatore, Processi (sixteenth century), busta
147, case 9; busta 290, case 3.
12. Stefano Tabacchi, "Buon Governo, Sacra Consulta e dinamiche dell'amminstra-
zione pontificia nel XVIII," *Dimensioni e problemi della ricerca storica* 1 (2004): 43–65.

surveillance over the territories of the state's central belt—Umbria and the Marches. But it was limited in the north, where the power of the legates of Ferrara, Bologna, and the Romagna was thoroughly sovereign, and delegated directly by the pope.

There were assorted attempts to define the tasks of the Consulta, to enhance its surveillance over magistrates on the periphery and to subject their work to periodic review, to organize their records, to register peace pacts in the place where they were made, and energize the assorted corps of *birri*.[13] At Rome, there were major efforts, by the congregations above all, to raise the level of instruction of the men who governed the periphery. This last was never easy. Under Alexander VII, the Sacra Consulta underwent changes that affected the structure of both the tribunal and the curia. Alexander's reforms made new prelates hold degrees in civil and canon law. This requirement stiffened theological training through legal education. The changes stressed the function of judges and administrators as interpreters and mediators; these functions looked to law for the principle of *equitas*.[14] The prefect of the congregation was no longer the cardinal nephew, as he had been in the pontificates of Clement VIII or Urban VIII, but a cardinal who had distinguished himself in service and who had concrete experience running legations, or in diplomacy. Such qualifications were necessary for presiding over a major congregation. In the Roman curia, any man, like all those in his circle of friends and clients, almost always held many jobs at once. This fact was at once a source of strength and a cause of weakness. There was strength because ties of friendship, fealty, and kinship helped coordinate the diverse congregations in governing matters spiritual and temporal. There was weakness because the holders could not specialize. This loose division of labor was not by any means a distinctive trait of the Papal State alone. The coordination of justice and administration and governance was assured by the presence of many of the same persons in the assorted congregations. But good government was impeded by the jealous defense of prerogatives and functions and of

13. BAV, Vat. lat. 12229, ff. 154r–157v.

14. For Alexander's reforms, see Ludwig von Pastor, *History of the Popes*, trans. Frederick Ignatius Antrobus and Ralph Kerr, 40 vols. (London: K. Paul, Trench, Trubner, 1891–1961), vol. 31, 127–29. (Original edition, Freiburg im Breisgau, 1928.) For pathways to papal careers, see Renata Ago, *Carriere e clientele nella Roma barocca* (Rome: Laterza, 1990).

the honor they afforded. Moreover, the constant piling of obscure new rules atop old ones that never really died, and the heaping up, in time and space, of competing tribunals braked and blocked reasonable administration.

In the middle of the seventeenth century, the *pratiche* (briefs) discussed by the Consulta concerned justice to the exclusion of almost everything else. There were queries over procedures and clarifications of uncertain cases. Judges on the periphery received from Rome endless pleas for moderation in torturing prisoners, and for taking further evidence about the "qualities of the person and of the excess" and for granting parties in a case more time to ready a defense. These are the same requests for precision, punctuality, and good scheduling that went out, as we have seen, from the Holy Office to the *vicari*, inquisitors, and bishops across the Papal State. There were also reiterated appeals to governors to register safe-conducts and to guarantee that exile, the most common sentence, be carried out. In this last matter, reform did more harm than good, for local justice knew well that exile broke the ties between the condemned and his family and community of origin. Exile meant, above all, loss of a reasonably secure occupation that could sustain a family. In a precarious economy, it was a powerful step, but exile also fed some of the very phenomena that the authorities hoped to curb—vagabondage and poverty. Local authorities knew this and often pointed out the need to control the consequences of exile for their communities. Here we see an example of the awkward clash between the logic of the capital's justice and local governments' practical good sense and expertise.

Rome tried many other ways of improving local justice. For instance, both governors and the Sacra Consulta were forever pressing communities to keep in good order, for easy consultation, their "book of peace agreements" *(libro delle paci)*. The aim of these pacts was to nip in the bud the frequent conflicts that set head to head perpetrators and the families of their recent victims. Whenever these private settlements toppled, it fell to Roman justice to pick up all the pieces. Moreover, in the provinces, official justice entailed hard slogging: the waits were long and contestants dug in their heels, and so people often preferred to turn straight to Rome, to the Consulta or the cardinal nephew. Cardinal Giovanni Battista De Luca, at the end of the seventeenth century, managed to praise this arrangement, and champion it as a model for other states:

And it is, in truth . . . a magistracy, which one can never contrive to praise sufficiently, as the good effects it produces are incredible, for the vigilance that is there, and, especially, in the matter of the oppression of subjects, who often suffer at the hand of officials and governors, and also of potent citizens, so that it should serve as an example to other princes, so long as they maintain and observe its old ways of doing business.[15]

Like many of De Luca's judgments on curial institutions, his appraisal here paints a cloying picture; it contrasts sharply with everything many observers and critics, decades earlier, had denounced.

BETWEEN STEREOTYPES AND REALITY

According to a *topos* widely current in old regime treatises and pamphlets, when they discussed state governance, authors tended to separate the responsibilities of a sovereign from those of the sovereign's ministers. A little tract, neither signed nor dated, proposed having "all the *podestà* and all the officials of the Sacra Consulta come up for a conduct review [*stare a sindacato*] at the end of their term of office . . . if we are ever to get out of this fix"; it also urged, yet again, stricter order in keeping the books and in informing Rome about procedures followed. Its author wanted the police strengthened, the better to scour the countryside, and suggested they be funded by all those who, on petitioning, won a pardon. He observed that

many crimes committed, for lack of witnesses, cannot be verified, as the witnesses fear they might be killed or harmed in assorted ways by these perpetrators, or by others who take orders from them. If they [the criminals] are liberated they give false witness, and witnesses are [then] persecuted, a thing that offends their souls, and sometimes they are put to torture by judges.[16]

Paul V's reform must have been slow in making its effects felt. Whenever a pontificate began, it was customary to flood the new ruler with a stream of writings, opinions, and discourses, invited or uninvited, aiming to inform and counsel him on *buon governo*. Justice was a favorite subject. These seventeenth-century writings constitute a motley genre we might call, in modern terms, "political counsel."

---

15. Giovan Battista De Luca, *Il Dottor volgare*, bk. 15, part 3: *Relazione della stessa Curia romana* I, ch. 22, vol. 4, 539 (Rome: G. Corvo, 1743).

16. BAV, Vat. lat. 12229, ff. 154r–157v: "Suggerimenti alla Sacra Consulta per tutto lo Stato Ecclesiastico."

Among them is a manuscript labeled "Discorso sopra il buon governo di Roma."[17] The anonymous author, who boasts of long international experience, not only observes the pope's city and the functioning of its courts. He also gives a picture of all the state's dysfunctions, not only justice's. The author may have done some diplomatic work for the pope. He remarks that, in Rome, civil justice works fairly well, thanks to the Rota. Meanwhile, criminal justice, whether "commutative or vindictive," has been applied with useless severity and has turned into cruelty. The popes, writes the author, seem to have lost contact with the fundamental gift that should always accompany justice: clemency, "the most beautiful virtue that can shine in a prince."[18] It is necessary, above all, to keep separate crimes against God and those against men. With the first, one must proceed without pity; with the others, greater discretion and clemency make sense. All in all, he writes, it is futile to weigh courts down with summonses, complaints, and lawsuits, and the use of "extreme rigor, especially in cases of brawls and angry outbursts, however light they chance to be, as in fist-fights and verbal insults even among the lowest classes and petty women." All this prosecution works to the financial advantage, says he, only of the advocates, notaries, and *birri*, or of those groups at the bottom of society against whom the popes have recently intervened. Things are even worse in the provinces. It is the fault of the Sacra Consulta, among others, for

it is so slow to ask governors of provinces to send it trials, that they, aware of where their advantage lies . . . often do not hesitate to change the case's story, making the crime graver, or lighter, in accordance with their passions and their interests.[19]

Arbitrary imprisonment, and remanding trials to other jurisdictions, to the harm of communities, let courts function, he says, "with an attitude of getting money by all possible means; one gives punishment these days not from zeal for justice, but to fill the purse."[20] The author condemns roundly the scandal of sentencing

17. Biblioteca Casanatense, Rome (henceforth BC), MS 2097, ff. 253r–290v.

18. Justice and clemency were the inseparable couple in the iconography of justice: see Mario Sbriccoli, "La benda della giustizia. Iconografia, diritto e leggi penali dal Medio Evo all' Età Moderna," in Mario Sbriccoli et al., eds., *Ordo Iuris. Storia e forme dell'esperienza giuridica* (Milan: Giuffrè, 2003), 42–95; Adriano Prosperi, *Giustizia bendata. Percorsi storici di un'immagine* (Turin: Einaudi, 2008).

19. BC, MS 2097, f. 265r.

20. BC, MS 2097, f. 267r.

delinquent clergy to the galleys alongside common criminals. They are abused by the "galley-drivers, who are the crudest generation nourished on this earth, having nothing human about them besides their faces. They treat the poor religious just like Turks and barbarian peoples." So the undated tract must have been written before the Ergastolo of Corneto tried to put an end to the unedifying spectacle of clerics in the galleys, by offering other punishments better suited to God's ministers. Here the author championed an opinion that had for some time circulated at Rome and elsewhere.

The anonymous critic was hardest on distributive justice; he took to task the whole court and courtier system for excluding virtuous, prepared persons from a career. Perhaps he had himself in mind.

How many men of worth and literary training are found outside the court and the city of Rome since they are neglected because unknown to the Prince and lack other persons who could bring them forward, men who would be very worthy of promotion to high offices and dignified positions![21]

Perhaps the author of these pages was a provincial, aware of poor governance far from Rome, and knowing how hard it was to repair disorders. Perhaps he had seen other lands and could risk a eulogy on the Low Countries, where republican governors and heretics "took extraordinary care to have good, and real information about meritorious subjects [i.e., persons] in general in the entire land."[22] These criticisms were nevertheless packaged with obligatory praise for the virtue and prudence of the new pope, Urban VIII, from whom, he said, one expected nothing but good.

⚜

All across Europe, everywhere, not just Italy, critics from Erasmus down to Traiano Boccalini (1556?–1613), who characterized the judges of Rome as corrupt butchers who had eyes only for their pay (he had himself once been a judge of the senator), targeted the maladministration of justice and the judiciary's corruption. Old saws notwithstanding, such comments expressed "a profound aversion toward the juridical system in place, which was overabundant, complex, and far indeed from the primitive simplicity of custom."[23]

---

21. BC, MS 2097, f. 267v.
22. BC, MS 2097, f. 290r–v.
23. Italo Birocchi, *Alla ricerca dell'ordine. Fonti e cultura giuridica nell'età moderna*, 275 (Turin: Giappichelli, 2002).

Critiques inspired utopian projects, designs for a world ruled by a fairer-minded justice. Although these denunciations are repetitious and unoriginal, they do hint at an unease born of the gulf between intention and reality, between an abstract idea of justice and the daily reality in which real justice took shape. They also express a widespread, deep-rooted mistrust of justice's courts, institutions, personnel, and practices. This mistrust made men and women shy away from courtrooms and invited private settlements of quarrels, via peace pacts and other bargains. Though in early modern times sovereigns, the pope included, made justice the cornerstone of their propaganda of good governance, their subjects sought other routes to assure peace and good order. But when they could no longer duck their day in court, other forms of mediation, tying subjects to sovereigns, also came into play. As we shall see, it was here that petitions came in; they adapted justice and made contracts with it. The confraternities were essential here; they facilitated the acceptance of petitions and helped set in motion the grace and clemency of rulers. The confraternities were accredited spokesmen for the organs of justice; they intervened best for their own members. These bodies helped build steps on the stairway that led from the subjects to their sovereign, or, so to speak, from earth to heaven.

11

Little Fatherlands
Local Identity and Central Power

"POPULAR OUTCRY"

Since most of the popular outcry and of the state's disorders is born of ministers' lacking clean hands, you should not only protect yourself from the least shadow of such a defect in your own person, but you should [also], particularly, keep it the main thing on your mind to ward off the extortions of your officials, who, generally setting themselves no other end than pecuniary gain, let pass no occasion to increase it, to the people's detriment.

These were recommendations to the men about to take a government position far from Rome.[1] But the project to establish more efficient justice did not clash solely with officials' shortcomings and procedure's leaden pace. Rather, alongside the letters local judges sent the Sacra Consulta, about working justice or procedures, the congregation also received memorials and petitions from subjects and—increasingly in the seventeenth century—from entire communities. These papers complained of the "excesses" committed by legal officials,[2] of their incapacity to carry out their tasks without giving scandal, and of their connivance in the very crime they were supposed to quell. When communities denounced their officials in hopes of quick riddance, alleging scandalous behavior or sexual crimes, the Roman tribunal responded slowly, careful to ascertain that the accusations were not born of private feuds, personal hatreds, or the actions of "adversaries" otherwise unspecified.

In 1652, the prefect of the Consulta wrote the governor of Perugia to find out if

it is true that the governor of Cannara, along with that *podestà* of Castel Buono, who is a priest, have for a short while had the company of a wom-

---

1. "Instruttione per Prelato che vada in governo" (sec. XVII): BAV, Chigiano, Q. I. 12, f. 151rv.

2. So, in 1652, the Consulta asked the governor of Perugia to consult with the priors of the village of Castiglion del Lago, "for the removal of the governor, given the wrongs that they claim to receive from him." BAV, Borg. lat. 729, f. 26r.

an who is married, but who has a bad moral reputation [*publica dishon-esta*], and that that woman then went off to Foligno. And that the [governor], in company of some young men . . . after having eaten and drunk well, went around his village making a ruckus in the night, and, as a joke, they went to the house of some peasant friends to get something to eat, but that the governor had first immorally requested that women be put under penalty. I found no foundation for this.[3]

In this case, the denunciations seem in fact to have come from "persons hardly friendly to the said governor": "for a little mortification [to put him in his place]" he was detained in Perugia for several days.[4] Here we see the state's caution and prudence before proceeding; hasty decisions and theatrical punishments could disturb delicate local equilibria and make the job of justice even harder.

To reach the pope, alongside the Sacra Consulta and the other curial bodies that ruled the state, the cardinal nephew was long a privileged channel. At least down to the middle of the seventeenth century, he remained both prominent and potent. In his capacity as the state's overseer, it fell to him to hear the "outcry of the populaces" who turned to him, and then respond either directly or via his faithful "ministers." For the men of the law, often sent to far corners of the state for the first steps of a career that frequently proved arduous and risky, the cardinal nephew was a lodestar. They wrote him for the right reading of the rules, especially if crime was on the docket, or to ask his opinion and instructions on when to torture, or to make him prompt local bishops to apply church censure. To write the cardinal nephew helped legitimate his role as an undisputed link between center and periphery, papal court and officialdom, and papal household and individual magistrates.[5] In their missives to the cardinal nephew, legates, governors, and officials of local tribunals expounded their expectations for their careers, their honor, and their power. Letters, in courtly fashion, stressed good "disposition" and fidelity to Rome's orders, but then, to excuse their authors' actual conduct, pointed out how hard it was to apply locally rigid rules needing prudent mediation and alert interpretation. Rome especially prized this local mediation; it was crucial to

---

3. BAV, Borg. lat. 729, f. 26v.

4. BAV, Borg. lat. 729, f. 26v.

5. On the role of the cardinal nephew, see two important studies: Antonio Menniti Ippolito, *Il tramonto della curia nepotista* (Rome: Viella, 1999); Birgit Emich, *Bürokratie und Nepotismus unter Paul V (1605–1621)* (Stuttgart: Hiersemann, 2001).

consensus. Inquisitorial activity, in state affairs, navigated mainly with an eye to the Holy Office in Rome, a monolithic presence
that set its rules; meanwhile, temporal justice, both civil and criminal, fixed its eyes not only on the assorted congregations but also
on the heads of divers tribunals, so its points of reference and its intermediaries were more abundant. Not only the cardinal nephew
and other cardinals, but also the women and other members of the
larger papal family, and the ambassadors all hearkened to the "outcry of the peoples" and agitated for justice on their behalf.

When a community felt it could argue that scandalous actions
were "enormous"—in the original, literal sense [e-*norm*-ous], meaning outside the bounds of behavior's norms—and intolerable, and
harmful to collective honor and the prince's sovereignty, it drafted a petition, rich in detail and richer yet in outrage, straight to
the pope or to his cardinal nephew, going over the heads of all local go-betweens. In Ascoli, in the fall of 1627, after scandals that
had shaken the city and undermined the wobbly credibility of papal governance, the city council members [*anziani*] wrote:

It gives this city infinite displeasure to inform your most illustrious lordship about what is happening with Captain Paolucci from Perugia, the
castellan of Rocca Pia [Ascoli's castle]. We had been hearing for some
months of many thefts and of how the castellan proved his guilt by open-
ly accepting stolen goods. And it seemed impossible that a minister of the
Holy Church should be carrying on in such a fashion, so we never gave
ear to such reports. Finally, some days ago, a merchant from the Kingdom [of Naples] was robbed of four loads of silk and five mules, worth
two thousand scudi and more, that he was transporting to L'Aquila for
sale. The merchant heard that it was all being held in the castle. He came
here [i.e., to the city council] and stayed several days and talked about this
with Monsignor Governor, and obtained permission to use due diligence
to learn all about that theft. He set up guard at the [city] gate that goes
toward Perugia, where, this morning, the castellan himself appeared,
with other armed men, to send off four horses with cargo. Among the
other goods was a bundle of silk. So it was all impounded, both the horses and the silk, and it all was put under the power of the officers of justice. And among those things, besides the others, he [the merchant] recognized the silk as part of his, stolen from him. And because there have
been many thefts in these parts since the day that the castellan arrived
in these parts, of horses, cattle, pigs and other animals, and of goods, as
has been claimed in public by varied and divers persons, it seems strange
indeed that this office, which should serve for the defense of the Holy

Church, should be the receiver of this thievery. Besides what has been told Monsignor Governor, it seemed proper to inform your most excellent lordship, to help you do what should be done in this matter.[6]

So the "foreigner" castellan's ongoing thievery was portrayed as a profound affront to the honor of the city, and to the justice and the authority that Ascoli hoped to represent. The disgrace also tainted the city's ancient castle, Rocca Pia, renamed for its modernizer, Pius IV—a papal symbol now transformed by its commander's skullduggery into a den of thieves. Ascoli was a restless town; it had rebelled not long ago. The castellan's failure to assure local order was a symptom of the bad governance that had sparked revolt.[7] The Ascolani chose to argue that the city's quiet, order, and *buon governo* depended on Rome's capacity to forestall such crimes and to respect and champion the idealized virtues of the citizens, as Ascoli's patriciate proclaimed them.

Down to the end of the seventeenth century, denunciations like Ascoli's reveal a panorama of tenacious obstacles to Rome's initiatives.[8] The town of Caprarola in 1679 complained that it had gone far too long without a governor, "at the discretion of a notary who has paid rent for that tribunal, where he continually extorts money." Caprarola's petition signaled the connivance of local prelates, including Abbot Francesco Caetani, a Roman noble, and listed the futile denunciations

brought to your holiness and to the Sacra Consulta, and although very just orders were issued for the removal of the aforesaid abbot and notary, they have never been put to effect, despite the gravest scandals, that have been explained other times, as above, in the matter of girls deflowered. For he [the abbot] is backed by the powerful patronage of some ministers.[9]

In their petitions aggrieved communities also stressed the deplorable "contempt for justice"—and thus for papal authority—that, they asserted, imbued the public behavior of legal officials, and charged them with lèse-majesté, a grave accusation. For instance, on 13 August 1679, Domenico Parenti was appointed by Veroli's town council as

6. BAV, Barb. lat. 8965, fol. 3r–v (13 October 1627).

7. For the revolt of Ascoli in the year 1555 see Irene Fosi, *La società violenta. Il banditismo nello Stato pontificio nella seconda metà del Cinquecento* (Rome: Ateneo, 1985), 54–58.

8. For a good example, ASV, Segreteria di Stato, Memoriali e biglietti, n. 18, folio unnumbered, label: "consulte," dated August and September 1679.

9. ASV, Segreteria di Stato, Memoriali e biglietti, n. 18 (13 August 1679).

exactor of the seed grain. When the exaction list was given him, with a judicial decree, first he rejected it with the greatest scorn for justice. And the second time, when it was presented to him by the same bailiff, in the presence of two witnesses, he rejected it with the same scorn, and, in the public square, he beat the bailiff.

Imprisoned, Parenti claimed to be a bailiff of a commissary of the Fabbrica di San Pietro, the office for the upkeep of Rome's greatest church. The town authorities rebutted his claim. The case was sent to the Consulta for further investigation.[10] Whatever the eventual result, the people of the town would have remained scandalized by the beating, an act of public contempt for a town official; in the town council's eyes, it was a contagious example of dire highhandedness, and, of course, an explicit offense to papal authority.

In 1656, over many cities, and over Rome itself, hung the peril of the plague that then was sweeping half of Italy. Authorities adopted strict security measures to prevent or limit the contagion, and laid heavy penalties on transgressors. But, in Rome and in the provinces, the system sometimes unraveled. Some persons, against the rules, cashed in on the epidemic. Like the plague itself, they were contagious, examples of a scorn for authority that undermined the health of all. The village of San Quirico, in the Marches, wrote to the Sacra Consulta that their *podestà*, Agostino Cecchini,

is making a business out of the guards, that at present they are keeping on account of rumors of plague. He has peasants from out of town give him whole cheeses to let them come in without tickets [to show they come from plague-free places], and he also takes money and other things. He has boasted that in this guards affair he can earn 100 scudi. . . . In every piece of community business, he tries to make a profit, and no one says no; here three or four peasants rule the village. But we petition, lest the poor be exploited by this man: we live without justice, in the Catalan fashion, paying fines without due process. He says, "This is what I want, and so that is how it has to be."

Begging for justice, the writer stressed, in a petition's standard formulae, how the *podestà* in his arrogance "does not care a bit about things divine or human."[11]

Communities did not limit themselves to denunciation. Not only did they deplore scandals, connivance, and bad governance by au-

10. ASV, Segreteria di Stato, Memoriali e biglietti, n. 18 (9 September 1679).
11. BAV, Borg. lat. 63, II, f. 393r.

thorities both lay and churchly, and even targeted bishops, accusing them of complicity or at least of conveniently closing their eyes to repeated crimes; towns also asserted their right to observance of the rules. They demanded respect for their statutes and for the proper conduct of council elections. They insisted that judicial officials pass under formal review (*sindicazione*) at a term's end, and complained of officers who were corrupt, lacked their doctorate, or stayed on well past their term of office. In stance and language, a memorial of the conservators of Imola is no exception. The document accused the archbishop of Bologna of "all the tricks, and continual conferring, and complicity" with the governor of Imola, "who commits these excesses, hating all the while the public and private steps taken against him last year, with the most excellent legate and with the Sacra Consulta. So every action [on his part] should be seen as suspect, for, in things of the greatest importance, he has shown us his mettle." This mix of low insinuations and high moral language reflected the play of urban politics. As for the real crux of the matter: the memorial merely accuses the archbishop, Girolamo Compagni, and the governor of Imola, Pietro Ettori, of backing a minority faction in the city council.[12] To give another example, the community of Cingoli petitioned the Sacra Consulta to require of the governor of the Marches "that he at once cause a new magistrate to be elected." The document recalled the town's earlier remonstrances, so far in vain, and denounced the governor's failure to vet the performance of local magistrates and to redraw the electoral lists of candidates eligible for city office.[13]

The entire seventeenth century resounded with civic outcry. Big or small, near or far, wherever papal power seemed tentative and compromising, or where personnel failed to meet the ideals propounded in treatises, briefs, instructions, and pamphlets, towns complained and made demands. In their *doléances*, the Papal State's communities reclaimed their identity and civic culture, which the Papal State, despite its sway, had half-tamed but never swept away.

THE DEFENSE OF CIVIC IDENTITY

The petitions and letters that peripheral towns sent the Consulta expound their idea of community. Places with a long past,

---

12. ASV, Segretaria di Stato, Memoriali e biglietti, n. 18.
13. BAV, Borg. lat. 63, II, ff. 349r–54r. The same year, Recanati, also in the Marches, sent in the same requests.

they defended themselves firmly and consciously, as social worlds with their own particular space and history. Moreover, local identity had a solid institutional base, rooted in customs and statutes, and attached to major civic monuments and well-defined communal spaces. Their boundaries could be reinforced by including or excluding outsiders, foreigners, and peasants.[14] Almost always, city consciousness matched that of the governing elites, who, by the seventeenth century, had shrunk to a small number of families who defended their privileges but claimed to speak for the whole town. Thus, claims to Rome doubtless fit the desires of the governing class.[15] Almost always, a petition's author belonged to a patrician or noble group whose power had been guaranteed in exchange for fidelity to the pontiff.[16] Moreover, in the larger towns especially, the Roman curia offered members of elite families a long shot at a career.

The defense of identity was thus a major communal project. For the early modern period, identity has complex connotations. It was strongest in communes that were distinguished by geographic position, civic traditions, or history. So, even for the communities of the Papal State, whose self-governance was weaker than in some other parts of Italy, one can speak of a collective identity as a "bond of belonging, dynamic, but endowed with a stability that is transmitted from one individual generation to a determinate social group, with the sharing of values, norms, and representations, and thus of ideologies and symbols."[17] In these Papal State petitions, individuals often choose to act as spokesmen for a collectivity, defending its norms and customs and demanding *buon governo* and justice in conformity with their own traditions, symbols, and local laws. So, for the communities of the pope's domains, "the con-

14. See Giovanni Tocci, *Le comunità in età moderna. Problemi storiografici e prospettivi di ricerca* (Florence: Nis, 1997); Edward Muir, "The Idea of Community in Renaissance Italy," *Renaissance Quarterly* 55 (2002): 1–18.

15. For the social transformation of Mediterranean communities, see Gérard Delille, *Le maire et la prieur. Pouvoir central et pouvoir local en Méditerranée occidentale (XVe–XVIIIe siècle)* (Paris: Ecole des Hautes Etudes en Sciences Sociales, 2003).

16. Marco Pellegrini, "Corte di Roma e aristocrazie italiane in età moderna. Per una letturatura storico-sociale della curia romana," *Rivista di Storia e Letteratura Religiosa* 30 (1994): 543–602.

17. Paolo Prodi, "Introduzione: evoluzione e metamorfosi delle identità collettive," in *Identità collettive tra Medioevo ed Età Moderna*, ed. Paolo Prodi and Wolfgang Reinhard, 11 (Bologna: Clueb, 2002).

sciousness of the place [*luogo*] as a seat of continual residence . . . gives origin to a class's identity."[18] Meanwhile, petitioners, picking terms with care, cited their native *civitas:* many letters to Rome invoked this resonant urban term, recalling an august history, with its glorious episodes and storied personages.

Identity and privileges were on the table because the communities, and their representatives—facing papal ministers, whether legates, governors, or judges of whatsoever rank or power—resisted Rome's campaign for integration and homogenization. Local elites, patrician and noble, strove to bog down Rome's march. To battle such social forces, from the mid-sixteenth century on, papal power forged alliances and struck enduring compromises, for rule's sake, to clinch consensus and legitimate its own authority. When such accords were threatened, when privileges looked scorned, protest resurfaced and the denunciations of Rome's incapacity flew thick. Up went the call for the recognition of urban privileges and customs.

The big towns were not the only ones to put in claims like these. The greater towns and cities could assert their rich history and firm identity forcefully. Smaller places were less wealthy, socially less stratified and varied, and, all told, poorer in history; they possessed just a plain story, not a glorious "history" but a humble chronicle of strung-out events unworthy of high rhetoric and a prestigious humanist label. Still, they claimed respect for their statutes and their civic customs, and demanded *buon governo* and a justice worthy of the distant, foreign sovereign. This is what happened, for example, with the scattered upland communes of the prefecture of the Montagna, between the Marches and the province of Umbria. It was also true of the communities in the north, in the legations of Ferrara, Bologna, and Romagna. And, if we scan the correspondence, the same is true for other parts of the state: everywhere, towns continually claim, protest, and petition. From 1592, the Congregazione del Buon Governo regulated and oversaw the economies and finances of the communities of the state, while the Sacra Consulta worked as high court, also for criminal affairs. This division of labor simplified administration. Nevertheless, even with this rationalization of the organs of curia and government, the communities and their representatives kept on writing straight to the pope,

18. Francesco Campennì, *La patria e il sangue. Città, patriziati e potere nella Calabria moderna* (Manduria: Lacaita, 2004), 27.

the cardinal nephew, and the other members of the papal family. In their eyes, personal, direct links best guaranteed justice, order, and *buon governo*.

The largest cities of the state, like Bologna and Ferrara, kept ambassadors at Rome. Other towns had agents to represent their needs to the curia or to members of the papal family.[19] Alongside this relatively stable official representation, on special occasions there were also missions by civic notables. The reasons for sending local representatives to Rome were extremely varied, and all such missions offered a splendid opportunity to dialogue directly with power, and to build networks that might in the future benefit both the community and its emissaries themselves. Ability and prudence were thus crucial. When in Rome, the bearers of messages from the *patria* could exploit common origin, familiarity, and friendship with fellow citizens now residing in the capital and, with luck, well connected at the curia. Go-betweens, both official and informal, listened to the voices of these emissaries, who spoke in the collective name.

A murmur of voices spread ceaselessly from the dominated territories in the direction of the center of power; in an epoch that had long canonized the necessity for men of the court to keep silent in the face of the prince, the possibility of speaking to power had been transformed by a great mutation and to speak out no longer served to persuade and convince, but rather to conquer the benevolence (and thus the protection) of the interlocutors.[20]

To speak as emissaries did was to recognize power and to legitimate its dominion over the periphery, for in speaking one acknowledged a basic trait of sovereignty. The oral side of these civic missions has almost entirely vanished, as observers seldom wrote down carefully ambassadors' spoken words. Nevertheless ambassadorial letters themselves bear witness to the pattern's continuity and utter consistency.

The defense of *buon governo* and justice was expressed in terms that shifted with the circumstances and the interlocutors who chanced to be involved. Communities declared their fealty to Rome,

---

19. For Perugia, see Erminia Irace, "Una voce poco fa. Note sulle difficili pratiche della comunicazione tra il centro e le periferie dello Stato Ecclesiastico (Perugia, metà XVI–metà XVII secolo)," in *Offices, écrits et papauté (XIIIe–XVIIe siècle)*, vol. 3, *Une culture exacerbée de l'écrit, Actes du colloque de Paris (Paris 2003, Avignon 2004)*, ed. Armand Jamme and Olivier Poncet, 273–99 (Rome: Ecole Française de Rome, 2007).

20. Ibid.

but sought respect for their statutes, laws, and practices of governance. They requested "suitable" ministers and honors for their fellow citizens with careers outside the *patria*. So negotiation seldom stopped, and the center, for the sake of consensus and fidelity, had to make concessions. In the seventeenth century, this was the dialogue that shaped relations. It proves that the old tension, revolt, repression, and mayhem that marked the sixteenth century had been overcome. So no more rebelling, but cities defended and respected tradition. That is what emerges from the letters sent ahead by courier or carried along in saddlebags to Rome. The stronger state, supported by the dual nature, spiritual and temporal, of papal power, tried to turn communities that were mindful of their own history, and kept on claiming privileges or trying for dialogue, into a sworn, corporate society bound by oaths. The towns aimed to align their own ideals of *buon governo* and justice with what Rome was trying to impose.

When they denounced misappropriation of wealth and official corruption, communities stressed to Roman authorities the violation of their fundamental values. Yet the exchange of information with Rome did not boil down to lamentations over *malgoverno*, incompetence, corruption, and the litany of other abuses that throng the memorials. There were also suggestions, proposals, and, above all, nominations of persons seen as talented and suitable for lay or spiritual careers in government. These were usually local sons. In postulants' eyes, they embodied the traits and virtues of the *patria*. One knew them, their families, their friendships, and their factional alliances. So, it followed, they were controllable. Prospering in careers, they were in a position to guarantee favors, and to hear and to understand what their fellow citizens requested. In sum, because not foreigners or outsiders, they were allies.

Nevertheless, communities generally defended, with one voice, any outsiders who, to their eyes, had done *governo* well, that is, who had guaranteed abundance, peace, and order, and pacified local enmities, conjuring away bloody vendettas fed by faction. So even a foreigner could fit in, if he knew and observed the rules, and an honest minister could receive testimonials to gratitude and esteem, proffered urgently whenever the community wrote Rome to beg a new minister no less worthy. Towns harped on their fidelity to signal how much it depended on Rome's own respect for the rules and its open ear to requests from below. For example, on 22 February 1641, the representatives of Corneto (now Tarquinia), wrote Cardinal Francesco Barberini that

Signor Agabito Gori, after having finished governing this city, has held a review of office [*sindicato*] in which he has not had any petition [against his rule], which is a sign that he has behaved laudably in his office. So it seemed good to accompany him, to your Excellency, with an ample testification both of his honored qualities and also of the affection of this Public toward him. We owe him a certain amount of obligation, for he has rid us of criminal persons, armed with firearms, who used to carry on around the city, and defended, with much spirit, our jurisdictions and other interests.[21]

At the lower levels, easy relations between the governors and the governed, the kind that modeled justice and proper sovereign power, were far from a sure thing. At Corneto, for instance, the conservators and captains had insisted again and again to their city's governor on the proper use of firearms. Such weapons were not symbols, but real instruments of power and defense. Violation of the rules on the part of the guarantors of public order seemed a danger to everybody. The accusations were explicit:

In the service of justice, in order to frighten and pursue some persons who on several days appeared here with double-barreled firearms, our lord Governor has used ten muskets taken from our armory, and he has always kept them in a room next to the armory, to have them, he says, more ready for urgent needs that might arise.

In reply, the governor justified his custody and personal use of the weapons for the sake, he said, of protecting justice and public order. Indeed, he asserted, "those arms are always ready, for his orders and for any occurrence, and he is keeping them only for the benefit of this city, as appears in the effects, for persons who are criminal, and armed with firearms never appear, as had been usual in the past."[22] In this story two concepts of order collide. The governor's, too personalized, is contrary to the interests of the community; to the bottom-up view of order and *buon governo* his vision seems dangerous, and antithetical.

---

21. BAV, Barb. lat. 9018, f. 62r.
22. BAV, Barb. lat. 9018, f. 61r–v.

"OUR CITY BEING BY NATURE FACTIOUS": ASCOLI

In April 1555, Ascoli was the theater of a bloody revolt led by several nobles, prominent among them Mariano Parisani, a man destined to symbolize the city's liberty and its opposition to papal power. He probably inspired the character Argillano in the epic *Gerusalemma Liberata*.[23] The revolt broke out in the vacant see after the death of Julius III. It aimed to free the city from papal rule, to remove the legation, and to return the power of governance to the local nobility. But the nobles, divided into quarrelsome factions, had for years shredded the social fabric and disturbed public order. In the spring of 1555, the Ascoli revolt ended with the killing of the vice-legate, Sisto Bezio da Treponzi, in the sacristy of the cathedral of Santa Maria Grande. While this was happening, Giovanni Alato, another head of the tumult, turned to the crowd to give a speech. As a trial witness reports, Alato described the vice-legate in colorful language and justified the "tyrannicide" as a step necessary for the recovery of liberty.

My citizens, be of good spirit and do not be dismayed by the death of Sisto da Treponzi, who was a lowly peasant born in a hut in Treponzi and who made himself a tyrant of this magnificent city. Be of good spirit that Sisto is dead; the tyrant is dead! And what do you think were the glories of Hercules and others like him, who killed the Centaurs, lions, bears, and other monsters, if not the death of similar tyrants. And monsters, what was a greater monster and bear than Sisto da Treponzi?[24]

The call to myth and history aimed to legitimate and sacralize the actions of the nobility and to soothe the populace of the city and countryside, discountenanced by decades of factional strife. In the middle of the sixteenth century, in Ascoli, as in other territories, to reestablish order meant to use every possible measure against a factious, rebellious nobility. The rebels, under ban one and all, suffered divers fates. To tame the sedition, establish lasting order, and reestablish papal rule, the authorities took a hard line. All the rules sent from Rome for the punishment of crimes, and especially the crime of lèse-majesté, were to be applied, neither altered nor interpret-

23. David Quint, "Political Allegory in the *Gerusalemme liberata*," *Renaissance Quarterly* 42 (1990): 1–29.

24. ASR, Tribunale Criminale del Governatore, Processi (16 secolo), busta 21, case 1, ff. 70v–71r. For the revolt of Ascoli, see Giuseppe Fabiani, *Ascoli nel Cinquecento*, vol. 1 (Ascoli Piceno: D'Auria, 1957), 284–321; Fosi, *La società violenta*, 54–58.

ed nor in any way softened. To the governors and other ministers sent to the city and the surrounding countryside went an injunction "that from now on they never make a compromise settlement [*compositione*] or commutation of ordinary punishment" without the pope's consent. These dispositions reflected the emergency, and the necessity of quelling both the revolts and the banditry that for years longer would still torment Ascoli and other zones of the state. But this rigor was destined, over the years, to lose its edge and to give way, in the next century, to mediation and dialogue.

Once the sixteenth-century rebellions against the popes had finally been tamed, Ascoli and its territory remained a reservoir of soldiers, but also of bandits.[25] Even in the seventeenth century, its position on the border with the Kingdom of Naples made it vulnerable to incursions by cross-border bandits who sacked the countryside. The town wrote to Rome about these disorders, and often asked the Sacra Consulta for help in restoring order, but in vain. At Ascoli as elsewhere, territorial control was all the harder, the further one went from Rome.

The city and its ruling class of nobles and patricians continued to defend civic identity, a tradition of governance now identified with patrician ways, and to demand the recognition of their privileges.[26] The election of a new pope was the occasion for renewing, ritually, both declarations of devotion and fealty and requests for the reaffirmation of civic traditions. After Maffeo Barberini was elected to the papal throne, on 11 December 1623, the *anziani* of Ascoli wrote his nephew, Francesco, recently made cardinal, on the occasion of their representatives' Roman mission:

To celebrate the assumption of your most meritorious uncle to the pontificate, and of your most excellent father [Carlo Barberini] to the highest rank of General of the Holy Church, and of Your Lordship to the title of grand cardinal . . . we have wished to charge Signor Lancellotti, our agent, to pass to you in the name of this city this due compliment and to ask you to listen willingly and to give faith to what he will say on behalf of this public.[27]

25. Giampiero Brunelli, *Soldati del papa. Politica militare e nobiltà nello Stato della Chiesa (1560–1644)* (Rome: Carocci, 2003).

26. For the identification of the city with its representatives, see Pietro Costa, *Civitas: Storia della cittadinanza in Europa*, vol. 1, *Dalla civiltà comunale al Settecento* (Rome: Laterza, 1999), 27; Peter Clark, *European Cities and Towns (400–2000)* (Oxford: Oxford University Press, 2008).

27. BAV, Barb. lat. 8965, f. 1r.

In effect, as we shall see, the repeated requests sent to Rome during the Barberini pontificate were almost always satisfied. Already, in April 1623, Anacleto Benedetti from Offida was named *podestà* of Ascoli, and immediately the *anziani* hastened to thank Francesco Barberini for hearing their request.

In letters sent to Rome, the respect for tradition, and affirmation of the "liberty" of the city, were an undying motif with concrete meaning. To the urban regime, to recognize the city's noble history meant, in fact, also to send Ascoli governors of high rank, perhaps even cardinals. On 23 November 1632, at the end of the mandate of Stefano Sauli, a Genoese, the *anziani* thanked the pope and asked that they be sent a minister no less worthy. Rome had always sent

to the governance of this [city] prelates of the highest worth. We recently had experience of the person of monsignor Sauli, governing for the space of two years, in which he has always shown himself most zealous in the maintenance of justice, and of peace, the rule over youth, vigilance over the food office [*abbondanza*], care for health, and shown every virtue that a people can hope for in an honored prelate.[28]

The next year there was sent to Ascoli, as a new governor, Brunoro Sciamanna, originally from Terni. He was a mere doctor in law and no prelate. The representatives of the community continued to request explicit signals of consideration, to obtain governors with a cardinal's title, or, at least, "a qualified prelate." They lamented the scanty esteem the pope had shown the city; he had declared he would send a mere *dottore* to Ascoli, while, in the meantime, "some cities that are usually governed by *dottori* are honored by prelates." So the city's agent in Rome was charged to lodge a protest, stressing that the *buon governo* of a "qualified prelate" could help guarantee the "devotion, faith, and quiet of this his most faithful and obligated city."

⚜

Ascoli's requests did not stop there. They also addressed the spiritual governance of the diocese. In December of 1638 the *anziani* wrote that

because we, as citizens, can see with our eyes our needs, we take it upon ourselves to represent to Your Beatitude that, our city being by nature factious, and as seething as ever with hatreds and rancors, and full of youth with time on its hands, it would be necessary to have a prelate who

28. BAV, Barb. lat. 8965, f. 6r.

could join to pastoral vigilance and pious and paternal zeal the authority to oppose by his own intervention those fires that in other times we have seen flare up among us. And this should be a bishop who is a cardinal.[29]

The next year, although declaring themselves satisfied with the designation of Cardinal Santacroce to the diocese of Ascoli, the town fathers nevertheless observed that his nomination "is looking murky" and feared that perhaps it would not come to pass. So they kept agitating to have a cardinal sent to be their bishop.[30] Sometimes requests would be more personal, to boost the career of a member of a powerful local family. By special courier, the *anziani* petitioned the cardinal nephew, Francesco Barberini, to intervene with the Knights of Malta to insert "our gentleman," Emiddio Saladini, into their ranks. The postulant had been refused the order's habit after the new rules of 1633 imposed more stringent proofs of noble birth.[31] From Ascoli, the *anziani*, offended and resentful, remarked:

A repulse like this manifestly detracts from the honor of this whole city, and not just of the families belonging to the [heraldic] quarters of the claimant.... It puts us in straits to see ourselves held in such low regard, even though there are encomia by writers, in every century, and the most noble pronouncements of many Supreme Pontiffs, emperors, kings, queens, and free republics, concerning the nobility of this *patria*. So there is no reason to credit a missive [containing the Knights' refusal] that arrived via a byway, and that has been rebutted, point by point, conclusively.[32]

To maintain good relations with Rome and its representatives, "to keep the province quiet," to realize Ascoli's desired *buon governo*, it was also necessary to fill canonicates and other benefices. Their economic value was not the only stake; there was also their social benefit, the honor and prestige in the eyes of the whole community. The distributive justice of the sovereign came into doubt: could he grasp and satisfy local aspirations? So, on 14 September 1632, the *anziani* sent to Rome two citizens with a petition to the pope. It buttered up the recipient, thanking him for "the honors that on every occasion he has seen fit to do this most faithful city, and particularly in the employment of so many of its citizens in past expedi-

---

29. BAV, Barb. lat. 8965, f. 13r–v.   30. BAV, Barb. lat. 8965, f. 16r.
31. Angelantonio Spagnoletti, *Stato, aristocrazie e Ordine di Malta nell'Italia moderna* (Rome: Ecole Française de Rome, 1988); H. J. A. Sire, *The Knights of Malta* (New Haven, Conn.: Yale University Press, 1996); Helen Nicholson, *The Knights Hospitaller* (London: Boydell Press, 2001), 116–37.
32. BAV, Barb. lat. 8965, f. 7r–v.

tions." Then it laid out precise requests, its tone shifting from obsequious to pushy.

> But, since for the conservation of quiet we think it necessary to add a bit of grace to the *toga*, the unhappiness of heaven not permitting it to be possible to offer a greater prize than a poor canonicate of this cathedral, [the *anziani* ask the pope to] order his ministers to see to it that the vacancies of these canonicates be provided with persons who are citizens of good birth and who have set out on the path of merit.[33]

To deny honors to local aristocrats, so went the plea, would open the door to disorders, compromise good governance and justice, and undermine yet further any consensus that upheld their city's precarious balance of power, neither stable nor permanent. Ascoli should not become a reservoir for benefices for "foreigners," as had happened with other southern Italian churches.[34] In the letters of the *anziani* the city and its church were a seamless unit, a symbol of a shared history to be asserted and defended in the face of Rome's logic of papal rule. Ascoli was not alone in this; seventeenth century correspondence abounds with negotiations between Rome and local oligarchies over matters of *buon governo* and territorial control.

Fidelity was a leitmotiv. Bad functionaries, if not up to their job, could undermine loyalty. This fidelity was not just a given; it was negotiated, with an eye to traditions, local balances of power, and everything that constructed the local identity that a town defended and deployed in the face of the center's might. So, for instance, Perugia, in the very middle of Urban VIII's profligate, futile Castro war to retake the Farnese lands, raised the issue of its fidelity, threatened by the soldiers' lust for loot. Their misconduct was "without true profit, rather, with inestimable damage to the Prince," said the city. It lashed out against bad governance, abuses, and "the negligence and grasping habits of the ministers."[35] The city totted up the usual havoc wrought by the unruly, grasping soldiery, lamenting the "scarcity of pay." Perugia, like Ascoli, was a subject town. Its protestations illustrate how, even under papal absolutism, all the communities of the papal state retained a degree of agency. Slow justice and imperfect administration left them both room and reason for self-assertion.

33. BAV, Barb. lat. 8965, f. 5r.
34. Mario Rosa, "La chiesa meridionale nell'età della Controriforma," in *Storia d'Italia, Annali*, vol. 9, *La Chiesa e il potere politico*, ed. Giorgio Chittolini and Giovanni Miccoli, 291–345 (Turin: Einaudi, 1986).
35. BAV, Chigiano, F. VI, ff. 85r–92v.

12

Rivers of Ink
Petitions, Memorials, Letters

THE EAR OF THE POPE

In the old regime's society, the commonest means of communication between subjects and their sovereign was the petition. It was an instrument for modulating and adapting justice, a device to narrow the gap between sentence and punishment; it spoke to power and, by grace of communication, recognized it and bestowed legitimacy. Petitions (*suppliche*) and memorials (*memoriali*), as sources, are both fascinating and enigmatic.[1] Although prone to repetition, they are often quirky and captivating. They offer an image of daily life, of collective and individual behavior; though sieved through a mesh of commonplaces and formulae, they are a device for self-representation and a medium of personal communication. But petitions are perilous sources, as their details distort society's image. Suppliants often appear older than their actual years; their offspring are always unbearably numerous, "unproductive [*inutili*], and at risk"; moreover, almost every petitioner complains of illnesses as dire as they are vague, and usually well beyond the ken of diagnosis. To round out this doleful scene, often richly painted, is the vague presence of assorted murky enemies more or less at fault for the petitioner's own misdeeds, whether actual or just ballyhooed by "rivals." These misdeeds have prompted, the petitions claim, excessive punishments which have flayed individual and collective honor, disturbed familial and communal peace, and troubled social order; all such woes the prince's own hand and justice might just now set right. All told, then, petitions are less likely than many other sources to tell us "the truth." Or, to be precise, they tell us a

---

1. In this book, we use petitions and memorials (*suppliche* and *memoriali*) as synonyms. In formal diplomatics, they were distinct; the *supplica* was an official document presented to authorities, while *memoriali* were unofficial and less fixed in destination: Thomas Frenz, *I documenti pontifici nel medioevo e in età moderna* (Vatican City: Archivio Segreto Vaticano, 1989), 74.

subjective "truth," intentionally freighted with signals that lay out a strategic reality of the author's devising, every utterance scheming to provoke the sovereign's gracious intervention. This self-image collides and tangles with another image—forged by power's institutions and broadcast by propaganda's words and images—one that vaunted order and justice.

Why then might a source so flawed seem still so valuable? How does it let us grasp essential aspects of old regime society, its vertical relationships of state and subjects, and its horizontal ones, among subjects, in their assorted hierarchies and groups? First of all, there is the source's bulk itself; it is, without exaggeration, well nigh endless. Petitions are even today ubiquitous, in the papers of civil and criminal, church and lay tribunals. They also appear in archived correspondence, where they often lurk in the guise of letters. Memorials and *suppliche* that implore papal justice—the nod of sovereign will—plead for changed relations between subjects and their lords. They also plead for a shift in the links between authorities themselves—judicial ones especially—in the center and periphery, as such relationships looked from down below, from the petitioner's own station and location. What do these records tell us? Do they better illustrate crime, or punishment and justice? Whichever the case, the papers are so abundant and repetitive that they give historians the illusion of confronting, over and over, the selfsame issues and protagonists. They also project an image, fluid and many-sided, of a running dialogue between the sovereign and his subjects, and also between the central and peripheral offices of state, obliged to apply the rules, but modifying and adapting them, chipping away the rigid bark of their promulgated form. Eyeing only petitions sent by subjects, one has the illusion of a monologue, a freshet of requests unheard by a distant power plainly unable to listen. But, in fact, these papers went just everywhere; on the one hand, they bear witness to belief, or at least hope, that one would be heard; on the other hand, they testify to the ability of the written word to jog power—in this case justice, but, ever more, institutions in general—into action on subjects' behalf. To petition was to establish a rapport with power, constraining it to listen, learn, and govern well. Meanwhile, petitioning served also to recognize and legitimate authority and to bolster its coercive power.

The old regime recognized subjects' capacity to appeal judgments on any level. One could petition decisions of civil and criminal courts of first and second instance. But the "second instance" did not exclude an even higher "final" instance with no appeal, like the *governatore* or the pope himself. A petitioner's appeal presupposed a hierarchy among judges. The recourse to a higher judge, here the pontiff as highest judge of all, belonged to the Roman tradition of *appellatio*, codified in the age of Augustus, and then passed on into medieval *ius commune* (common Roman law). When, in petitions and memorials, subjects demanded justice from a higher judge, or indeed, directly, from the highest judge, they tended to subject him to higher principles, and to free him from any contingencies that might harm and hem his work; all told, they held him to the proper administration of justice. So said the ancien régime's juridical theory.[2] The double nature of papal monarchy, sacred and secular, certainly reinforced both the image and the real capacity of the pope as a just highest magistrate; canon law, after all, made openness to petition an attribute not of the pope alone, but of any bishop. This papal capacity looked both back and forward; if on the one hand it evoked the basic traits of sovereign absolutist power, on the other hand it anticipated modernity. As noted above, when the highest authority accepted a petition and, in its judgment, showed its *auctoritas* over a *res iudicata* (a matter that had been judged), it helped set off a revolution in governance that "foretold, and imposed, to use modern language, new relations between citizens and the state."[3]

WRITING, AND COMMISSIONING WRITING

Precise rules regulated the composition of the memorials and petitions that beseeched a pontiff's help. They must be directed to the pope himself; always, "Most Blessed Father" were the unmistakable first words. They had to present the postulant, attaching all information that flagged identity and position. They must also expound the facts of the case clearly, beg grace, and lay out all reasons for higher justice's intervention. The subject's right to this *appellatio* traced back to rules enshrined in the laws of ancient Rome. In medieval and early modern Europe, these rules became more precise and richer in detail—on the one hand to satisfy the ever more com-

2. Riccardo Orestano, "Appello, (Diritto Romano)," in *Novissimo Digesto Italiano*, I, i, 723–25 (Turin: UTET, 1974).
    3. Ibid.

plex workings of the papal chancery and the pope's evolving bureaucracy, and on the other hand to assuage the characteristic Italian "need to write" that found an outlet in these petitions, as often
elsewhere.[4] Petitions infiltrated the chanceries and bureaucratic organs of the state; their diffusion illustrates the acceleration of written communication so characteristic of early modern times. There
was a "writing revolution" with more to it than just its flood of paper. Petitioning was an activity, with its times, movements, and
purposes, and, along with other papers, it contributed to what Armando Petrucci, historian of writing, calls the "rapid transformation of public administration, into bureaucratic structures always
more complex, more widespread, and better linked together; the
centrality of the role of a new intellectual-bureaucrat, the secretary,
and the multiplication, in kind and number, of written documentation, in the form of letters."[5]

In petitions one cannot hear subjects' authentic voices; they are
normally masked by stereotypes: in the bid for sovereign pity and
grace, the supplicant, on paper, is almost always poor, needy, and
honest. Nor can one see the subject's authentic hand, and thereby gauge education, for the script itself was seldom the petitioner's own. Nor does it suffice to consider petitions as just a literary
genre.[6] In form, in the church state as elsewhere, they are best seen
less as works of literature than as an expression of the culture of notaries—a culture sometimes a little rough, conservative, and scle-
rotic—for, to access tribunals, judges, and the curia, one normally

4. Daniele Marchesini, *Il bisogno di scrivere. Usi della scrittura nell'Italia moderna*
(Rome: Laterza, 1992). For the manuals, which in early modern Italy dictated the rules
for composing memorials and letters of every sort, see Amedeo Quondam, *Le "carte
messaggiere." Retorica e modelli di comunicazione epistolare. Per un indice dei libri di lettere
del Cinquecento* (Rome: Bulzoni, 1981); Stefano Iucci, "La trattatistica sul segretario tra
la fine del Cinquecento e il primo ventennio del Seicento," *Roma moderna e contemporanea* 3 (1995): 81–96. Even in the early eighteenth century, the rules for drafting memorials still followed this centuries-old design: Francesco Parisi, *Istruzioni per la gioventù
impiegata nelle Segretarie, specialmente in quelle della Corte romana* (Rome: I. Fulgoni,
1781).

5. Armando Petrucci, "Introduzione alle pratiche di scrittura," *Annali della Scuola Normale Superiore di Pisa*, Classe di Lettere e Filosofia, series 3, vol. 23, no. 2 (1993):
549–62. For works translated into English, see Armando Petrucci, *Writers and Readers in Medieval Italy: Studies in the History of Written Culture* (New Haven, Conn.: Yale
University Press, 1995); Petrucci, *Public Lettering: Script, Power, and Culture* (Chicago:
University of Chicago Press, 1993).

6. Natalie Zemon Davis, *Fiction in the Archives: Pardon Tales and Their Tellers in
Sixteenth-Century France* (Stanford, Calif.: Stanford University Press, 1987).

had recourse to notaries.[7] Often for the drafting one turned not to notaries but to mere scribes, who knew their formulae, seldom polished the prose, and worked from the supplicants' own spontaneous, often garbled dictation. Many street scribes drafted letters on a bench at the crossroads. But they had some colleagues with higher literary pretensions, and others with even lower—some barely literate, as we see from petitions written for convicts in prison or the galleys beseeching a sentence's remission.[8] The scribal formulae, however, were no mere rigid containers of frozen commonplaces. Postulants could use and adapt them, as could, especially, their scribe-intermediaries, who, despite weak writing skills, often strove to snatch echoes of actual facts, in a quest for images and turns of phrase to enliven and empower their timeworn tropes.

IN THE LABYRINTH OF THE CURIA

While the medieval itinerary of papal petitions is well known, for the early modern era things are far less clear.[9] There were chancery rules, but what actual route did petitions take? It was the pope himself who decided a case, said the rules, as listening was itself an act of sovereignty. So, in the Middle Ages, a petition was presented, aloud, to the pope himself, especially when church benefices were at stake. This action was a powerful, explicit symbol of the pope's sovereignty and the sacrality of his office.

In the fifteenth century, however, there arose a new office, the Segretaria dei memoriali.[10] From then on, petitions were read, scrutinized, and summarized in the office of the referendary of memorials and only later, in extraordinary cases, laid before the pope, who then decided by virtue of his *viva voce* authority. The referendary, a secretary of memorials, had the pope's confidence, and was usually

7. "Below the threshold of letters, one writes, and is constrained. The paradox of the society of the Old Regime lies in this: on the one hand, one wrote a lot, and written communication invaded every corner of social life; but, on the other hand, that did not mean that common individuals had to have an active rapport with writing; on the contrary, it eliminated it." Attilio Bartoli Langeli, *La scrittura dell'italiano* (Bologna: il Mulino, 2000), 109. For notaries, see also Attilio Bartoli Langeli, *Notai. Scrivere documenti nel Medioevo* (Rome: Viella, 2006); Laurie Nussdorfer, *Brokers of Public Trust: Notaries in Early Modern Rome* (Baltimore: Johns Hopkins University Press, 2009).

8. For petitions from prison, see Laura Chiarotti, "La popolazione del carcere nuovo nella seconda metà del XVII secolo," *Archivio della Società Romana di Storia Patria* 115 (1992): 147–79.

9. Frenz, *I documenti pontifici*, 72–75.

10. For surviving records see ASV, Segretaria dei Memoriali, vols. 1–19 (1636–1667).

linked to him by fealty, friendship, kinship, or shared birthplace. It
was his duty to refer to the pontiff, on the appointed days, *in exten-
so* or in brief, all written requests for grace and justice. At the end
of his audience, he carried back the pope's decision, written on the
petition's reverse.[11] The secretary became crucial to the process; in
treatises on the curia, he came to figure as the link between subjects and their sovereign: there was no going around him. But, late
in the sixteenth century, starting with Sixtus V, many congregations
of cardinals were invested with the authority to deliberate on their
own on matters befitting their competence. This change was typical of the curial reforms of Sixtus V, who championed specialization
and expertise.

The pope's sovereign function of hearing petitions, codified in
the Middle Ages with precise rules, ceremonies, and symbolic actions, all in the curia, had awakened and broadcast trust in his direct protection of his subjects and his ear for their requests. But the
elaboration of papal bureaucracy, from the fifteenth century on, removed the pope ever more from this fundamental function, from
then on in practice performed by curial officials. The evolution also
swelled the ranks of potential patrons, conferring ever greater power of intercession upon members of the pope's own family, upon the
cardinals, and, with Sixtus V, upon the congregations' prefects. The
fragmentation of the powers to judge and to distribute benefices
explains why, from the late sixteenth century, though petitions still
address the pope himself, at the same time they also signal an actual addressee: the office or person at the curia best placed to accept
or thwart the plea. When a petition aimed for justice, or for grace,
the decisions of the relevant departments seldom settled matters.
Things took their good time: not rarely someone asked for a supplementary inquiry, often granted, or the admission of new defense
arguments. In other cases, the final decision was written on the
bottom or back of the folio. A request was more likely to succeed if
it dealt with release from a penalty already largely paid—exile, out-
lawry, the galleys—in exchange for a cash settlement, its size left to
the magistrate's discretion.

It was crucial, as notarial formulae of liberation at page-bottom
often stress, that one have made one's peace with the offended par-

11. Gaetano Moroni, *Dizionario di erudizione storico-ecclesiastica*, vol. 43 (Venice:
Tipografia Emiliana, 1847), 18–92.

ties. The petitions themselves hastened to stress the pursuit of this ritual of pacification, essential to resolving a conflict and to recomposing the social order a crime had troubled, restoring the honor of injured parties, and legitimating an offender's reinsertion into both community and good legal standing after some breach of the law and of the social rules. The peace agreement had to be concluded before a notary or a tribunal, and the certificate itself sometimes arrived attached to the petition. Nevertheless, in the absence of notarial proofs, judges not rarely interrogated reliable witnesses or probed "public voice and fame" (a legal term for public reputation) to prove a reconciliation.[12]

The pope's subjects had a hard time seeing clearly this complex, piecemeal pathway through chancery. Especially when one lived far from Rome, it was not easy to understand the itinerary a request should follow. From the beginning of the seventeenth century, the heads of tribunals and of congregations received more and more petitions directed straight to them.[13] These papers were then forwarded to the many Roman confraternities, some of which, thanks to papal privilege, had the power to spare a person condemned to death or free a prisoner. There was a veritable battle among petitioners for the chance to line up for such a benefit. It was a struggle for a bit of grace, a whiff, via confraternal mediation, of that essence of sovereign power, usually so distant and oppressive. One needed a good word put in by one's parish priest, and the protection of the local powerbrokers and perhaps also of powers in Rome. Public reputation (*publica fama*) played a crucial role, but chief of all was peace with the offended party. Meanwhile, grace, via confraternities, seldom came free of charge; very often, with the petition, the brothers wanted alms, often ample ones. When one lacked funds, grasping hands might obstruct an already thorny path to forgiveness.[14]

Petitioners reacted slowly to the growing complexity of the papal court. In the seventeenth century the curia grew ever more strati-

12. Girolamo Casanate, governor of Ancona, consulta of 1 February 1657, BC, MS 1355, f. 91r, for this procedure.

13. ASR, Tribunale Criminale del Governatore, Atti vari di cancelleria, busta 127–133 (1656–1668).

14. Cecilia Nubola, "Liberazioni per privilegio. Confraternite e grazia nella prima età moderna (secoli XVI–XVIII)," in *Chiesa e mondo moderno. Scritti in onore di Paolo Prodi*, ed. Adriano Prosperi, Pierangelo Schiera, and Gabriella Zarri, 235–56 (Bologna: Il Mulino, 2007).

fied and complex, but subjects, notaries, scribes, and all communication's other intermediaries were not always quick to accept the fact. Many subjects kept right on writing to the pope himself, and strove to meet him face to face to hand him their requests. But by this time the curial apparatus had taken a very different path. Innocent XII (1691–1700) did try in vain to bring "audiences" back to life; within a few years the attempt went under. Innocent did not portray his campaign, part of his major reforms of the curia and the justice system, as an innovation. Rather, it was an anachronistic move, the resumption of a medieval custom, abandoned more than a century earlier, but retaining its powerful symbolism.[15]

Among the state's subjects, faith in direct relations with the pope, font of justice and grace, remained strong. This was true not only of the Eternal City's inhabitants, who took advantage of the solemn processions to present petitions, especially at the *Possesso* ceremony, the newly elected pontiff's cavalcade from Saint Peter's to the Lateran.[16] Note this story by Faustina Stella, an elderly Roman woman who gave her petition directly to Clement VIII "in his going to San Giovanni." Addressing the pope with the formal, impersonal "you" one reserved for superiors, she lamented her poverty and her need to pawn to the Jews some of her goods, for first fifty and then twenty scudi

to be able to sustain us in these penurious and calamitous times. But the poor supplicant [*oratrice*: literally, pray-er], having three times gone to your palace when you were cardinal, when, finally, you were going into the conclave, predicted to you that you were going to assume such a dignity [i.e., the papacy], was not able to have the favour of speaking to you; she petitions you today, once more; she petitions and beseeches you to give her sufficient aid, so that the aforesaid fifty and twenty scudi be paid her, lest the poor supplicant be forced to go around begging.[17]

Clearly, Faustina's try for direct contact with the pope failed, for, as this petition shows, after the *Possesso* she continued to push her claims via the curia's tortuous meanders.

15. Claudio Donati, "'Ad radicitus submovendum': materiali per una storia de progetti di riforma giudiziaria durante il pontificio di Innocenzo XII," in *Riforme, religione e politica durante il pontificio di Innocenzo XII (1691–1700)*, ed. Bruno Pellegrino, 159–78 (Galatina: Congedo, 1994).

16. Irene Fosi, "Court and City in the Ceremony of the Possesso in the Sixteenth Century," in *Court and Politics in Papal Rome, 1492–1700*, ed. Gianvittorio Signorotto and Maria Antonietta Visceglia, 31–52 (Cambridge: Cambridge University Press, 2002).

17. ASV, Segreteria di Stato, Memoriali e biglietti, busta 1.

POTENT INTERMEDIARIES

A request's happy outcome, in justice and other matters, depended on many things; certainly chief among them was the role of the petition's patron. It was no easy matter to find the right potentate to solicit via back channels. Petitions and oral requests came in from the whole state, even from the furthest villages, as well as from Rome itself. As the seventeenth century wore on and more and more persons close to the pope's own family, and to the cardinal nephew's, were sought out as intermediaries, a veritable assembly line sprang up. From the parish priest via the bishop, or via a local notable, one might arrive at a cardinal or, via shortcut, at some fellow townsman who had made his career in Rome, in the curia or at the pope's court. A patron's intervention could clinch a case. So the choice of a patron brought into play aspects of old regime interpersonal relations, both vertical and horizontal—ties of shared birthplace, service, fealty, and feudal loyalty.

In 1622, "moved by mercy," Giannantonio Orsini, duke of San Gemini, wrote the pope on behalf of a vassal who had been condemned to exile but was allowed to be confined for two years to Ferrara (a papal city). He was "poor, and burdened with family, and more worthy of compassion than are others because he was seduced by a priest, his kinsman, who was condemned to the galleys for five years." The duke's request, for a three-month safe-conduct "to see his family again and to provide them with sustenance," was passed to the governor and accepted. Nobles' requests were usually effective; they often settled matters, especially when the author could cash in on prestigious positions at the curia held by churchmen in the family or among its allies. Belardino Veniero from Ferrara, "coachman in Rome," accused of stealing a harness and sentenced to perpetual exile, turned to the governor himself to have the ban overturned. He reminded him, among other things, how he had served in Rome "most honorably, as his patrons themselves have reported, and in particular Monsignor Laudivio Zacchia" (jurist, cardinal, and member of the Holy Office court that tried Galileo). On the back of the petition, the deliberators endorsed the revocation of his exile. Geronimo Colonna, a Venetian, had the same success with a request to get out of jail. He wrote the governor, "to remedy his bad fortune, knowing that Signor Mario Caffarelli paid people in the name of Signor Marchese Vitelli to serve the Holy

See, he had enlisted as heavy cavalry soldier." Colonna asserted that he had been jailed unjustly for carrying arms, and alleged that he had the *bollettino* (permit) for bearing weapons and declared himself "ready to lay my life on the line for the Holy See."[18] Colonna leveraged his two patrons, one a Roman noble and the other a cardinal, plus his military service, to extract his pardon from the pope. The patron, as intermediary, had on earth the same roles, as intercessor and protector, that the saints and Virgin had in heaven when they stepped in to serve terrestrial providence or eternal salvation.[19] A successful petition could remedy the imbalance between actual guilt and harsh official punishment; it could reduce banishment, a punitive device that the Papal State abused and that, as we have seen, uprooted men, broke up families, and set off a tidal wave of social dislocation that caused further crime.

Often hidden, though no less effective than male patrons and often called on by petitioners, were the women of the pope's own family. Petitioners turned, for instance, to Costanza Magalotti Barberini, Urban VIII's sister-in-law, invoking the "mantle" of her powerful protection. This sartorial metaphor evoked the famous, widespread image of the Madonna as protectress, sheltering a gathering of huddled faithful beneath her cloak. Pompilia, "a poor old woman, and a widow, who has been the wet nurse for the Signor Prince Aldobrandino and has also been most devoted to his service," wrote Costanza asking her intercession for a son in prison:

Under the pretext that he had committed many thefts, he has already been condemned to death. Interpose yourself with your authority and see to it that the aforesaid Giovanni Battista, her son, not die so ignominious a death, but be sent to the galleys to pay the penalty for his ill deeds.[20]

Costanza passed Pompilia's petition to the Confraternita del Suffragio, where the sentence was reduced to three years in the galleys. Women who sought the patronage of ladies of the Roman court, and of kinsfolk of the pope, rummaged in their pasts for good proof of connections, even if thin and evanescent, that suggested a

18. ASR, Tribunale Criminale del Governatore, Atti vari di cancelleria, busta 85, nos. 56 and 58.

19. Albrecht Burckardt, *Les clients des saints. Maladie et quête du miracle à travers les procés de canonisation de la première moitié du XVIIe siècle en France* (Rome: Ecole Française de Rome, 2004).

20. ASR, Tribunale Criminale del Governatore, Atti vari di cancelleria, busta 84, no. 21.

link with the patron's person, or with her family. Domestic service however brief, wet-nursing, or marriage to a past servant might secure a good result. Such memories meant very different things for the petitioner and the patron; they were fragments of the past that, for the unfortunate, kindled hopes of a better future.

TO TELL TALES, AND TELL ONE'S OWN STORY

Petitions were partisan self-portraits, hardly objective, where the self often had its helpers. To escape the oar or banishment, disingenuous blasts at "enemies" and florid catalogues of the petitioner's own supposed merits laid a thick double smokescreen across what really happened. Very often, as we have seen, the petition was written by someone else; seldom were the author and the grace-seeker one and the same. Usually, it was kinfolk who initiated the plea. Mothers wrote, and wives and sisters—or, rather, had a letter written—for sons, husbands, and brothers. These petitioners portrayed themselves as poor, laden with unproductive offspring, and with daughters teetering on the verge of sin. Sometimes, for greater impact, the request for justice took pains to muster group solidarity. Thus Dorotea and Domenica di Lugnano, "very poor and burdened with family," denounced to the governor what they called the irregularity of the trial against their husbands, at the hands of one Angelo Nardi, a notary of the governor's court.

The poor husbands are innocent and the trial is false, utterly false. We petition in the name of the Viscera of Our Lord to assign them another notary. We allege that the said Angelo Nardi is suspect, utterly suspect, for he has always shown himself to be both party and judge in the said case, and, to keep it so, he has controlled who appears in court and has arranged the steps of the proceedings.

At the outset, the two petitioners alleged, there had been impostures, and acts of revenge by a fellow villager, who had later been denounced and "turned over to the court and condemned to five years in the galleys."[21] Other petitions had male authors, usually pleading for family: brothers, sons. They narrate the events that led to the offense and stress extenuating circumstances—the defense of honor, youth, "foolishness" (*poco cervello*), legitimate self-defense against "enemies"—and they are careful to unload the

21. ASR, Tribunale Criminale del Governatore, Atti vari di cancelleria, busta 85, no. 8.

blame for the misdeed on these ubiquitous "adversaries." Such petitions stress, instead, the sentence's severity, the good behavior of the delinquent—or the innocent unjustly condemned—and the peace with all injured parties that guaranteed respect for order when the course of justice at last came around at the end. Thus, male petitions differed somewhat from female ones in their strategies of self-presentation, even where the woman used male scribes. The men stressed hard work, good service, loyalty, and the generous and politic willingness to concede a peace. The women, meanwhile, summoned up the language of piety and mercy, and reminded readers of their own solid, familial morality, as faithful, honest household members. But, above all, petitions, male and female, stressed the benefits, or harm, at stake, not only for the postulant but also for the whole community, for family, and for wider kin; a petition was no mere solo, but an implicit chorus.

In 1622, Cesare Ricci wrote the pope a detailed story. Five years before, he had been

assaulted by Annibale the potter . . . not once but many times. The petitioner was unarmed, and, with his own weapons [and those of] the aforesaid Sinibaldo killed him [Annibale], as appears in the legal papers of Monsignore Governor of Rome, who condemned the petitioner to death, in absentia, for he had fled [*in contumacia*]. But the petitioner, who is very poor, and is burdened with a family without any financial support, having now obtained peace from the opposing party, supplicates Your Holiness to deign to do him grace, that he be given remission freely. For he has no way of gaining remission while in the countryside, for he is very poor. And so that his family not be scattered, given that he is outside the State of the Church.

At the bottom of Cesare's petition appears the decision: even though it is a homicide, since the culprit has already spent five years on the run, his liberation would be entrusted to the Confraternita di Santa Maria del Carmine, in Rome's Trastevere district.[22]

Despite the readiness to petition on behalf of kin, family solidarity had its limits. Family members might turn to justice seeking protection against violence, death threats, and vendettas by their own kinfolk. Often, mothers implored a firm intervention against unruly sons, or wives against violent husbands. Arigo Giletti, who

22. ASR, Tribunale Criminale del Governatore, Atti vari di cancelleria, busta 84, no. 3.

had been jailed at Corte Savelli, was turned in by his own mother because

the aforesaid son tried to hit her on the head with a big cudgel. Had she not retreated, he would have carried out his evil intention. Because he has ill will against the said petitioner, and has declared his intention to harm her property, and has made a pact with others to destroy her vineyard and to harm her in her income . . . all told he does not want to do what is right, but to go amuse himself, and he does not want to be a gentleman under the control of his mother and his stepfather.

The mother went on: "He should not be set free under any pretext whatsoever, for fear that he has it in him to do wrong, for one sees he is a bad character [*tristo*]."[23] Arigo's mother seems to have wanted to defend her family's new equilibrium, a certain economic security guaranteed by a second marriage that, clearly, her son rejected. The tribunal's decision seems not to have favored the mother; on the back are the words "there is no reason [*non c'è mente*]." The community itself may have looked askance at the widow's second marriage and new ménage. Still, the mother's request for the court's forceful intervention into the family sphere reveals society's frequent incapacity or unwillingness to resolve domestic conflicts without the state's intervention. Sometimes, for families, the state, as "sovereign guardian," seemed the one desperate last chance to restore domestic relations. Not only did mothers and widows resort to law; there were even fathers who felt threatened in their role and local honor by the actions of unruly or delinquent sons.[24]

If, as we have seen, male and female narratives were different, and built identity in different ways, not always did gender set the voice. Men, like women, portrayed themselves as poor, with families in peril should the petition go unheeded. In such plaints, male strength is masked, and the defense of honor, though implicitly at stake, goes undiscussed. Men needed to identify themselves by their work, be it, with luck, service in the train of a potentate at court or a crusade for Christendom in the many wars against heretics or Turks. For women, meanwhile, identity lodged in domestic rhythms and household labor. Petitions, especially female ones,

23. ASR, Tribunale Criminale del Governatore, Atti vari di cancelleria, busta 85, no. 63.

24. Luca Mannori, *Il sovrano tutore: pluralismo istituzionale e accentramento amministrativo nel principato dei Medici, secc. 16.–18* (Milan: Giuffrè, 1994).

often refer, directly or obliquely, to local personages, parish priests especially, who could vouch for the respectable background and good conduct of the supplicants, victims of abuse and violent acts deleterious to honor.

Maddalena was a Roman courtesan, or perhaps one of those many women who from day to day navigated the slippery boundaries between marriage and other sexual bargains and who therefore seemed more dangerous because, unlike official, public prostitutes, they evaded authorities' surveillance and control. Turning to the governor, she told her story:

> Some days back, she had gone to bed, and certain young men from Savoy arrived, and they made her get dressed and they took her out to have fun around Rome, and when they were near the house of a certain Fulvia, the said young men fired off a pistol loaded with bullets and hit the window of the said Fulvia.

After Fulvia's denunciation, Maddalena stayed in jail for eighteen days, and then was released and exiled from Rome. Having made peace with Fulvia, she declares in her petition that she lives from alms alone and alleges a voucher, a *fede*, by the parish priest of San Biagio della Fossa, a Roman church:

> Maddalena is of a good father and a good mother, who died in my parish, and I hope that the said petitioner will rededicate herself to a virtuous life, staying in Rome, for she has found a respectable old man who will give her bread and wine every day until she marries.

On the back of Maddalena's petition appears the formula *concedatur non gravetur*—let her not be burdened.[25] It proves that the tribunal preferred to reinsert Maddalena into her community on the basis of precise guarantees furnished by trustworthy patrons, above all "her own parish priest," vigilant custodian of order and morality, as the Council of Trent had wished. Moreover, Maddalena's peace pact and the offer, from a man who seemed well past sin, of material support, an alternative to sexual commerce, guaranteed social tranquility and moral order and also freed up the cluttered legal docket.

25. ASR, Tribunale Criminale del Governatore, Atti vari di cancelleria, busta 85, no. 36.

THE INJUSTICES OF JUSTICE

What, for subjects, was injustice, and what were the instruments, rhetorical and other, to denounce and repair it? Injustice meant to punish too severely. It also meant to let go free those who besmirched themselves with crime, scandal, or irremediable offense to sovereign justice. Injustice also meant offense to the statutory rights and customary laws of towns and villages. And injustice, too, was blatant, irremediable corruption by local judicial personnel. Injustice was also the frequent disproportion between crime and punishment. So, when they confronted the injustices of everyday justice, and the failed attempts at extrajudicial settlement via composition and private reconciliation, subjects across the state turned to Rome, to the sovereign superior justice incarnated in the pope, to correct abuses and furnish tangible examples of *buon governo*.

In 1620, for instance, Fulvio Ionio, from Cerreto, a village near Spoleto, wrote the pope, complaining

how some years back Sellante Arducci, for an intentional homicide [*homicidio con assassinio*] committed on the person of Giulio, brother of the petitioner, was banished and condemned in the tribunal of Florence and of Norcia [near Spoleto], and for other crimes by the Principality of Massa, with a death sentence. And having later been put in prison for other crimes [*eccessi*] in the State of Milan, he was by that Senate condemned to the galleys, from where, on orders of Your Beatitude, he was brought to Rome on orders of the Auditor of the Camera. By way of powerful favors his death sentence was commuted to perpetual galley slavery and he was transported to Civitavecchia. For about two years not only has he not rowed, but also, thanks to favors from those ministers, he is treated like a gentleman, just going in chains with all his ease, and he is transferred from one galley to another, without ever leaving port in sailing season, with little honor to justice, for he is not carrying out the intentions of the Patrons [the state], nor is he suffering the mortifications that so atrocious a crime deserves. He is cocky, as if he had not committed any crime at all, making a bad example and scandal for all to see, and what is worse, he has been put on the list of incurable invalids, and it seems likely that he is actually to be set free.[26]

The suppliant's words do not limit themselves to describing the injustice suffered by him and by his family. They widen the pic-

26. ASR, Tribunale Criminale del Governatore, Atti vari di cancelleria, busta 83, no. 3 (1620–1621).

ture to embrace the whole social context in which he lived, and the communal rules so brashly scorned and broken, the transgressions tolerated, and the scandalous actions of the ministers of justice. He wishes to voice his claim upon his lord, summoning him to his duty, as sovereign and as father and protector of his subjects.

The image of the just judge, attached to the pontiff by both treatises and iconography, also featured in petitions' formulae. It appeared both in the freer prose, sometimes in the author's own hand, of educated persons, *dottori* or clerics, and also in texts that owed their phrasing to a notary's formulary, adapted to the case at hand. Requests for, and expectations of, severe just punishment and due clemency did not come from individual subjects only. Often, the family or even the entire community sought protection from crimes that had upset their internal balance and social bonds. Left unpunished, said petitioners, such things could set a dreadful example. In 1623, Francesco da Baldo wrote the pope in the name of his community, the village of Palazzo di Assisi. He spared no details of a scandalous case, said he, that offended the collectivity and besmirched the image of Rome's justice in the provinces. The petition favored an accusatory style that rolled confidently from point to marshaled point; it was less a solo song than an oratorio of blame:

Some days back a complaint was registered before Monsignor Governor of Perugia against Evangelista di Tommaso, who is also from the same village of Palazzo, for several excesses. And, among the others, for a homicide committed against Bernardo di Morellino. Item: for having played host continually to men banished under pain of death, and to their servants, for other homicides, assassinations, and robberies. . . . Item: for having fired an harquebus at two other men, father and son, to kill them both; [even] if, in fact, it did not succeed because, as pleased the Lord, the harquebus failed to fire. Item: for having stolen a virgin from her mother and deflowered her by force, who, a few days later, died. Item: having broken and robbed the mill of the community of Assisi. Item: having stolen a shirt and other goods to a value of twenty-five scudi from the curate priest of the said village of Palazzo and for other crimes mentioned in the trial. And even though all the aforesaid accusations have been proved, still the said Evangelista, cited here, has never been in prison, and this for no other reason than that he is very rich and finally, that, in the belief that he could go scot-free, he has obtained an order from this court, directed to Monsignor Governor, that he [the governor] proceed no further in this case, so that the petitioner is afraid that, alongside his other offenses, he will break the neck of justice and that such a man will get off unpunished.

The petitioner asked the pope to remand the case to the governor of Rome, who here figures not as an intruder, but as the best instrument to overcome the connivances and unfairness of local justice.

For the authorities in Rome, these writings, flooding toward the curia daily, were a way to know the state's realities. But they also served as a means to influence the workings of local justice, to adjust its rules and correct the operations of its organs, which often were not up to the complexity and diversity of conditions in the provinces. Petitions expressed and manipulated inequality, in vertical relationships. They also showed subjects' faith in the value of personal connections, and in the usefulness of the papal court's milieu. So they influenced governance, at the state's most important junctures, mediating the power of local elites, thanks to governors and legates. In power's endless back and forth, center and periphery were not opposites. In their use of language, the subjects participated in the construction of the state and in the legitimization of authority.[27] The periphery suggested, communicated, supplicated; central authority responded not as a monolith, but as a complex system of forces mediated by a plethora of figures, institutions, and bodies, all of them important cogs in the machinery of early modern papal monarchy.

27. Peter Blickle, "Conclusions," in *Resistance, Representation and Community* (Oxford: Clarendon Press, 1997), 336–38.

13

Justice Represented,
Justice Recounted

The campaign for effective justice had its own elaborate imagery, much of which can be traced to the sixteenth century. At mid-century, justice and *buon governo* confronted an infinite variety of situations and unforeseen problems. Good rule had to compromise with forces it would much rather have tamed or squelched outright. It had to make do with "ministers" who fell far short of treatises' ideals and rules Trent set. Nevertheless, in this very era, in Rome, justice and *buon governo* were presented, and extolled, in a new way, in a variety of idioms—in ceremonies and painted picture cycles, and on coins and medals. Justice basked in panegyrics of paltry literary merit and in the praise of renowned authors of dense treatises defending the supremacy of the church of Rome. By 1550, themes of peace, abundance, and justice were no longer statecraft novelties; already, Leo X (1513–1521) famously had presented himself as heir to the prosperity of ancient Rome, in line with the Medici legend that celebrated a renewed Golden Age back when his father, Lorenzo the Magnificent, presided over Florence.

In the first decades of the sixteenth century, the dramatic, dangerous Italian Wars shifted the themes of the pontiff's celebration far from intimations of Augustan Rome. This change reflected not only the accidents of diplomacy, but also heresy's rapid spread. Symbols of force and war, not of justice or clemency, festooned papal policies toward the foreign sovereigns, French and Spanish Imperial, contending for supremacy on Italian soil. Lasting peace came to Italy in 1557, and to France and Spain, its rivalrous chronic disturbers, in 1559. So it was in the century's second half that justice really took over, utterly, as symbol of papal sovereignty. The papacy had by then conquered its own well-bounded territory and had taken to governing it, ideally, with severity, justice, and clemency, a mix of traits that reflected, evoked, and summed up the double nature of the pontiff's power. It is thus no accident that images celebrating the triumph of justice, like Vasari's *Giustizia Farnese* (1543), attached to an ambitious project: the paintings feted the family of Paul III and reaffirmed papal power to a Europe roiled by heresy, frightened by advancing Turkish armies, and unsettled by internal instability.[1] At the *Possesso*, when the new pope went in procession from Saint Peter's to the Lateran to assume his bishopric of Rome, the celebratory plaster and papier-mâché triumphal arches along the route sported symbols and metaphors of justice. They were designed to show the city the substance of the new regime and to stress the new pope's differences from his predecessor. Whether marking continuity or break, the swift message strove to address the lively play of factions and families always active in an elective monarchy. The messages to the pope's own city, and to his other cities, now conquered and docile, and to the rest of Europe and the whole Catholic globe, embraced a new idiom, of peace, justice, and *buon governo*. This new line was forged and championed from Sixtus V (1585–1590) onward.

"PERFECT SECURITY"

Sixtus's regime, though decisive for the development of papal monarchy, was nevertheless marked by grave internal problems: hunger, banditry, and political tension with Spain. But brief as his reign was, five years only, it elaborated a comprehensive program that we can call "the ideology of *buon governo*." Long thereafter, good administration remained a theme in Rome's propaganda. The whole of Sixtus's own political propaganda centered on high justice, absolute in zones both spiritual and material, solidly built and sagely directed by the pope's own hand or by men tightly bound to him. Historians have usually depicted Sixtus as a great restorer of public peace, an unrelenting scourge of scandal, vice, and crime, and a keen administrator of the papal fisc. He was, so goes the pic-

1. For the painting, created for Cardinal Alessandro Farnese and now at Capodimonte museum, and reflecting the opening of the Council of Trent, see Monica Grasso, "L'allegoria della Giustizia dipinta da Giorgio Vasari per il cardinale Alessandro Farnese," in *I cardinali di Santa Romana Chiesa: collezionisti e mecenati*, ed. Harula Economopoulos, 55–67 (Rome: Shakespeare and Company, 2003); Stefano Pierguidi, "Sulla fortuna della 'Giustizia' e della 'Pazienza' di Vasari," *Mitteilungen des Kunsthistorischen Instituts in Florenz* 51, 2007 (2009): 576–95.

ture, the pontiff who finally restored peace and abundance to his subjects, and who concluded a useful religious peace with Catholic princes in a Europe torn by confessional strife. Although partly true, this historical consensus has its mythic streak.

The main traits of the image of Sixtus, fateful for his story and his myth, arose in the very first months of his papacy. Sixtus, who used the arts to defend the faith, teach catechism to the ignorant, and battle heresy, also exploited iconography to present his own persona. He stressed the attributes of his personal power, using the symbols of his family and of royal sovereignty, and, especially, the insignia of his role as Grand Inquisitor. For his icon, Sixtus chose the lion, royal and powerful. In heraldic art, he was a proud lion, vigilant and threatening, perched atop many a painted or sculpted mountain, and nothing escaped his eye, while in his paw he clutched a pear tree branch. These pears were an easy visual pun, as Sixtus, by birth, was a Peretti, and his name means "little pears." This iconography left little to the imagination; it offered the Peretti pope a simple, obsessive symbolism that flooded not only the paintings of his reign but also literary effusions—poems, diaries, and his many biographies.

In political propaganda—the expression is anachronistic when applied to a pre-ideological realm, but hard to improve on—reality blended with image, myth, and rhetoric. The rich mixture of meanings illustrates well the character of sixteenth-century papal monarchy, and the evolving nature of its self-representation. Indeed, when it came to justice, myth preceded and encouraged reality: political propaganda, centering on the realization of justice here on earth and celebrating the pope's success in nailing down public order, ran well ahead of hard facts on the ground. The construct's artifice displays the seeming modernity of the papal monarchy's use of language.

In 1587, not quite two years into the reign, a medal celebrated a crucial mission accomplished, or so went the claim—the reestablishment of order and public quiet. The medal's inscription announced in triumphal tones *"perfecta securitas"* and presented an idyll, a pilgrim resting on the ground, in the shadow of a tree. The medal was a curial original destined to carry a precise political message to civic magistrates, nobles, and the cardinals themselves, many of them hostile to the pope ever since his election. This medal was only one of many such images, not always numismatic, exalting the "perfect" realization of a program of governance that made justice a central plank, as part of a general campaign to strengthen central government. The medals, coins, and many biographies, both printed and in manuscript, and the sonnets, madrigals, prints, and paintings of *buon governo*—these last best seen in the frescoes at the Vatican Library and Lateran Palace—all seem forged from a single template. They all celebrate a new reign of Saturn, a time of mythic peace and plenty, thanks to Sixtus's decisive campaign of repression and moral rigor.

Sixtus's propaganda stressed his policy's novelty. A political regime claiming with or without reason to be doing something new, often legitimates itself by stressing its innovations and its capacity to bring peace and good administration after a turbulent, unstable past. In Sixtus's regime, the only truly new thing was the person of the pope in power. But his government, in its propaganda, trumpeted novelty and rupture with traditional governance, stressing Sixtus's role as *pastor angelicus*. It did not revert to old, classical symbols, like those that Julius II, for instance, had made his own, early in the century, to solemnize his project of *renovatio imperii* (restoration of the empire), or the swaggering devices by which Paul III Farnese vaunted his "Roman" bellicosity. Sixtus's own bellicosity was not political but moral, and inquisitorial, as befitted a severe chastiser of sin and crime.

In the spring of 1585, when Sixtus took the throne, public order was far from tranquil. Accordingly, Sixtus felt, papal justice should present itself to public eyes as new, extraordinary, and effective. The ticklish internal situation made decisive propaganda necessary; celebrate his deeds forthwith and champion their results as effective from the start and perfect. So began the idealization and the myth. The pope desired a sharp contrast with the stasis and inertia of his predecessor, Gregory XIII, with his feeble reputation for justice and order.

At the beginning of the summer of 1585 came drastic measures to evoke the quick repression of crime and swift social moralization. Sixtus's political design was taken up at once in sundry literary, iconographic, and numismatic images. Three symbols—of justice, peace, and abundance entwining with the papal coat of arms—celebrate the alleged completion of Sixtus's program. An upturned sword, holding scales in perfect balance—an image of justice resting on force and resolve—appears in many apologetic minor writings, and in poems in press. One image—the boast was premature—shows the state purged of bandits, with commerce and prosperity restored. It appears not only on the medals, which had limited circulation, but also on the minted currency, carrying the message straight to anyone who could read Latin or puzzle out the imagery. For example, two *testoni* (large silver coins) from 1587 had inscriptions: *publicae quietis parens Roma* (Rome is the parent of public quiet) and *securitas populi Romani* (the security of the Roman people). Meanwhile, on the Capitoline Hill, the dedicatory inscription to a new statue celebrating the pope's restoration of privileges to the city's magistrates extolled the renewal of *publica quies*. The privileges celebrated in stone were more sham than real, but the city still guarded them jealously, as a pale shadow of civic liberty, crushed ever more completely, all century long, by the curia's policy of centralization.

Sixtus's propaganda offered a prospectus for continental change. It contended that, after the first years of his rule, thanks to the fruits of his policy, Rome would assume a new complexion, a model for all, of peace, morality, and devotion. Once his own domains were quelled, the pope would turn his attentions outward, settle Europe, troubled by heresy and religious strife, and export Rome's own model, a shining example of a new spirituality and a society based on true justice.

The most complete celebration of the theme of *buon governo*, so tenaciously propounded, appears in the frescoes of the Salone Sistino at the Vatican Library, painted between 1587 and 1589. High on the walls under the ceiling's vaults are broad lunettes, each with a single scene emblematic of the regime's aspirations. The paintings exalt the internal pacification, now accomplished, they claimed, with the extermination of the bandits, portrayed allegorically as so many wolves fleeing the Sistine lion, symbolic pear in paw, at whose feet huddle the faithful sheep. They also feature the reform of finances and of the grain office, the shutting away in convents of poor girls and mendicant nuns, and, abroad, peace with princes. As for Rome itself, the frescoes show the pope's striking urbanism, his bold and fateful interventions in the city's fabric, laying out across great stretches of the city broad, straight streets that receded, like the methodical backdrops in high-Renaissance paintings, to a dis-

FIGURE 7. Two coins from 1587 crediting Sixtus V with the reestablishment of public order: testone with legend "Securitas pop[u]li romani"; and testone with legend "public[a]e quietis parens roma."

tant, enticing vanishing point. All these new papal streets survive to this day, with proud Egyptian obelisks at their points of intersection. An Augustinian, Angelo Rocca, left a detailed description of these frescoes; he had inspired their themes and symbols and his writings illustrate clearly how artistic expression readily followed the pedagogical dictates of the Counter Reformation.[2]

Sixtus's accomplishments found their final, synthetic, and densest expression in the pope's funeral monument in Santa Maria Maggiore. In a splendid domed chapel he commissioned, it faces the monument to Pius V, calling to mind, concretely, how much, for Sixtus, this severe predecessor had been a model. Here too *buon governo* reigns, as a central theme of two of the five rectangular relief panels flanking the pope's own enormous statute; one celebrates justice and peace, and the other charity and abundance. Victory over

2. Bibliotheca Vaticana a Sixto 5. pont. max. in splendidiorem commodioremq. locum traslata, et a fratre Angelo Roccha a Camerino, ordinis Eremitarum S. Augustini, sacrae theologiae doctore, commentario variarum artium, ac scientiarum materijs curiosis, ac difficillimis, scituq. dignis refertissimo, illustrata, Romae, ex typographia Apostolica Vaticana, 1591.

FIGURE 8. Figure of Justice from a bas relief on the tomb of Sixtus V in the Basilica of Santa Maria Maggiore, Rome.

the bandits appears in the first, one more reminder of the repression of crime and restoration of order necessary for further progress. Soldiers clutching the severed heads of bandits camp on the Roman Campagna. In the background rise the arches of the Acqua Felice, named for the pope (Felice Peretti before his elevation). His aqueduct is a concrete memento of his effort to revive the wide, empty wasteland around Rome that ten years earlier had made so strong an impression on the traveling essayist Michel de Montaigne. Reality was far less tidy than the image the pope projected. In reality, it was Sixtus's successor, Clement VIII, who through clever military policy succeeded in defeating banditry.[3] Nevertheless, after Sixtus, the representation of justice, tied tightly to each pope's exploits and to his family's celebration, would, throughout the seventeenth century, remain a dominant motif. Paul V would flaunt the themes, symbols, and allegories of justice, peace, and abundance. In 1612, at the Vatican, he celebrated his reform of the tribunals and, in his painting programs across town at the Quirinal palace, he made generous use of personages from sacred history to exalt papal power's consolidation. No sooner was Paul V elected, in 1605, than he set in motion the construction at Santa Maria Maggiore of a chapel dedicated to the Virgin Mary, an architectural pendant to the chapel built there by Sixtus. In this "new papal mausoleum" before the tombs of Pius V, Sixtus V, and Clement VIII, "the popes appear as defenders of the faith, vanquishers of heresy, dispensers of justice, and reconcilers of discord."[4]

FLATTERING PAPAL RULE

Propaganda did not travel by images alone. Between the late sixteenth century and the early decades of the seventeenth, the sharpened pens of first-rank political theorists, polemicists, and pamphleteers were mobilized to defend the primacy of the Roman pontiff and to compose eulogies to his temporal power, based on superior, and absolute justice.

A veil was raised and there appeared the sacred two-edged sword in the midst of the divinity of spiritual and temporal authority, resplendent like the brightest sun, a weapon of highest heaven sent to the popes. For that reason it is a thing of such great value that it cannot be weighed by human judgment; with the mind alone, it was honored, adored, and admired by all.

With these words, Traiano Boccalini (1556?–1613), although he had had direct experience of Roman justice and did not hesitate to call his judicial colleagues "butchers," nevertheless exalted the dual pow-

---

3. Irene Fosi, *La società violenta. Il banditismo nello Stato pontificio nella seconda metà del Cinquecento* (Rome: Ateneo, 1985),195–226.

4. Antonio Menniti Ippolito, *I papi al Quirinale. Il sovrano pontefice e la ricerca di una residenza* (Rome: Viella, 2004), 111–26; Steven F.Ostrow, *Art and Spirituality in Counter Reformation Rome* (Cambridge: Cambridge University Press, 1996), 258.

ers of Paul V's justice.[5] His was not the first such celebration. Fabio Albergati, in his *Discorsi politici*, a polemic against the political theories of Jean Bodin, had stressed how, in general, rewards and punishments were not the only useful means to conserve and maintain a realm.[6] In his *Il Cardinale*, where he celebrated "the nobility of the cardinal's position and the excellence of ecclesiastical government, both in temporal and in spiritual matters," he extolled the superiority of the Papal State, above other kingdoms and above republics, on account of the double nature of papal power. Based as it was on justice and clemency, said he, the Papal State resembled God's own realm. If highest equity was manifested in distributive justice, commutative justice too responded perfectly to the principle of *mediocritas*, the golden mean, newly celebrated and appropriated at the end of the sixteenth century by Neo-Stoic thought. Albergati indeed affirmed that, like a good physician, a good state counselor would advise that

the laws of the State of the Church should aim for the conservation of *mediocritas* [moderation] among the subjects. . . . Furthermore, they [the laws] should not part company with it [*mediocritas*], by imposing penalties and hurts that are harsher than is due, by taking property, or sending persons into banishment for a petty failing, nor should they lightly pardon the gravest of excesses. If they do such things, on the one hand the people, out of desperation, take to the road and fill the countryside with robbery, making the state ungovernable and uninhabitable, and on the other hand overweening clemency, inviting scoundrels to do new misdeeds, renders life in villages and the cities more dangerous than the woods.[7]

In reality, in the everyday administration of justice, in the very years when Albergati wrote his meditation, what happened was just the opposite. Banishment was dealt out unsparingly, and capital punishment, often just to warn others, ran rampant, while the houses of families who collaborated with banished men were razed. Some writings and images exalted this severity, but it did not escape attentive observers, like the Venetian ambassador Paolo Paruta, that such

5. Traiano Boccalini, *Pietra del paragone politico tratta dal monte Parnaso, dove si toccano i governi delle maggiori monarchie dell'universo* ("Cosmopoli" [actually Venice]: Giorgio Teler, 1615). No numbered pages.

6. *De i discorsi politici di Fabio Albergati libri cinque ne i quali viene riprovata la dottrina politica di Gio. Bodino, e defesa quella d'Aristotele, all'Ill.mo Sig. Pietro card. Aldobrandino* (Rome: L. Zanetti, 1602), 497–99.

7. Ibid., 137–38.

measures were disruptive and futile. In a confidential dispatch to his masters, the diplomat wrote:

Nevertheless one sees that this extreme rigor has not helped to extirpate these people [the bandits]. On the contrary, it has done harm. Whenever one single person from among them, who has been in some way guilty of having been in the company of exiles, falls to the forces of justice, it causes many to go into the countryside and turn themselves into exiles, because, knowing that one proceeds with the greatest severity against everyone, others too become afraid, when some deed has been discovered, that they will fall into suspicion of complicity with the crime, or of giving aid and favor to the person who committed it. Of their own accord, they choose banishment and join other outlaws and men of similar condition. And, indeed, one proceeds with such rigor, that, among other things, there is a rule in the cities of the Church State that all members of a family and kin group, even cousins across to the fourth degree, are held to make good the damages done in the village where they live. Nevertheless, things have gone worse than ever, as the bandits have become bolder at doing harm.[8]

These criticisms cut to the quick. And they matched the laments from subjects and villages, less elegant and politically astute than the ambassador, in letters, memorials, and petitions. On the other hand, a leading intellectual among the cardinals and the pope's theologian, the Jesuit Robert Bellarmine, was inspired by Holy Scripture and by the Fathers of the Church, Jerome especially, to defend the severity of the pope's justice. It expressed his even hand; it was necessary for the suppression of quarrels and disturbances of public tranquility, and for the defense of the common good. Bellarmine, on these grounds, legitimated the harshest of means, "lest the parts corrupt the whole." He did not even exclude the doctrine of the state's revenge, at the hands of "a legitimate judge."[9] Bellarmine expressed this idea, in concord with other theorists of his time, like Mariana, in his most famous work, *Controversiae*, conceived as an attack on Protestants and a defense of the pope's *potestas indirecta*.[10]

---

8. "La Relazione di Roma di Paolo Paruta (1595)," in *Relazioni degli ambasciatori veneti al Senato durante il secolo decimosesto*, ed. Eugenio Alberi, series 2, vol. 4, 393 (Florence: Società Editrice Fiorentina, 1857).

9. Roberto Bellarmino, *Scritti politici*, ed. Carlo Giacon (Bologna: Zanichelli, 1950), 248–51. On the subject of a vendetta which was not private, but was waged by a judge, he argued that "it is certainly for a good end, as when there is the hope to emend the malefactor by this punishment, and to impede his badness, and he would continue to do harm if he was allowed to go about unpunished."

10. *De controversis christianae religionis adversus huius temporis haereticos* (Paris: ex

THE CRUEL JUSTICE OF THE POPE

In the very years when Bellarmine's sober treatise praised tough justice, the severity of the courts acquired connotations of cruelty in another, very different literary genre that transmitted, to Rome and much of early modern Europe, an enduring image of the pope's bloodthirsty justice. From the late sixteenth century, in Rome as elsewhere in Europe, justice stories started to make the rounds, famous tales, stories of blood crime, family vendettas, whose protagonists, at the beginning, in Rome were almost always nobles, members of a caste targeted by the severe justice of popes like Pius V, Sixtus V, and Clement VIII. In the stories, they are dissolute figures, adulterers, parricides, matricides, unmasked by the vigilant hand of justice. Ending up in papal courts, they perish at the hangman's hand. Before their execution, almost always a public spectacle—the better to warn and cow the audience, or so went the belief—they are redeemed by the tireless labors of the pious comforters at their sides. Among the protagonists of these turbid tales, to name the more famous, are the adulterers Vittoria Accoramboni and Duke Paolo Giordano Orsini (these two, despite Paolo's many crimes, escaped the scaffold), and the Marchese di Altemps, executed under Sixtus V. There were also the turbulent Troilo Savelli, denounced by his own mother and beheaded, and the parricide Beatrice Cenci, and Onorio Santacroce, killer of his mother. Other tales of trials and executions at the pope's inflexible hand soon followed. There were accounts of abjuring foreigners tarred with heresy, and the condemnations of scandalously lubricious churchmen, not to mention adulterous wives and poisoners of hapless spouses, and of corrupt cleric-forgers, like Francesco Canonici, alias il Mascambruno, and of plotters against the pope and papal family, like Giacinto Centini. Throughout the seventeenth century and into the early decades of the eighteenth, fresh accounts enriched the trove of gory or sordid tales.

To tell of justice and of executions was by no means just Roman, or Italian. In England, for instance, gallows stories had a long tradition and lively trade.[11] Public taste in all places bespoke the curi-

---

officinis Tri-Adelphorum bibliopolarum via Iacobaea, & in monte d. Hilarij, 1613), especially vol. 1, *De potestate Summi Pontificis in rebus temporalibus;* vol. 2, *De laicis ac potissimum de magistrato politico.*

11. See Jeremy A. Sharpe, "'Last Dying Speeches': Religion, Ideology and Public Ex-

osity of those who flocked to executions in squares and other parts of townscape designated as justice's stage and backdrop. Crime stories in circulation usually stood on a foundation of trial papers, perhaps spirited back by some officer of the court itself, and then enriched by details bandied about by *publica fama*, which embellished the tale of current interest. These stories served to make the machinery of justice widely known and to champion its rigor and rigidity. Most authors were anonymous; some may have been from the court's own orbit, perhaps from among the many spies, the so-called "friends of the court." Style was simple and efficient. Tales were quick to stress gore—putting protagonists in the worst possible light, especially if they committed crimes inside the family, as did parricides, infanticides, and some supposed witches—but were also swift to trumpet justice's triumph, routing evil and squelching sin. In Rome, it was a controlled literature, an instrument of propaganda, championed in its early decades by figures at the curia who knew well its value. These stories were known, read, and heard, and above all copied and recopied, with additions and corrections, in a whirl of manuscripts, and were sometimes anthologized in fat volumes of judicial miscellany, still on hand in many libraries in Rome and elsewhere.[12] At the beginning of the eighteenth century, print joined manuscript, often in the form of a single case, just a few pages, sometimes with a good execution on the cover. They were cheap productions, probably destined for wide circulation at fairs and markets, for reading silently or aloud for the delectation of all who loved to hear tales of violence, star-crossed loves, and bloody feuds. The printed broadsheets echoed oral tales enriched in their particulars by public gossip, and helped to fix both fact and fiction in popular memory. They were tales read and recounted in both town and country in easy company; their telling marks were repetition and zest for piquant detail.

   Rome's justice literature had an afterlife and second fate. Later

---

ecution in Seventeenth-Century England," *Past and Present* 107 (1985): 144–67; Lincoln B. Faller, *The Forms and Functions of Criminal Biography in Late Seventeenth- and Early Eighteenth-Century England* (Cambridge: Cambridge University Press, 1987); Frances E. Dolan, *Dangerous Familiars: Representations of Domestic Crime in England, 1550–1700* (Oxford: Clarendon Press, 1994).

   12. British Library: MS Add. 8408: "Descriptions of Trials of Heretics and Other People" (eighteenth century); MS Add. "Avvenimenti tragici in Roma sotto diversi pontefici" (eighteenth century); MS Eg. 1100 has records of executions under Sixtus V; MS Eg. 1101, "Giustizie seguite in varii tempi."

generations elaborated and reworked it, using it to portray conditions that marked Italy's image for Europe. Manuscripts found by chance by travelers and writers—this is a famous topos in countless books—were then improved on, by novelists, for instance, such as Stendhal in his *Chroniques italiennes*, to paint a dramatic fresco of Italian decadence, where the image of a bloodthirsty, immoral Rome fills the foreground. These images were fated to recur in travel literature, to animate and feed stereotypes that died hard.[13] At the end of the nineteenth century, eager scholars, archivists, and erudite amateurs began to interest themselves in this tradition, and blended the tales with their own new research. New details from archives began to enrich the old stories of justice and of famous trials. And some of these tales turned into novels; the case of young Beatrice Cenci, who with her mother had her vicious father killed, is a fine example.[14] She by now has inspired a play by the poet Shelley, treatises, short stories, and a mid-twentieth-century opera as well. Other protagonists of Roman justice were conscripted into the ranks of the martyrs of free thought, less famous comrades of the philosopher Giordano Bruno, burned in 1600 at the orders of the Inquisition. They too figure, for their champions, as innocent victims of the obscurantism and cruelty of papal justice. These tales add no small piece to the structure of the black legend that, for many years, surrounded not only the Inquisition, but the whole purported "decadence" of baroque Italy.

13. Attilio Brilli, *Il viaggio in Italia. Storia di una grande tradizione culturale* (Bologna: il Mulino, 2006).

14. *Beatrice Cenci. La storia, il mito*, ed. Mario Bevilacqua and Elisabetta Mori (Rome: Viella, 1999). Alberto Moravia, *Beatrice Cenci*, trans. Angus Davidson (New York: Noonday Press/Farrar, Strauss and Giroux, 1966); for an earlier history, Corrado Ricci, *Beatrice Cenci*, trans. Morris Bishop and H. L. Stuart (London: Heinemann, 1926); Berthold Goldschmidt, *Beatrice Cenci: Opera in 3 Acts*; libretto by Martin Esslin based on *The Cenci* by Shelley (1819) (London: B. Goldschmidt, 1994). The score dates from 1949.

Conclusion

Sweeping across a span of more than two centuries, this study has tried to capture the fundamental traits of justice in the Papal State. The phenomenon took many forms and was riddled with contradictions; justice cut a splendid figure but had feet that sometimes looked like clay. So, on the one hand, one reading of the rules, institutions, tribunals, and men of law might portray sovereign justice as sitting easy in the saddle. Justice served the papal resolve to build and bolster an ever more cohesive, coherent, and unitary territorial state, in the face of geographic particularism, local patriotism, and nobles' resistance. The justice Rome desired and embraced, the justice championed in assorted media—treatises, pamphlets, and visual arts—was meant to be the cornerstone of state construction. Throughout the whole early modern period popes pursued such policies. Their exact ways and means might vary, both because papal monarchy was not hereditary but elective, and because recalcitrant internal conditions and the shifting balance of international politics sometimes hampered papal statecraft. That reading, in sum, is the view from above, which in large part stresses the pope's strong arm, fortified by justice. Then there is the contradictory second view, from below, and from the side, which shows justice sitting a lot less firmly in that same saddle. When we look at society and politics, at the stories of the men and women who found themselves in court, and read the letters from the jurists and the governors, we see the reality of justice at work, face to face with local situations and concrete problems. In this daily work, justice clashed with other lively powers still present on the landscape and strove hard, but not always successfully, to dike and discipline the stubborn violence and disorder that marked the everyday relations among subjects, whether in town or out on the land.

Our exploration of strengths and weaknesses took us to the grimmer side of papal justice. Cruelty, a play for strength, was so drastic because in fact it tried to compensate for weaknesses in the judicial apparatus. When almost all malefactors got away, it was tempting indeed to apply *inquisitio* and torture to the few one caught, to collect evidence and extort confessions, and then to use macabre spectacles like capital punishment to deter the others. None of these devices were peculiar to the justice of the popes, as some historians of the eighteenth and nineteenth century for polemic's sake contended. Rather, such things were the common coin of old regime justice, anywhere. Nowhere was there any great push to make punishment fit the crime; disproportion was an operating principle. But Rome had its own complexities: the double nature of papal monarchy made it hard to distinguish and sever, in the modern way, ecclesiastical from lay justice. To make things even harder, many jurists and governors who had to put Rome's abundant laws into practice were clergy. In the pope's state, from the end of the sixteenth century, bureaucracy assumed clearer shape and firmer power; it was governed by congregations that grew ever better organized, whose job it was to survey and direct from the center the work of those who governed the periphery. The state's evolving machinery made use of men of state who, thanks to their training in civil and canon law, knew how to balance the tricky double task of ruling subjects and guiding souls. But there are risks in looking only at the center, at Rome, with its curial apparatus, congregations, and courts: at the Sacra Consulta, and the tribunals of the governor and of the Inquisition. Such a picture would be partial and distorted. For a wider view, it is important to cast an eye to the full range of sources.

So, this book has argued that it is crucial to study the correspondence between the organs at the center and those lodged at the periphery. Petitions reveal strategies the state's subjects used, singly or collectively, to put justice to work, and to seek grace, often from the pope himself. The endless stream of letters flooding in from the edges of the Papal State, from cities and isolated villages, often remote and poor, arrived at the doorstep of the Roman congregations and of members of the pope's own family, the cardinal nephew especially. This correspondence reveals the periphery's endeavor to cope with Rome. It abounds in requests by local administrators for the clarification of rules, and for recommendations as to how to do justice, secure order, and effect *buon governo*, thereby creating a local consensus supporting state power. And, from the center, from Rome, they tried to write back, to answer, to solve the problems, and to broadcast the perennial call for collaboration.

One place where the gap between aspiration for justice and reality was wide was in staffing. Alongside well-trained and capable officials were the ignorant, corrupt, and immoral, the antithesis of the image of the worthy administrator, good father of his state family, broadcast by countless treatises imbued with pious Counter Reformation culture. The same contrast and complexity appears among the clergy, both secular and regular. The shepherds of the flocks of souls, often far removed from Trent's model, were thus in no shape to discipline the faithful and pry them away from vice or superstition, or other behaviors that, to the Inquisition's eye, were now becoming sins.

Justice, we have seen here, also had its structural problems. There were far too many tribunals. In one or another territory or town, or in Rome itself, there was a multitude of courts, some old, some new. There were rivalries between assorted judges, each defending his prerogatives, power, and pay, in the face of Rome's demands that they all work together in happy harmony, with edifying, useful synergy. The mail back and forth with Rome shows, beyond the least doubt, the gap between theory and practice and between propaganda and real conditions. Ideals spoke of *buon governo*, discipline, the control of souls and bodies, and the imposition of a kind of order just as moral as it was social or political. These themes figured in the celebration of the doings of the major popes of the sixteenth and seventeenth centuries: Sixtus V, Paul V, Alexander VII, and Innocent XII, to cite the most important and consequential. Meanwhile, reality entailed a constant effort to take the measure of real problems of resistance and disorder, and to overcome them. Ever so gradually, justice did gain ground, but, at the time when our study ends, its march was far from over.

BIBLIOGRAPHY

Archival Sources

Archivo della Congregazione per la Dottrina della Fede, Vatican City
(ACDF)
Decreta 1565–1566
S. O., St. St. D 6-e; DD 2-b; DD 1-e; EE 3-a; HH 2-e; H 6-f; I 2-d; L 3-f;
   LL 5-c, h; LL 1-a; M 5-a, b, p; M 4-l; M 2-m; Q 3-a, d; R 2-m; UV 11, 12.

Archivio Caetani, Rome (AC)
nn. 65394; 4923

Archivio Colonna, Monastero di Santa Scolastica, Subiaco (Rome) II, A. 12.

Archivio Segreto Vaticano, Vatican City (ASV)
Curia Savelli, Investigazioni, vol. 1
Fondo Bolognetti, vol. 156
Misc. Arm. II, vol. 80; Misc. Arm. III, t. 15
Segreteria dei Memoriali, vols. 1–19 (1636–1667)
Segreteria di Stato, Memoriali e biglietti, nn. 1, 18

Archivio Stato, Rome (ASR)
Tribunale Criminale del Governatore, Atti vari di cancelleria, buste 127, 131,
   133, 84, 85
Tribunale Criminale del Governatore, Processi, 16 secolo, buste: 10; 11; 21,
   case 1; 76, case 6; 116, case 3; 126; 147, case 9; 159, case 19; 201, case 14; 223;
   290, case 3; 309
Tribunale Criminale del Governatore, Processi, 17 secolo, buste: 55, case 3;
   67, case 1; 84, case 5; 86, case 29; 88, case 9; 99, case 23; 114, case 6; 115,
   case 19; 135, case 27; 147, case 15; 158, cases 14, 18, 19; 225–227
Tribunale Criminale del Governatore, Relazioni dei birri, 17 secolo, buste
   104; 20
Tribunale Criminale del Governatore, Registrazione d'atti, busta 152

Archivio Storico del Vicariato di Roma (ASVR)
Tribunale Criminale del Vicario, Costituti, vol. 102

Archivio di Stato, Florence (ASF)
Archivio Capponi, buste 166–168; 173; 175
Mediceo del Principato, filze 492; 533; 2776

Biblioteca Apostolica Vaticana, Vatican City (BAV)
Barb. lat. 8925; 8994; 8965; 9018

Borg. lat. 63, II; 729
Chigiano, F. VI; Q. I. 12
Ottob. Lat. 1113; 2349;
Urb. lat. 1040; 1049
Vat. lat. 12229
Microfilm Trinity College Dublin (MF, for microfilm), held at the Vatican
     Library
MF 25 (Ms 1248); 26 (Ms 1252); 36 (Ms 1259)
MF 26 (Ms 1251)

Biblioteca Casanatense, Rome (BC)
BC, MSS 1355, 2097

British Library, London (BL)
MS Add. 8408;
MSS Eg. 1100; 1101

Haus-, Hof- und Staatsarchiv, Vienna, Judicialia latina nn. 399/14; 400; 401

Printed Sources

Albergati, Fabio. *Trattato del Signor Fabio Albergati del modo di ridurre a pace
     l'inimicitie private.* Rome: Francesco Zannetti, 1583.
———. *De i discorsi politici di Fabio Albergati libri cinque ne i quali viene ri-
     provata la dottrina politica di Gio. Bodino, e defesa quella d'Aristotele,
     all'Ill.mo Sig. Pietro card. Aldobrandino.* Rome: Luigi Zannetti, 1602.
Bellarmino, Roberto. *Scritti politici.* Edited by Carlo Giacon. Bologna:
     Zanichelli, 1950.
Boccalini, Traiano. *Pietra del paragone politico tratta dal monte Parnaso, dove
     si toccano i governi delle maggiori monarchie dell'universo.* "Cosmopoli"
     [Venice]: Giorgio Teler, 1615.
Botero, Giovanni. "Delle cause della grandezza delle città." In *Della Ragion
     di Stato libri X.* Venice: Gioliti, 1598.
———. *The Cause of the Greatnesse of Cities.* London: E. P. for Henry Seile,
     1635.
*Bullarum diplomatum et privilegiorum Sanctorum Romanorum Pontificum
     Taurinensis Editio.* Vol. 6. Turin: Dalmazzo, 1850.
*Bullarum diplomatum et privilegiorum Sanctorum Romanorum Pontificum
     Taruinensis Editio.* Vol. 7. Turin: Dalmazzo, 1862.
Carena, Carlo. *Tractatus de modo procedendi in causis S. Officii.* Cremona:
     M. A. Belpierum, 1636.
De Luca, Giovan Battista. *Il Dottor volgare.* Rome: G. Corvo, 1743.
Farinacci, Prospero. *Consilia.* In *Opera Omnia,* vol. 7. Antwerp: apud
     J. Keeberquium, 1618.
Fenzonio, Giovanni Battista. *Adnotationes in Statuta, sive ius municipale
     Romanae Urbis.* Rome: Camera Apostolica, 1636.
Firpo, Massimo, and Dario Marcatto, eds. *I processi inquisitoriali di Pietro*

Carnesecchi (1557–1567). Vatican City: Archivio Segreto Vaticano, 1998, 1999.

Giannone, Pietro. *Vita scritta da lui medesimo*. Edited by Sergio Bertelli. Milan: Feltrinelli, 1960.

Guazzini, Sebastiano. *Tractatus de pace, tregua, verbo dato alicui principi*. Macerata: A. Grisei eredi, 1669 (original edition, Rome, 1610).

Morone, Nicolò. *Tractatus aureus. De fide, tregua, et pace. In quo omnia fere continentur, quae in civilibus et criminalibus iudiciis*. Venice: Z. Damiano, 1574.

Parisi, Francesco. *Istruzioni per la gioventù impiegata nelle Segretarie, specialmente in quelle della Corte romana*. Rome: I. Fulgoni, 1781.

Paruta, Paolo. "La Relazione di Roma di Paolo Paruta (1595)." In *Relazioni degli ambasciatori veneti al Senato durante il secolo decimosesto*. Edited by Eugenio Alberi. series 2, vol. 4. Florence: Società Editrice Fiorentina, 1857.

Raynaldi, Gian Domenico. *Obvservationes criminales, civiles et mixtae*. Rome: Corbelletti, 1690.

Rocca, Angelo. *Trattato per la salute dell'anime e per la conservatone della robba, e del denaro contra i giuochi di carte e dadi*. Rome: G. Facciotto, 1617.

Roccha, Angelo. *Bibliotheca Apostolica Vaticana a Sixto 5. pont. max. in splendidiorem, commodioremq. locum translata, et a fratre Angelo Roccha a Camerino, ordinis Eremitarum S. Augustini, sacrae theologiae doctore, commentario variarum artium, ac scientarum materijs curiosis, ac difficillimis, scituq. dignis refertissimo, illustrata*. Rome, ex typographia Apostolica Vaticana, 1591.

Rocciolo, Domenico, ed. *Della giurisdittione e prerogative del Vicario di Roma. Opera del canonico Niccolò Antonio Cuggiò segretario di Sua Eminenza*. Rome: Carocci, 2004.

Scaramella, Pierroberto, ed. *Le lettere della Congregazione del Sant'Ufficio ai tribunali di fede di Napoli 1563–1625*. Triest: Edizioni Università di Trieste—Istituto Italiano per gli Studi Filosofici, 2002.

Spada, Giovanni Battista. *Racconto delle cose più considerabili che sono accorse nel governo di Roma*. Edited by Maria Teresa Bonadonna Russo. Rome: Società Romana di Storia Patria, 2004.

Volpelli, Orazio. *Tractatus de pace*. Venice: Giovan Battista Guerra, 1573.

Secondary Sources

Ademollo, Alessandro. *Le giustizie a Roma dal 1674 al 1739 e dal 1796 al 1840*. Rome: Forzani, 1881.

Ago, Renata. *Carriere e clientele nella Roma barocca*. Rome: Laterza, 1990.

Alessi, Giorgia. *Il processo penale: un profilo storico*. Rome: Laterza, 2004.

Angelozzi, Giancarlo. "Il tribunale criminale di Bologna." In *La Legazione di Romagna e i suoi Archivi. Secoli XVI–XVIII*, edited by Angelo Turchini, 737–74. Cesena: Il Ponte Vecchio, 2006.

Angelozzi, Giancarlo, and Cesarina Casanova. *La nobiltà disciplinata: vio-*

lenza nobiliare, procedure di giustizia e scienza cavalleresca a Bologna nel XVII secolo. Bologna: Clueb, 2003.

———. *La Giustizia criminale in una città di antico regime. Il tribunale del Torrone di Bologna (secc. XVI–XVII).* Bologna: Clueb, 2008.

Anselmi, Alessandra. *Il palazzo dell'ambasciata di Spagna presso la Santa Sede.* Rome: De Luca, 2001.

Arcangeli, Alessandro. *Passatempi rinascimentali: storia culturale del divertimento in Europa (secoli XV–XVII).* Rome: Carocci, 2004.

Auricchio, Sabrina. "'La ronda di notte': Le Relazioni dei Birri nella Roma del Seicento." Laurea thesis for l'Università di Roma "La Sapienza," 1994–1995.

Baernstein, Renée. *A Convent Tale: A Century of Sisterhood in Spanish Milan.* London: Routledge, 2002.

Baldassari, Marina. *Bande giovanili e "vizio nefando." Violenza e sessualità nella Roma barocca.* Rome: Viella, 2005.

Baldini, Ugo. "The Roman Inquisition's Condemnation of Astrology: Antecedents, Reasons and Consequences." In *Church, Censorship and Culture in Early Modern Italy,* edited by Gigliola Fragnito, 79–110. Cambridge: Cambridge University Press, 2001.

Bartoli Langeli, Attilio. *La scrittura dell'italiano.* Bologna: il Mulino, 2000.

———. *Notai. Scrivere documenti nel Medioevo.* Rome: Viella, 2006.

Behringer, Wolfgang. *Witches and Witch-Hunts: A Global History.* Cambridge: Polity Press, 2004.

Bellabarba, Marco. "Informazioni e fatti. Casi di storia del processo penale nell'Italia centro-settentrionale." *Storica* 20–21 (2001): 155–75.

———. "Pace pubblica e pace privata: linguaggi e istituzioni processuali nell'Italia moderna." In *Criminalità e giustizia in Germania e in Italia. Pratiche giudiziarie e linguaggi giuricidici tra tardo medioevo ed età moderna,* edited by Marco Bellabarba, Gerd Schwerhoff, and Andrea Zorzi, 189–213. Bologna: il Mulino; Berlin: Duncker and Humblodt, 2001.

———. *La giustizia nell'Italia moderna.* Rome: Laterza, 2008.

Benedetti, Roberto. "Tribunali e giustizia a Roma nel Settecento attraverso la fonte delle liste di traduzione alla galera (1749–1759)." *Roma moderna e contemporanea* 12, no. 3 (2004): 507–38.

Beretta, Francesco. *Galilée devant le Tribunal de l'Inquisition. Une relecture des sources.* Fribourg: Université de Fribourg-Suisse, 1998.

Bethencourt, Francisco. *L'Inquisition à l'epoque moderne. Espagne, Portugal, Italie, XV–XIX siècle.* Paris: Fayard, 1996.

Bever, Edward. *The Realities of Witchcraft and Popular Magic in Early Modern Europe: Culture, Cognition and Everyday Life.* Basingstoke: Palgrave Macmillan, 2008.

Bevilacqua, Mario, and Elisabetta Mori, eds. *Beatrice Cenci. La storia, il mito.* Rome: Viella, 1999.

Birocchi, Italo. *Alla ricerca dell'ordine. Fonti e cultura giuridica nell'età moderna.* Turin: Giappichelli, 2002.

Black, Christopher F. *Church, Religion, and Society in Early Modern Italy.* New York: Palgrave, 2004.

Blastenbrei, Peter. "La quadratura del cerchio. Il bargello di Roma nella crisi sociale tardocinquecentesca." *Dimensioni e problemi della ricerca storica* 1 (1994): 5–37.

———. *Kriminalität in Rom.* Tübingen: Max Niemeyer Verlag, 1995.

———. "Violence, Arms, and Criminal Justice in Papal Rome, 1560–1600." *Renaissance Studies* 20, no. 1 (February 2006): 68–87.

Blickle, Peter. "Conclusions." In *Resistance, Representation and Community,* 336–38. Oxford: Clarendon Press, 1997.

Boiteux, Martine. "Dérision et déviance: à propos de quelques coutûmes romaines." In *Le Charivari,* edited by Jacques Le Goff and Jean Claude Schmitt, 237–49. Paris: Mouton-EHESS, 1981.

Bossy, John. *Peace in the Post-Reformation: The Birkbeck Lectures 1995.* Cambridge: Cambridge University Press, 1998.

Bouwsma, William J. *Venice and the Defense of Republican Liberty: Renaissance Values in the Age of the Counter-Reform.* Berkeley and Los Angeles: University of California Press, 1968.

Brambilla, Elena. *Alle origini del Sant'Uffizio. Penitenza, confessione e giustizia spirituale dal medioevo al XVI secolo.* Bologna: il Mulino, 2000.

———. "I poteri giudiziari dei tribunali ecclesiastici nell'Italia settentrionale e la loro secolarizzazione." In *Le secolarizzazioni nel Sacro Romano Impero e negli antichi Stati italiani: premesse, confronti, conseguenze,* edited by Claudio Donati and Helmut Flachenecker, 99–112. Bologna: il Mulino; Berlin: Duncker & Humblodt, 2003.

———. "La polizia dei tribunali ecclesiastici e le riforme della giustizia penale." In *Corpi armati e ordine pubblico in Italia (XVI–XIX sec.),* edited by Livio Antonielli and Claudio Donati, 73–111. Soveria Mannelli: Rubbettino, 2003.

Brilli, Attilio. *Il viaggio in Italia. Storia di una grande tradizione culturale.* Bologna: il Mulino, 2006.

Broggio, Paolo, and Maria Pia Paoli, eds. "Stringere la pace. Teorie e pratiche della conciliazione nell'Europa moderna (secoli xv–xviii)." Rome: Viella (forthcoming).

Brunelli, Giampiero. *Soldati del papa. Politica militare e nobiltà nello Stato della Chiesa (1560–1644).* Rome: Carocci, 2003.

Burckhardt, Albrecht. *Les clients des saints. Maladie et quête du miracle à travers les procés de canonisation de la première moitié du XVIIe siècle en France.* Rome: École Française de Rome, 2004.

Burke, Peter. *The Historical Anthropology of Early Modern Italy.* Cambridge: Cambridge University Press, 1987.

Caetani, Gelasio. *Domus Caietana.* Vol. 2: *Il Cinquecento.* San Casciano Val di Pesa: Stianti, 1933.

Caffiero, Marina. *Battesimi forzati. Storie di ebrei, cristiani e convertiti nella Roma dei papi.* Rome: Viella, 2004.

Caffiero, Marina, and Maria Antonietta Visceglia, eds. "Congiure e complotti." Special issue of *Roma moderna e contemporanea* 11, nos. 1–2 (2003).

Calzolari, Monica, Michele Di Sivo, and Elvira Grantaliano, eds. "Giustizia e criminalità nello Stato Pontificio." *Rivista storica del Lazio* 9, no. 4 (2001).

Campennì, Francesco. *La patria e il sangue. Città, patriziati e potere nella Calabria moderna.* Rome: Lacaita, 2004.

Carroll, Stuart. "The Peace in the Feud in Sixteenth- and Seventeenth-Century France." *Past & Present* 178 (2003): 74–115.

Casanova, Cesarina. *Gentiluomini ecclesiastici. Ceti e mobilità sociale nelle Legazioni pontificie (sec. XVI–XVIII).* Bologna: Clueb, 1999.

———. "L'amministrazione della giustizia a Bologna. Alcune anticipazioni sul Tribunale del Torrone." *Dimensioni e problemi della ricerca storica* 2 (2004): 267–92.

———. "La giustizia penale in Romagna e a Bologna nella seconda metà del Seicento. Alcune ipotesi e molte incertezze." In *La Legazione di Romagna,* edited by Angelo Turchini, 699–735. Cesena: Il Ponte Vecchio, 2006.

Castiglione, Caroline. *Patrons and Adversaries: Nobles and Villagers in Italian Politics.* New York: Oxford University Press, 2005.

Chiarotti, Laura. "La popolazione del carcere nuovo nella seconda metà del XVII secolo." *Archivio della Società Romana di Storia Patria* 115 (1992): 147–79.

Clark, Peter. *European Cities and Towns (400–2000).* Oxford: Oxford University Press, 2008.

Cohen, Elizabeth S. "'Courtesans' and 'Whores': Words and Behaviour in Early Modern Rome." *Women's Studies* 19, no. 2 (1991): 201–8.

———. "Seen and Known: Prostitutes in the Cityscape of Late Sixteenth-Century Rome." *Renaissance Studies* 12, no. 3 (1998): 392–409.

———. "The Trials of Artemisia Gentileschi: A Rape as History." *Sixteenth Century Journal* 31, no. 1 (2000): 47–75.

———. "Back Talk: Two Prostitutes' Voices from Rome c. 1600." *Early Modern Women: An Interdisciplinary Journal* 2 (2007): 95–126.

———. "To Pray, to Work, to Hear, to Speak: Women in Roman Streets, c. 1600." *Journal of Early Modern History* 12, no. 3–4 (2008): 289–31.

Cohen, Thomas V. "The Case of the Mysterious Coil of Rope: Street Life and Jewish Persona in Rome in the Middle of the Sixteenth Century." *Sixteenth Century Journal* 19, no. 2 (Summer 1988): 209–21.

———. "A Long Day in Monterotondo: The Politics of Jeopardy in a Village Rising (1558)." *Comparative Studies in Society and History* 33 (1991): 639–68.

———. "Three Forms of Jeopardy: Honor, Pain and Truth-telling in a Sixteenth-Century Italian Courtroom." *Sixteenth Century Journal* 29, no. 4 (1998): 975–98.

———. *Love and Death in Renaissance Italy.* Chicago: University of Chicago Press, 2004.

———. "Communal Thought, Communal Words, and Communal Rites in a Sixteenth-century Village Rebellion." In *Sociability and Its Discontents: Civil Society, Social Capital, and Their Alternatives in Late Medieval and Early Modern Europe*, edited by Nicholas Epstein and Nicholas Terpstra, 23–50. Leiden: Brill, 2009.

Cohen, Thomas V., and Elizabeth S. Cohen. *Words and Deeds in Renaissance Rome*. Toronto: University of Toronto Press, 1992.

———. "Open and Shut: The Social Meanings of the Renaissance Italian House." *Bard Graduate School of Design Journal* 9, no. 1 (Fall–Winter 2001–2002): 61–84.

Comino, Caterina. "La prefettura di Montagna come esempio di distrettuazione periferica." *Archivi per la storia* 13, nos. 1–2 (2000): 231–41.

Costa, Pietro. *Dalla civiltà comunale al Settecento*. Vol. I of *Civitas: Storia della cittadinanza in Europa*. Rome: Laterza, 1999.

D'Amelia, Marina. "Il buon diritto, ovvero dell'accesso alla giustizia per i poveri. Prime riflessioni su un problema rimosso." In *Povertà e innovazioni istituzionali in Italia. Dal medioevo ad oggi*, edited by Vera Zamagni, 335–54. Bologna: Clueb, 2000.

Dandelet, Thomas. "Between Two Courts: The Colonna Agents in Italy and Iberia, 1555–1600." In *Your Humble Servant: Agents in Early Modern Europe, 1500–1800*, edited by Hans Cools, Marika Keblusen, and Badeloch Noldus. Hilversum: Verloren, 2006.

Dandelet, Thomas, and John Marino, eds. *Spain in Italy: Politics, Society, and Religion 1500–1700*. Leiden: Brill, 2006.

Davis, Natalie Zemon. *Society and Culture in Early Modern France*. Stanford, Calif: Stanford University Press, 1975.

———. *Fiction in the Archives: Pardon Tales and Their Tellers in Sixteenth-Century France*. Stanford, Calif.: Stanford University Press, 1987.

De Benedictis, Angela. *Repubblica per contratto. Bologna, una città europea nello Stato della Chiesa*. Bologna: il Mulino, 1995.

De Boer, Wietse. "The Conquest of the Soul: Confession, Discipline, and Public Order." In *Coniugi nemici. La separazione in Italia dal XII al XVIII secolo*, edited by Silvana Seidel Menchi and Diego Quaglioni. Bologna: il Mulino, 2000.

De Franceschi, Sylvio Hermann. *Raison d'état et raison d'église. La France et l'Interdit vénitien (1606–1607): aspects diplomatiques et doctrinaux*. Paris: H. Champion, 2009.

De Vivo, Filippo. "Dall'imposizione del silenzio alla *Guerra delle scritture*. Le pubblicazioni ufficiali durante l'interdetto del 1606–1607." *Studi Veneziani* 41 (2002): 179–213.

———. *Communication and Culture in Renaissance Venice*. Oxford: Oxford University Press, 2007.

Dean, Trevor. *Crime in Medieval Europe. 1200–1550*. Harlow: Longman, 2000.

———. *Crime and Justice in Late Medieval Italy*. Cambridge: Cambridge University Press, 2007.

Del Col, Andrea. *Domenico Scandella known as Menocchio: His Trials before the Inquisition (1583–1599)*. Binghamton, N.Y.: Medieval and Renaissance Texts and Studies, 1996.

———. *L'Inquisizione in Italia dal XII al XXI secolo*. Milan: Mondadori, 2006.

Del Re, Niccolò. *Monsignor Governatore di Roma*. Rome: Istituto Nazionale di Studi Romani, 1972.

———. "Prospero Farinacci giureconsulto romano (1544–1618)." *Archivio della Società Romana di Storia Patria* 98 (1975): 135–220.

———. *La Curia capitolina e tre altri antichi organi giudiziari romani*. Rome: Fondazione Marco Besso, 1993.

Delille, Gérard. *Le maire et le prieur. Pouvoir central et pouvoir local en Méditerranée occidentale (XVe–XVIIIe siècle)*. Paris: École des Hautes Etudes en Sciences Sociales, 2003.

Delumeau, Jean. *Vie économique et sociale de Rome dans la seconde moitié du XVIe siècle*. Vol. 1. Paris: De Boccard, 1959.

Deventer, Jörg. "Zwischen Ausweisung, Repression und Duldung: die Judenpolitik der 'Reformpäpste' im Kirchenstaat (ca. 1550–1605)." *Aschkenas: Zeitschrift für Geschichte und Kultur der Juden* 14, no. 2 (2004): 365–85.

Dewald, Jonathan. *The European Nobility 1400–1800*. Cambridge: Cambridge University Press, 1996.

Dezza, Ettore. *Accusa e inquisizione dal diritto comune ai codici moderni*. Vol. 1. Milan: Giuffrè, 1989.

Di Simplicio, Oskar. *Storia di un Anticristo. Avidità, amore e morte nella Toscana medicea*. Siena: Il Leccio, 1996.

———. *Autunno della stregoneria. Maleficio e magia nell'Italia moderna*. Bologna: il Mulino, 2005.

Di Sivo, Michele. "Il tribunale criminale capitolino nei secoli XVI–XVII: note da un lavoro in corso." *Roma moderna e contemporanea* 3 (1995): 201–16.

———, ed. *I Cenci: nobiltà di sangue*. Rome: Colombo, 2002.

———. "'Rinnoviamo l'ordine già dato': il controllo sui birri a Roma in antico regime." In *La polizia in Italia e in Europa: Punto sugli studi e prospettive di ricerca*, edited by Livio Antonielli, 13–24. Soveria Mannelli: Rubbettino, 2006.

———. "Sulle carceri dei tribunali penali a Roma: Campidoglio e Tor di Nona." In *Atti del Convegno (Somma Lombardo, 14–15 dicembre 2001) Carceri, carcerieri, carcerati. Dall'antico regime all'Ottocento*, edited by Livio Antonielli and Claudio Donati, 9–22. Soveria Manelli: Rubbettino, 2006.

Dolan, Frances Elizabeth. *Dangerous Familiars: Representations of Domestic Crime in England, 1550–1700*. Oxford: Clarendon Press, 1994.

Donati, Claudio. "'Ad radicitus submovendum': materiali per una storia dei progetti di riforma giudiziaria durante il pontificio di Innocenzo XII."

In *Riforme, religione e politica durante il pontificio di Innocenzo XII (1691–1700)*, edited by Bruno Pellegrino, 159–78. Galatina: Congedo, 1994.

Dülmen, Richard van. *Crime and Punishment in Early Modern Germany.* Cambridge: Cambridge University Press, 1990.

Egmond, Florike. "Execution, Dissection, Pain and Infamy—A Morphological Investigation." In *Bodily Extremities: Preoccupations with the Human Body in Early Modern European Culture*, edited by Florike Egmond and Robert Zwijnenberg, 92–128. Burlington, Vt.: Ashgate, 2003.

Elias, Norbert. *The Civilizing Process.* 2 vols. Oxford: Blackwell, 1969–1982.

Emich, Birgit. *Bürokratie und Nepotismus unter Paul V (1605–1621)*. Stuttgart: Hiersemann, 2001.

———. "Bologneser libertà, ferrareser decadenza: Politische Kultur und päpstliche Herrschaft im Kirchenstaat der Frühen Neuzeit." In *Staatsbildung als kultureller Prozess. Strukturwandel und Legitimation von Herrschaft in der Frühen Neuzeit*, edited by Ronald G. Asch and Dagmar Freist, 117–34. Vienna: Böhlau, 2005.

Ernst, Germana. *Tommaso Campanella. Il libro e il corpo della natura.* Rome: Laterza, 2002.

Evangelisti, Claudia. "Gli 'operai delle liti': funzione e status sociale dei procuratori legali a Bologna nella prima età moderna." In *Avvocati, medici, ingegneri. Alle origini delle professioni moderne*, edited by Maria Luisa Betri and Alessandro Pastore, 131–44. Bologna: Clueb, 1997.

Fabiani, Giuseppe. *Ascoli nel Cinquecento.* Vol. 1. Ascoli Piceno: D'Auria, 1957.

Faller, B. Lincoln. *The Forms and Functions of Criminal Biography in Late Seventeenth- and Early Eighteenth-Century England.* Cambridge: Cambridge University Press, 1987.

Fanciulli, Pietro. *La contea di Pitigliano e Sorano nelle carte degli Archivi Spagnoli di Simancas e Madrid e dell'Archivio di Stato di Firenze (Mediceo del Principato).* Pitigliano: A.T.L.A., 1991.

Feci, Simona. "The Death of a Miller: A Trial *contra hebreos* in Baroque Rome." *Jewish History* 7, no. 2 (1993): 9–27.

Ferraro, Joanne M. *Nefarious Crimes, Contested Justice: Illicit Sex and Infanticide in the Republic of Venice, 1557–1789.* Baltimore: John's Hopkins University Press, 2008.

Firpo, Luigi. *I processi di Tommaso Campanella.* Edited by Eugenio Canone. Rome: Salerno Editore, 1998.

Forclaz, Bertrand. "Les tribunaux du seigneur. L'administration de la justice dans les fiefs du Latium au XVIIe siècle." In "Attori sociali e istituzioni in Antico Regime." Special issue of *Dimensioni e problemi della ricerca storica* 1 (2004).

———. *La famille Borghese et ses fiefs. L'authorité négociée dans l'Etat Pontifical d'ancien régime.* Rome: Ecole Française de Rome, 2006.

Fosi, Irene. *La società violenta. Il banditismo nello Stato pontificio nella seconda metà del Cinquecento.* Rome: Ateneo, 1985.

250 Bibliography

———. "Pietà, devozione, politica: due confraternite fiorentine nella Roma del Rinascimento." *Archivio Storico Italiano* 149 (1991): 119–62.

———. "Signori e tribunali. Criminalità nobiliare e giustizia pontificia nella Roma del Cinquecento." In *Signori, patrizi, cavalieri in Italia centro-meridionale nell'Età moderna*, edited by Maria Antonietta Visceglia, 214–30. Rome: Laterza, 1992.

———. *All'ombra dei Barberini. Fedeltà e servizio nella Roma barocca*. Rome: Bulzoni, 1997.

———. "'Parcere subiectis, debellare superbos': la giustizia nelle cerimonie di possesso a Roma e nelle legazioni dello Stato Pontificio nel Cinquecento." In *Cérémonial et rituel à Rome (XVIᵉ–XIXᵉ siècle)*, edited by Maria Antonietta Visceglia and Catherine Brice, 90–115. Rome: Ecole Française de Rome, 1997.

———. "Tribunali, giustizia e società nella Roma del Cinquecento e Seicento." Special issue edited by Irene Fosi, *Roma moderna e contemporanea* 5, no. 1 (1997): 7–184.

———. "Il banditismo e i Caetani nel territorio di Sermoneta (secoli XVI–XVII)." In *Atti del Convegno "Sermoneta e i Caetani. Dinamiche politiche, sociali e culturali di un territorio tra medioevo ed età moderna*," edited by Luigi Fiorani, 213–25. Rome: L'Erma di Bretschneider, 1999.

———. "Court and City in the Ceremony of the Possesso in the Sixteenth Century." In *Court and Politics in Papal Rome, 1492–1700*, edited by Gianvittorio Signorotto and Maria Antonietta Visceglia, 31–52. Cambridge: Cambridge University Press, 2002.

———. "Il governo della giustizia nello Stato Ecclesiastico fra centro e periferia (secoli XVI–XVII)." In *Offices et Papauté (XIVᵉ–XVIIᵉ). Charges, hommes, destins*, edited by Armand Jamme and Olivier Poncet, 216–21. Rome: École Française de Rome, 2005.

———, ed., with the collaboration of Andrea Gardi. *La Legazione di Ferrara del Cardinale Giulio Sacchetti (1627–1631)*. 2 vols. Rome: Archivio Segreto Vaticano, 2006.

———, ed. "La peste a Roma (1656–1657)." *Roma moderna e contemporanea* 1–2 (2006).

———. "Niccolò Orsini ribelle al papa e a Cosimo I (1561–1568)." In *Les procés politiques (XIV–XVII siècles)*, edited by Yves Marie Bercé, 273–89. Rome: École Française de Rome, 2007.

Frenz, Thomas. *I documenti pontifici nel medioevo e in età moderna*. Vatican City: Archivio Segreto Vaticano, 1989.

Gardi, Andrea. *Lo stato in provincia. L'amministrazione della Legazione di Bologna durante il regno di Sisto V (1585–1590)*. Bologna: Istituto per la Storia di Bologna, 1994.

———. "L'amministrazione pontificia e le province settentrionali dello Stato (XIII–XVIII secolo)." *Archivi per la storia* 13, nos. 1–2 (2000): 43.

———. "Il mutamento di un ruolo. I legati nell'amministrazione interna dello Stato Pontificio dal XIV a XVII secolo." In *Offices et Papauté*

(*XIVᵉ–XVIIᵉ*). *Charges, hommes, destins*, edited by Armand Jamme and Olivier Poncet. Rome: Ecole Française de Rome, 2005.

Garnot, Benôit, ed. *L'infrajudiciaire du Moyen Âge à l'époque moderne*. Dijon: Presses universitaires de Dijon, 1996.

Gatrell, Vic A. C. *The Hanging Tree: Execution and the English People 1770–1868*. Oxford: Oxford University Press, 1994.

Gauvard, Claude, and Robert Jacob, eds. *Les rites de la justice. Gestes et rituels judiciaires au Moyen Age occidental*. Paris: Léopard d'or, 2000.

Gerard, Kent, and Gert Hekma, eds. *The Pursuit of Sodomy: Male Homosexuality in Renaissance and Enlightenment Europe*. New York: Haworth Press, 1989.

Ginzburg, Carlo. *The Cheese and the Worms: The Cosmos of a Sixteenth-Century Miller*. Baltimore: Johns Hopkins University Press, 1980.

——. "Saccheggi rituali. Premesse ad una ricerca in corso." *Quaderni Storici* 22 (1987): 615–36.

——. *Il filo e le tracce. Vero, falso, finto*. Milan: Feltrinelli, 2006.

Golden, Richard M., ed. *Encyclopedia of Witchcraft*. 4 vols. Los Angeles: ABC-Clio, 2006.

Goldschmidt, Berthold. *Beatrice Cenci: Opera in 3 Acts*. Libretto by Martin Esslin based on *The Cenci* by Shelley (1819). London: B. Goldschmidt, 1994. (The score dates from 1949.)

Grasso, Monica. "L'allegoria della Giustizia dipinta da Giorgio Vasari per il cardinale Alessandro Farnese." In *I cardinali di Santa Romana Chiesa: collezionisti e mecenati*, edited by Harula Economopoulos, 55–67. Rome: Shakespeare and Company, 2003.

Grendi, Edoardo. Foreword to "Fonti criminali e storia sociale." *Quaderni storici* 66 (1987): 695–700.

——. "Sulla 'storia criminale': risposta a Mario Sbriccoli." *Quaderni storici* 73 (1990): 269–75.

Groebner, Valentin. "Describing the Person, Reading the Signs: Identity Papers, Vested Figures, and the Limits of Identification 1400–1600." In *Documenting Individual Identity: The Development of State Practices in the Modern World*, edited by Jane Caplan and John C. Torpey, 15–27. Princeton, N.J.: Princeton University Press, 2001.

——. *Der Schein der Person. Steckbrief, Ausweis und Kontrolle im Europa des Mittelalters*. Munich: C. H. Beck Verlag, 2004.

Hanlon, Gregory. *The Twilight of a Military Tradition: Italian Aristocrats and European Conflicts, 1560–1800*. London: Taylor and Francis, 1988.

——. *Human Nature in Rural Tuscany: An Early Modern History*. New York: Palgrave Macmillan, 2007.

Hunt, John. "Violence and Disorder in the Sede Vacante of Early Modern Rome." Doctoral dissertation for Ohio State University, 2009.

Irace, Erminia. *La nobiltà bifronte. Identità e coscienza aristocratica a Perugia tra XV e XVII secolo*. Milan: Unicopli, 1995.

——. "'L'Atlantico peso del Pubblico.' Patriziato, politica e amministrazione a Perugia tra Cinque e Settecento." *Archivi per la storia* 13, nos. 1–2 (2000): 177–90.

———. "Una voce poco fa. Note sulle difficili pratiche della comunicazione tra il centro e le periferie dello Stato Ecclesiastico (Perugia, metà XVI–metà XVII secolo)." In *Offices, écrits et papauté (XIIIe–XVIIe siècle)*, vol. 3, *Une culture exacerbée de l'écrit, Actes du colloque de Paris (Paris 2003, Avignon 2004).* Edited by Armand Jamme and Olivier Poncet, 273–99. Rome: Ecole Française de Rome, 2007.

Iucci, Stefano. "La trattatistica sul segretario tra la fine del Cinquecento e il primo ventennio del Seicento." *Roma moderna e contemporanea* 3 (1995): 81–96.

Krug-Richter, Barbara, and Ruth. E. Mohrmann, eds. *Praktiken des Konfliktaustrags in der Frühen Neuzeit.* Münster: Rhema, 2004.

Kuehn, Thomas. "Reading Microhistory: The Example of *Giovanni and Lusanna*." *Journal of Modern History* 61 (1989): 514–31.

Kurzel-Runtscheiner, Monica. *Töchter der Venus. Die Kurtisanen Roms im 16. Jahrhundert.* Munich: Beck, 1995.

LaCapra, Dominick. "*The Cheese and the Worms:* The Cosmos of a Twentieth-Century Historian." In *History and Criticism.* Ithaca: Cornell University Press, 1985, 45–70.

Langdon, Helen. *Caravaggio, a Life.* London: Pimlico, 1999.

———. "Gypsies, Tricksters and Whores: The Street Life of Caravaggio's Rome." In *Darkness and Light: Caravaggio and His World*, 22–25. Sydney: Art Gallery of New South Wales, 2003–4.

Laven, Mary. *Virgins of Venice: Enclosed Lives and Broken Vows in the Renaissance Convent.* London: Viking, 2002.

Luzzati, Michele, ed. "Ebrei sotto processo." *Quaderni storici* 99 (1998).

Mancini, Roberto. *I guardiani della voce: lo statuto della parola e il silenzio nell'Occidente medievale e moderno.* Rome: Carocci, 2002.

Manconi, Francesco, ed. *Banditismi mediterranei Secoli XVI–XVII.* Rome: Carocci, 2003.

Marchesini, Daniele. *Il bisogno di scrivere. Usi della scrittura nell'Italia moderna.* Rome: Laterza, 1992.

Martini, Alberto. "Dal tribunale al patibolo: il teatro della giustizia a Roma in antico regime." In *I Cenci: nobiltà di sangue*, edited by Michele Di Sivo, 255–308. Rome: Colombo, 2002.

Mazzacane, Aldo. *Farinacci, Prospero.* In *Dizionario biografico degli Italiani*, vol. 45, 1–5. Rome: Istituto dell'Enciclopedia Italiana, 1995.

Menniti Ippolito, Antonio. *Il tramonto della curia nepotista.* Rome: Viella, 1999.

———. *I papi al Quirinale. Il sovrano pontefice e la ricerca di una residenza.* Rome: Viella, 2004.

Merzario, Raul. *Anastasia, ovvero la malizia degli uomini. Relazioni sociali e controllo delle nascite in un villaggio ticinese.* Rome: Laterza, 1992.

Messina, Pietro. "Del Monte, Ippolito." Vol. 38 of *Dizionario Biografico degli Italiani*, 138–41. Rome: Istituto dell'Enciclopedia Italiana, 1990.

Moravia, Alberto. *Beatrice Cenci*. Translated by Angus Davidson. New York: Noonday Press/Farrar, Strauss and Giroux, 1966.

Moroni, Gaetano. *Dizionario di erudizione storico-ecclesiastica*. Vol. 43. Venice: Tipografia Emiliana, 1847.

Muir, Edward. *Mad Blood Stirring: Vendetta in Renaissance Italy*. Baltimore: Johns Hopkins University Press, 1998.

———. "The Idea of Community in Renaissance Italy." *Renaissance Quarterly* 55 (2002): 1–18.

Muir, Edward, and Guido Ruggiero, eds. *Microhistory and The Lost People of Europe*. Baltimore: Johns Hopkins University Press, 1991.

———, eds. *History from Crime: Selections from Quaderni Storici*. Baltimore: John's Hopkins University Press, 1994.

Murphy, Caroline. *The Pope's Daughter: The Extraordinary Life of Felice della Rovere*. New York: Oxford University Press, 2006.

Niccoli, Ottavia. "Rinuncia, pace, perdono. Rituali di pacificazione della prima età moderna." *Studi storici* 40 (1990): 219–61.

———. *Rinascimento anticlericale*. Rome: Laterza, 2005.

———. *Perdonare. Idee, pratiche, rituali in Italia tra Cinque e Seicento*. Rome: Laterza, 2007.

Nicholson, Helen. *The Knights Hospitaller*. London: Boydell Press, 2001.

Noto, Maria Anna. *Tra sovrano pontefice e Regno di Napoli. Riforma cattolica e Controriforma a Benevento*. Rome: Lacaita, 2003.

Nubola, Cecilia. "Liberazioni per privilegio. Confraternite e grazia nella prima età moderna (secoli XVI–XVIII)." In *Chiesa e mondo moderno. Scritti in onore di Paolo Prodi*, edited by Adriano Prosperi, Pierangelo Schiera, and Gabriella Zarri, 235–56. Bologna: il Mulino, 2007.

Nussdorfer, Laurie. "The Vacant See: Ritual and Protest in Early Modern Rome." *Sixteenth Century Journal* 18, no. 2 (1987): 173–89.

———. *Civic Politics in the Rome of Urban VIII*. Princeton, N.J.: Princeton University Press, 1992.

———. *Brokers of Public Trust: Notaries in Early Modern Rome*. Baltimore: Johns Hopkins University Press, 2009.

Orestano, Riccardo. "Appello: Diritto Romano." In *Novissimo Digesto Italiano*, vol. 1. Turin: UTET, 1974.

Ortalli, Gherardo, ed. *Bande armate, banditi, banditismo e repressione di giustizia negli Stati europei di antico regime*. Rome: Jouvence, 1986.

Ostrow, Steven F. *Art and Spirituality in Counter-Reformation Rome*. Cambridge: Cambridge University Press, 1996.

Paglia, Vincenzo. *La morte confortata. Riti della paura e mentalità religiosa a Roma nell'età moderna*. Rome: Edizioni di Storia e Letteratura, 1982.

Pastor, Ludwig von. *History of the Popes*. Translated by Frederick Ignatius Antrobus and Ralph Kerr. London: K. Paul, Trench, Trubner, 1891–1961, 40 vols. (Original edition, Freiburg im Breisgau, 1886–1933.)

Pastore, Alessandro. "Tra giustizia e politica: il governo della peste a Genova e a Roma nel 1656–7." *Rivista storica italiana* 100 (1988): 126–54.

———. Introduction to *Avvocati, medici, ingegneri. Alle origini delle profes-*

sioni moderne, edited by Maria Luisa Betri and Alessandro Pastore. Bologna: Clueb, 1997.

Pellegrini, Marco. "Corte di Roma e aristocrazie italiane in età moderna. Per una letturatura storico-sociale della curia romana." *Rivista di Storia e Letteratura Religiosa* 30 (1994): 543–602.

Petrucci, Armando. "Introduzione alle pratiche di scrittura." *Annali della Scuola Normale Superiore di Pisa.* Classe di Lettere e Filosofia. Series 3, vol. 23, no. 2 (1993): 549–62.

———. *Public Lettering: Script, Power, and Culture.* Chicago: University of Chicago Press, 1993.

———. *Writers and Readers in Medieval Italy: Studies in the History of Written Culture.* New Haven, Conn.: Yale University Press, 1995.

Pierguidi, Stefano. "Sulla fortuna della 'Giustizia' e della 'Pazienza' di Vasari." *Mitteilungen des Kunsthistorischen Intstitutes in Florenz* 51, no. 3 (2007): 576–95.

Pizzorusso, Giovanni. "Una regione virtuale: il Lazio da Martino V a Pio IV." In *Atlante storico-politico del Lazio.* Rome: Laterza, 1996, 63–87.

Preto, Paolo. *"Persona per hora secreta." Accusa e delazione nella Repubblica di Venezia.* Milan: il Saggiatore, 2003.

Prodi, Paolo. *The Papal Prince. One Body and Two Souls: The Papal Monarchy in Early Modern Europe.* Cambridge: Cambridge University Press, 1987.

———. *Una storia della giustizia. Dal pluralismo dei fori al moderno dualismo tra coscienza e diritto.* Bologna: il Mulino, 2000.

———. "Introduzione: evoluzione e metamorfosi delle identità collettive." In *Identità collettive tra Medioevo ed Età Moderna*, edited by Paolo Prodi and Wolfgang Reinhard. Bologna: Clueb, 2002.

Prosperi, Adriano. *Tribunali della coscienza. Inquisitori, confessori, missionari.* Turin: Einaudi, 1996.

———. *Dare l'anima. Storia di un infanticidio.* Turin: Einaudi, 2005.

———. "Morire volentieri: condannati a morte e sacramenti." In *Misericordie. Conversioni sotto il patibolo tra Medioevo ed età moderna.* Pisa: Edizioni della Normale, 2007.

———. *Giustizia bendata. Percorsi storici di un'immagine.* Turin: Einaudi, 2008.

"'Pro tribunali sedentes.' Le magistrature giudiziarie dello Stato Pontificio e i loro archivi." *Archivi per la Storia* 4, nos. 1–2 (1991). Published as a monograph.

Quint, David. "Political Allegory in the *Gerusalemme liberata*." *Renaissance Quarterly* 42 (1990): 1–29.

Quondam, Amedeo. *Le "carte messagiere." Retorica e modelli di comunicazione epistolare. Per un indice dei libri di lettere del Cinquecento.* Rome: Bulzoni, 1981.

Reinhardt, Nicole. "Bolonais à Rome, Romains à Bologna? Carrières et stratégies entre centre et périphérie. Une esquisse." In *Offices et Papauté (XIVe–XVIIc). Charges, hommes, destins*, edited by Armand Jamme and

Olivier Poncet, 237–49. Rome: Ecole Française de Rome, 2005.

Ricci, Corrado. *Beatrice Cenci*. Translated by Morris Bishop and H. L. Stuart. London: Heinemann, 1926.

Ricoeur, Paul. *Memory, History, Forgetting*. Translated by Kathleen Blamey and David Pellauer. Chicago: University of Chicago Press, 2004.

Rietbergen, Peter. "Pausen, Prelaten, Bureaucraten, Aspekten van de geschiedenis van het Pausschap en de Pauselijke Staat in de 17e Eeuw." Academic thesis, University of Nijmegen, 1983.

Rocke, Michael. *Forbidden Friendship: Homosexuality and Male Culture in Renaissance Florence*. New York: Oxford University Press, 1996.

Romeo, Giovanni. *Inquisitori, esorcisti, streghe nell'Italia della Controriforma*. Florence: Sansoni, 1990.

———. *Aspettando il boia. Condannati a morte, confortatori e inquisitori nella Napoli della Controriforma*. Florence: Sansoni, 1993.

Rosa, Mario. "La chiesa meridionale nell'età della Controriforma." In *La Chiesa e il potere politico*, edited by Giorgio Chittolini and Giovanni Miccoli, 291–345. Vol. 9 of *Storia d'Italia. Annali*. Turin: Einaudi, 1986.

———. "La Santa Sede e gli ebrei nel Settecento." In *Dall'emancipazione a oggi*, edited by Corrado Vivanti, 1067–87. Vol. 2 of *Storia d'Italia. Gli ebrei in Italia*. Turin: Einaudi, 1997.

Roscioni, Lisa. *Il governo della follia. Ospedali, medici e pazzi nell'età moderna*. Milan: Mondadori, 2003.

Ruff, Julius R. *Violence in Early Modern Europe*. Cambridge: Cambridge University Press, 2001.

Ruggiero, Guido. *Machiavelli in Love: Sex, Self and Society in Italian Renaissance*. Baltimore: Johns Hopkins University Press, 2007.

Santoncini, Gabriella. "Il groviglio giurisdizionale dello Stato ecclesiastico prima dell'occupazione francese." *Annali dell'Istituto Storico Italo-Germanico in Trento* 20 (1994): 82–102.

———. *Il Buon Governo. Organizzazione e legittimazione del rapporto fra sovrano e comunità (secc. XVI–XVIII)*. Milan: Giuffrè, 2002.

Sbriccoli, Mario. "Storia del diritto e storia della società. Questioni di metodo di ricerca." In *Storia sociale e dimensione giuridica. Strumenti di indagine e ipotesi di lavoro*, edited by Paolo Grossi, 127–48. Milan: Giuffrè, 1986.

———. "Fonti giudiziarie e fonti giuridiche. Riflessioni sulla fase attuale degli studi di storia del crimine e della giustizia criminale." *Studi storici* 29 (1988): 491–501.

———. "Giustizia criminale." In *Lo stato moderno in Europa. Istituzioni e diritto*, edited by Maurizio Fioravanti, 163–205. Rome: Laterza, 2002.

———. "La benda della giustizia. Iconografia, diritto e leggi penali dal Medio Evo all'Età Moderna." In Mario Sbriccoli et al., eds., *Ordo Iuris. Storia e forme dell'esperienza giuridica*, 42–95. Milan: Giuffrè, 2003.

Schmidt, Peter. "De Sancto Officio Urbis: Aspekte der Verflechtung des Heiligen Offiziums mit der Stadt Rom im 16. und 17. Jahrhundert."

Quellen und Forschungen aus italienischen Archiven und Bibliotheken 82 (2001): 404–89.

Serio, Alessandro. "Pompeo Colonna tra papato e 'grandi monarchie,' la pax romana del 1511 e i comportamenti politici dei baroni romani." In *La nobiltà romana*, edited by Maria Antonietta Visceglia, 63–87. Rome: Carocci, 2001.

——. *Una gloriosa sconfitta. I Colonna tra Papato e Impero nella prima età moderna (1431–1530)*. Rome: Viella, 2008.

Sharpe, Jeremy A. "'Last Dying Speeches': Religion, Ideology and Public Execution in Seventeenth-Century England." *Past and Present* 107 (1985): 144–67.

Siebenhüner, Kim. "'M'ha mosso l'amore' Bigami e inquisitori nella documentazione del Sant'Uffizio romano (secolo XVII)." In *Trasgressioni: seduzione, concubinato, adulterio, bigamia (XIV–XVIII secolo)*, edited by Silvana Seidel Menchi and Diego Quaglioni, 503–33. Bologna: il Mulino, 2004.

——. *Bigamie und Inquisition in Italien*. Paderborn: F. Schöningh, 2006.

——. "Conversion, Mobility and the Roman Inquisition in Italy around 1600." *Past & Present* 200 (2008): 5–35.

Sire, H. J. A. *The Knights of Malta*. New Haven, Conn.: Yale University Press, 1996.

Sluhovsky, Moshe. "The Devil in the Convent." *American Historical Review* 107, no. 5 (2002): 1379–1411.

Smail, Daniel Lord. *The Consumption of Justice: Emotions, Publicity, and Legal Culture in Marseille, 1264–1423*. Ithaca, N.Y.: Cornell University Press, 2003.

Spagnoletti, Angelantonio. *Stato, aristocrazie e Ordine di Malta nell'Italia moderna*. Rome: École Française de Rome, 1988.

Spierenburg, Pieter. *The Spectacle of Suffering: Executions and the Evolution of Repression: from a Preindustrial Metropolis to the European Experience*. Cambridge: Cambridge University Press, 1984.

——. *The Prison Experience: Disciplinary Institutions and Their Inmates in Early Modern Europe*. New Brunswick, N.J.: Rutgers University Press, 1991.

Spierenburg, Pieter, and S. Body-Gendrot, eds. *Violence in Europe: Historical and Contemporary Perspectives*. New York: Springer, 2008.

Stephens, Walter. *Demon Lovers: Witchcraft, Sex, and the Crisis of Belief*. Chicago: University of Chicago Press, 2002.

Stolleis, Michael. *Das Auge des Gesetzes. Geschichte einer Metaphor*. Munich: C. H. Beck Verlag, 2004.

Storey, Tessa. *Carnal Commerce in Counter-Reformation Rome*. Cambridge: Cambridge University Press, 2008.

Stow, Kenneth. *The Jews in Rome (1536–1551)*. 2 vols. New York: Brill, 1995.

——. *Theatre of Acculturation: The Roman Ghetto in the Sixteenth-Century*. Seattle: University of Washington Press, 2001.

Tabacchi, Stefano. "Buon Governo, Sacra Consulta e dinamiche dell'amministrazione pontificia nel XVIII." *Dimensioni e problemi della ricerca storica* 1 (2004): 43–65.

———. *Il Buon Governo. Le finanze locali nello Stato della Chiesa (secoli XVI–XVIII)*. Rome: Viella, 2007.

Tedeschi, John. *The Prosecution of Heresy: Collected Studies on the Inquisition in Early Modern Italy*. Binghamton, N.Y.: Medieval and Renaissance Texts and Studies, 1991. (Italian edition: *Il giudice e l'eretico. Studi sull'Inquisizione romana*. Milan: Vita e Pensiero, 1998.)

———. "Inquisitorial Law and the Witch." In *Early Modern European Witchcraft: Center and Peripheries*, edited by Bengt Ankarloo and Gustav Henningsen, 83–118. Oxford: Clarendon Press, 1993.

Tedeschi, John, and Gustav Henningsen, in association with Charlies Amiel, eds. *Studies in Sources and Methods: The Inquisition in Early Modern Europe*. Dekalb: Northern Illinois University Press, 1996.

Tocci, Giovanni. *Le comunità in età moderna. Problemi storiografici e prospettive di ricerca*. Florence: Nis, 1997.

Torres Sans, Xavier. "El bandolerismo mediterraneo: una visión comparativa (siglos XVI–XVII)." In *Los grupos sociales*. Vol. 2 of *Felipe II y el Mediterraneo*. Coordinated by Emanuel Belenguer Cebriá, 397–423. Madrid: Sociedad estatal para la commemoración de los centenarios de Felipe II y Carlos V, 2001.

Turchini, Angelo. *Istituzioni, comunità, mentalità*. Vol. 1 of *La Romagna nel Cinquecento*. Cesena: Il Ponte Vecchio, 2003.

Villard, Renaud. "L'homme du secret du pape: un gouverneur de crise dans l'État pontifical au XVIe siècle." In *Attori sociali e istituzioni in Antico Regime*, edited by Bertrand Forclaz. Special issue of *Dimensioni e problemi di ricerca storica* 1 (2004): 15–42.

Visceglia, Maria Antonietta, ed. *La nobiltà romana in età moderna. Profili istituzionali e pratiche sociali*. Rome: Carocci, 2001.

Volpi, Roberto. *Le regioni introvabili. Centralizzazione e regionalizzazione nello stato Pontificio*. Bologna: il Mulino, 1983.

Waquet, Jean-Claude. *Corruption: Ethics and Power in Florence, 1600–1770*. Translated by Linda McCall. University Park: Pennsylvania State University Press, 1991 (original edition: *De la Corruption: morale et pouvoir à Florence*. Paris: Fayard, 1984).

Yates, Frances A. *Astrea: The Imperial Theme in the Sixteenth Century*. London: Routledge and Kegan Paul, 1975.

Zarri, Gabriella. *Recinti. Donne, clausura e matrimonio nella prima età moderna*. Bologna: il Mulino, 2000.

Zarri, Gabriella, and Gianna Pomata, eds. *I monasteri femminili come centri di cultura fra Rinascimento e Barocco*. Rome: Edizioni di Storia e Letteratura, 2005.

Papal Justice: Subjects and Courts in the Papal State, 1500–1750
was designed and typeset in Jenson by Kachergis Book Design of
Pittsboro, North Carolina. It was printed on 55-pound Natural
and bound by Versa Press of East Peoria, Illinois.